Philosophy of Personal Identity and Multiple Personality

Routledge Studies in Contemporary Philosophy

1. Email and Ethics
Style and Ethical Relations in Computer-Mediated Communication
Emma Rooksby

2. Causation and Laws of Nature
Max Kistler

3. Internalism and Epistemology
The Architecture of Reason
Timothy McGrew and Lydia McGrew

4. Einstein, Relativity and Absolute Simultaneity
Edited by William Lane Craig and Quentin Smith

5. Epistemology Modalized
Kelly Becker

6. Truth and Speech Acts
Studies in the Philosophy of Language
Dirk Greimann & Geo Siegwart

7. A Sense of the World
Essays on Fiction, Narrative, and Knowledge
Edited by John Gibson, Wolfgang Huemer, and Luca Pocci

8. A Pragmatist Philosophy of Democracy
Robert B. Talisse

9. Aesthetics and Material Beauty
Aesthetics Naturalized
Jennifer A. McMahon

10. Aesthetic Experience
Edited by Richard Shusterman and Adele Tomlin

11. Real Essentialism
David S. Oderberg

12. Practical Identity and Narrative Agency
Edited by Catriona Mackenzie and Kim Atkins

13. Metaphysics and the Representational Fallacy
Heather Dyke

14. Narrative Identity and Moral Identity
A Practical Perspective
Kim Atkins

15. Intergenerational Justice
Rights and Responsibilities in an Intergenerational Polity
Janna Thompson

16. Hillel Steiner and the Anatomy of Justice
Themes and Challenges
Edited by Stephen de Wijze, Matthew H. Kramer, and Ian Carter

17. Philosophy of Personal Identity and Multiple Personality
Logi Gunnarsson

Philosophy of Personal Identity and Multiple Personality

Logi Gunnarsson

Routledge
Taylor & Francis Group
New York London

First published 2010
by Routledge
270 Madison Ave, New York, NY 10016

Simultaneously published in the UK
by Routledge
2 Park Square, Milton Park, Abingdon, Oxon OX14 4RN

Routledge is an imprint of the Taylor & Francis Group, an informa business

Typeset in Sabon by IBT Global.
Printed and bound in the United States of America on acid-free paper by IBT Global.

Library of Congress Cataloging-in-Publication Data

Gunnarsson, Logi.
Philosophy of personal identity and multiple personality / by Logi Gunnarsson.
p. cm.—(Routledge studies in contemporary philosophy ; 17)
Includes bibliographical references and index.
1. Self (Philosophy) 2. Identity (Philosophical concept) 3. Identity (Psychology) 4. Multiple personality. 5. Individuation (Philosophy) 6. Individuation (Psychology) I. Title.
BD438.5.G86 2010
126—dc22
2009006523

ISBN10: 0-415-80017-X (hbk)
ISBN10: 0-203-87263-0 (ebk)

ISBN13: 978-0-415-80017-4 (hbk)
ISBN13: 978-0-203-87263-5 (ebk)

Contents

Figures

Tables

Preface

I recently read in a German newspaper that you should thank your enemies in the preface: the reason is that once they are thanked, they are disqualified from reviewing your work, at least in the North American tradition. I won't be thanking my enemies. So, any way you look at it, it seems that I am in trouble.

I don't really know when I started working on this project. My guess is that it was sometime in 1998 or 1999. It doesn't really matter, but it is a problem that I am no longer sure who helped me in the long process. I'll take notes next time and ask for forgiveness this time. In 2000–2001, I spent a year at the University Center for Human Values at Princeton University and I am grateful to the center for awarding me a Laurance S. Rockefeller Fellowship. (This project was also supported by the Icelandic Center for Research in 2000 and 2002.) By the end of my year at Princeton, I had a long paper in English that included many of the basic ideas of this book, though they have been revised and developed in various ways. I would like to thank my colleagues at Princeton and elsewhere in the U.S.—in particular at the conference of the International Society for the Study of Dissociation in San Antonio in 2000—who talked with me about my ideas during that year: Stephen Braude, Harry Frankfurt, Mark Johnston, Sean Kelly, Béatrice Longuenesse, Richard Moran, Alexander Nehemas, Jennifer Radden, Margo Rivera, Carol Rovane, Peter Singer, and Leif Wenar. In particular, I would like to thank Heda Segvic (1957–2003) for her written comments on the paper I delivered at the University Center for Human Values.

After returning to the Humboldt University in Berlin, I began the task of turning the material into a book. By the beginning of 2005, I had a complete draft in German. During this period, I profited most from discussions with R. Jay Wallace, who read drafts of most of the chapters, though he had left Berlin for Berkeley. Rolf-Peter Horstmann's research colloquium, in which I presented my work on several occasions, was another important forum. Of the people in this circle, special thanks go to Dina Edmundts, Rolf-Peter Horstmann, and Ulrich Schlösser, who all also discussed my work with me outside the colloquium. In addition, Olaf Müller read drafts of several chapters and I profited greatly from his comments and the discussion at a meeting of his research seminar.

After taking up a position at the University of Liverpool in 2005, I started revising parts of the manuscript in English. I received valuable written comments from my colleagues at Liverpool (Barry Dainton, Jonardon Ganeri, Stephen McLeod) and from Jennifer Whiting. A "fourth phase" began after I joined the TU Dortmund University in 2006. Since then, I have benefited from comments by Stephen Braude, Christian Budnik, Robin Celikates, Nadja El Kassar, Martina Herrmann, Stefan Kübler, Res Mettler, Jennifer Radden, and Michelle Wüthrich. I gained a great deal of insight from several discussions with Lutz Wingert on my work. I also received important impetus from the discussion of my papers with Michael Quante and others in his research colloquium in Cologne in 2007 and with Monika Betzler and others in her research seminar in Bern in 2008. Finally, I would like to express my gratitude to all the audiences at the different places I have given talks on these topics in the past ten years.

Some of the rewritten parts were in English, others in German. I decided to have the remaining German sections translated and was provided with excellent translations of Chapters 1–3 by Mitch Cohen and Chapters 1, 8–9, and most of Chapters 13–14 by Joann Skrypzak. Since I worked on these chapters after receiving the translations, I bear responsibility for the final text. I am indebted to Isabell Donner for diligent work on the references and to her, Nadja El Kassar and Lena Ljucovic for valuable help with the proofs and the index. Before the final submission, the whole manuscript was carefully edited by Adam Blauhut. I am grateful to Erica C. Wetter at Routledge for taking on the project and would also like to thank her and Elizabeth J. Levine for all their help along the way. Thanks also go to the two anonymous reviewers for Routledge for their helpful comments.

The material in some parts of the book originates from papers I have published elsewhere and is reprinted here with the kind permission of the respective publishers (see the bibliography for more details): "What Is Constituted in Self-Constitution?" *Papers of the 25th International Wittgenstein Symposium* (2002) (with permission of the Austrian Ludwig Wittgenstein Society); "Trapped in a 'Secret Cellar': Breaking the Spell of a Picture of Unconscious States," *Philosophical Investigations* (2005) (with permission of Blackwell Publishing); "Festlegungstheorie zur Frage personaler Identität," *Deutsche Zeitschrift für Philosophie* (2008) (with permission of Akademie Verlag); "Sharing My Body," *SATS: Nordic Journal of Philosophy* (2009) (with permission of SATS). Material from *Amongst Ourselves* by Tracy Alderman and Karen Marshall (see bibliography) is reprinted with the permission of New Harbinger Publications, Inc., *Amongst Ourselves*, Alderman and Marshall (www.newharbinger.com). Material from *Fight Club* by Chuck Palahniuk (see bibliography) is reprinted with the permission of Donadio & Olson, Inc., copyright 1996 Chuck Palahniuk.

There is only one philosopher who has continually discussed this project with me since I started working on it: Eva Klingenstein. Although I have already used up a lot of thanks in this preface, she should get the last and largest chunk.

Part I

Introduction

1 Am I Alone in My Body?

Imagine this: You are in an unfamiliar city, but can't remember having traveled there. Or you don't know where you were yesterday. Or the day before. And people you have never heard of keep calling you up and reproaching you for not having kept an appointment that you never made. On the floor of your own apartment you regularly find your favorite clothing, cut to pieces. You can't explain it. You receive credit card bills that you can't pay, for things you didn't purchase—but find in your closet. You are held responsible for damaging property in clubs that you've never frequented, in cities you have never visited. Finally you go to a psychiatrist, and the diagnosis is: you suffer from multiple personality disorder. You have several personalities and it is the other personalities who have cut up your favorite clothes, bought the designer items, made the appointments with strangers, and smashed the furniture in unknown nightclubs.

Imagine it. Now ask yourself what you would think about it. Would you think, "I'm a different person than I thought!" or "That wasn't me! I don't cut my favorite clothes to pieces. I don't hang out in shabby clubs and I don't buy expensive designer goods. I obviously share my body with other persons, but I am no more identical to these persons than I am to my brother. In fact, I have more in common with my siblings than with the persons with whom I apparently share my body!" What would you think?

If you are ready for it, then also imagine this situation: The police break into your apartment. You are arrested and accused of having committed several kidnappings, rapes, and armed robberies, though you can't remember them. Precisely this happened to Billy Milligan on October 27, 1977, in his apartment in Reynoldsburg, Ohio. And it was indeed proven that this person, Billy Milligan, committed these crimes. In the course of a sensational trial, however, he was diagnosed with multiple personality disorder and acquitted.[1] If you had been charged, would you have considered yourself guilty, or would you have thought, "I'm innocent; the rapes were committed by another person in my body"?

You have probably asked yourself similar questions before. After all, my examples are modeled on real cases of multiple personality disorder, or dissociative identity disorder, as it is officially known today. And our times are downright obsessed with questions of identity and the theme of multiple personality. All of this has penetrated our culture to the point that it is hardly possible not to have encountered this theme in some form. Following the publication of the bestseller *Sybil* in 1973, the biography of a woman with sixteen personalities, more and more cases of multiple personality disorder were diagnosed[2] until, in the late 1980s and early 1990s, North America saw a true explosion of such diagnoses.[3] Since the early 1970s, countless biographies and autobiographies of multiple personalities have emerged,[4] along with extensive research literature on multiple personality disorder.[5] The media report on the topic sympathetically and critically. The phenomenon also finds an echo in television series, of course. For example, in Germany, the main character in *Dr. Stefan Frank—The Doctor Women Trust* had to deal with a multiple personality on July 20, 2001, at 8:15 p.m. on the station RTL. Recent Hollywood films like *Fight Club* (1999), *I, Me and Irene* (2000), and *Identity* (2002) have tapped into the complex drama of this phenomenon. But multiple personality disorder is not the only thing that fascinates us. The classical doppelganger motif is also undergoing a renaissance in contemporary novels and stories—*New York Trilogy* (1990), *Endlich Stille* (2005), and *Lunar Park* (2005) are just a few examples.

What captivates us so about multiple personalities and doppelgangers? What are we looking for and why can't we resist these themes? The short and general answer is: we want to understand ourselves and get to the bottom of our identity. One part of this interest is philosophical: is it possible that we are not alone in our bodies? This is a question central to this book, one I will answer with yes. More precisely, I will defend the following thesis: each of us is a kind of entity, of which more than one could exist in the same body. But the fascination with the subject is not purely philosophical. It also has to do with whether such phenomena actually exist. Are there really cases in which several persons are present in one body? Moreover, it is about understanding our culture and our fellow human beings: What does it mean when someone says about himself or somebody else that he is one of several personalities or persons in one body? This cluster of questions concerning multiple personality forms one of the main subjects of this study. The second chapter offers a systematic introduction to these issues.

The other basic topic of this monograph is the classical philosophical question of personal identity over time. Let us consider the following case: In 1970, a woman awakes from a six-month coma following a severe traffic accident. She cannot speak, eat, sit, or walk. She cannot do anything. And she remembers nothing. She must relearn every human capacity. To this day she cannot remember her life before the accident. Her emotional and cognitive ties to the person existing before the accident are like those to a third person. She now calls herself "Katharina Beta."[6] What has happened? Is Katharina Beta identical to the person who had the accident, or did she start to exist only after the coma? The philosophical discussion of diachronic personal identity attempts to clarify such disturbing questions. More on them in the third chapter.

A reader's guide: This book is written as a unified study of multiple personality and personal identity. However, some readers may be interested only in multiple personality. The following parts present them with an independently understandable treatment of this topic: Chapters 2–4, 7–9, and 12–14. Others may be interested only in the philosophical topic of personal identity. These readers might want to limit their attention to Chapters 2–7 and 9–12.

2 Multiple Personality

Most people equate the concept of *multiple personality* with the psychiatric diagnosis of *multiple personality disorder* or *dissociative identity disorder.* In this study, however, *multiple personality* is understood as a concept that has relevance beyond psychiatric contexts, as will become clear in the following. I will start by stating five theses that I intend to defend.

1 FIVE THESES

The bestseller *Sybil* retells how a psychotherapist discovers several personalities in her patient Sybil.[1] One of these personalities is named "Vicky." The doctor has the following conversation with her:

> "I did tell Sybil that she is subject to fugue states during which she is unaware of what's happening." [Dr. Wilbur]
> "I know," Vicky asserted, "but that's very different from telling her that she's not alone in her own body."
> "I think it will reassure Sybil to know that she is functioning even though she doesn't know it."
> "She, Doctor?" Vicky asked quizzically. "Isn't the pronoun *we*?"
> The doctor paused and made no direct answer. It was a thoughtful Vicky who broke the silence, saying, "I suppose you can tell Sybil. But I repeat: is it *she* who is functioning?" Without waiting for the doctor to reply, Vicky asserted, "We're people, you know. People in our own right."[2]

From the doctor's perspective, the situation is as follows: Sitting across from her is a patient who suffers from multiple personality disorder. One of the ways multiple personality disorder expresses itself is that, at different times, different personalities control the patient's life. Some time ago, the patient came to her in therapy as one of these personalities—as Sybil. In the preceding dialog, however, Vicky, one of the patient's other personalities, speaks with her. One of the ways the patient's two personalities differ at the time of the dialog is that the patient, as Vicky, is aware of the personality Sybil, but as Sybil the patient has no inkling of Vicky. When Vicky acts, Sybil is not aware of what is happening. For example, Vicky regularly goes to concerts and museums with her friend Marian Ludlow, about whom Sybil knows nothing.[3] When Sybil assumes control again, she can no longer recall these happenings—she simply has complete amnesia about the time period in question. Dr. Wilbur does not understand her patient as *several persons in one body*, but as *one person* who has various personalities.[4] Other therapists who work with the diagnosis of multiple personality disorder or dissociative identity disorder also usually assume this.[5]

But in the dialog, Vicky rejects this assumption vehemently. In another passage, when Dr. Wilbur asks her if she doesn't realize that the various personalities could be "different aspects of the same person," Vicky answers emphatically: "No . . . I don't see. You, you're just you. You're Dr. Wilbur and no one else . . . And I'm just Vicky."[6] Vicky's position is thus: she and Sybil are not merely personality facets of one person. Just as Dr. Wilbur is a person in her own right, so too are Vicky and Sybil two autonomous persons.[7]

Vicky's position is intriguing and disturbing—and also typical of characters in cases of multiple personality.[8] But what does Vicky really mean when she makes such claims? And is she right or at least could she be right? Is she one of several persons in one body, and is that even possible in principle?

> *Thesis 1*: Vicky and similar characters in cases of multiple personality understand themselves as one of two or more fundamental entities in one body—not as one personality facet of a single fundamental entity.

The philosophical concept of fundamental entity will not be more precisely elucidated until the next chapter, but the thesis can be roughly explained here: When Saul turned into Paul on the way to Damascus, he became another person, if you will. If that is correct, then Paul could have said: "Before my conversion I was another person." But this statement implies that *he* was the person before his conversion. One could express this by saying that, in the case of Saul/Paul, there exists only *one fundamental entity*, but *two persons*.

If Vicky merely meant that she and Sybil were two persons the way Paul and Saul were two persons, her position would be uninteresting. But she takes a much more radical position: just as Saul and Paul are *one* fundamental entity, she and Sybil are *two* fundamental entities, not merely two personalities or two persons in the sense of Saul and Paul. This interpretation of Vicky and similar characters is defended in detail in Chapters 8, 13, and 14.

> *Thesis 2*: Each of us is a fundamental entity, of which there could exist two or more in one body (coexistence thesis).

This is a purely philosophical thesis that could be maintained independently of any concern with the phenomenon of multiple personality. If one accepts it, one agrees with Vicky and similar characters on an important point: It is *possible* that she is one of several fundamental entities in one body. According to the next thesis, this is possible, but *never really* the case:

> *Thesis 3*: The conditions for the presence of two or more fundamental entities in one body are never fulfilled in reality.

This is an empirical thesis. According to it, Vicky is not in reality one of several fundamental entities in one body. The conditions necessary for this are in fact never fulfilled. Since this study is not an empirical investigation, I cannot prove this thesis. But I can pursue the philosophical question of what conditions must be met for two or more fundamental entities to exist in one body. It will turn out that these conditions are very difficult to fulfill in reality.

> Logi is a murderer! I am not Logi! Well, he hasn't killed anybody yet. But he wants to and he intends to. He is set on killing ME. In fact, the sole purpose of this book is to get rid of me. Erase, eliminate, and extinguish. Those are his three maxims when it comes to me. DON'T BUY INTO HIS MASQUERADE! Yes, this is, I suppose, a theoretical book. Yes, it is composed of words, and these words are printed, and you can read these words, and you think that he wrote them for you to ask yourself whether his theory is true. Yes, yes, sure. But no! From the first page to the last, he is spinning a web around me and with the last word I'll be dead. I won't let it happen. But if it does, I want you to be my witness. So remember: this it not a theory, this is a killing.

Here is my next thesis:

> *Thesis 4*: Multiple personality involves philosophical concepts whose analysis is indispensable for an adequate understanding of this phenomenon.

This thesis means that engagement with the phenomenon of multiple personality must lead to philosophy. It expresses a cornerstone of my methodological approach. In contrast, the next thesis underscores the fact that one must also move in the opposite direction, namely, from the philosophical investigation of personal identity to the theme of multiple personality:

> *Thesis 5*: The interpretation of multiple personality is an important basis for philosophical conceptions of personal identity.

Because this thesis concerns arguments for theories of personal identity, it will not be discussed until the next chapter. This chapter deals with multiple personality, i.e., with theses 1 and 4. But first the concept of multiple personality must be explicated.

2 THE CONCEPT OF MULTIPLE PERSONALITY

Even if the concept of multiple personality cannot be equated with multiple personality disorder or dissociative identity disorder, this diagnosis should not remain unexplained. A discussion of this psychological disturbance can also serve to illustrate possible forms of multiple personality. In the text revision of the fourth edition of the *Diagnostic and Statistical Manual of Mental Disorders* (DSM-IV-TR), dissociative identity disorder is defined by the following symptoms:

A. The presence of two or more distinct identities or personality states (each with its own relatively enduring pattern of perceiving, relating to, and thinking about the environment and self).
B. At least two of these identities or personality states recurrently take control of the person's behavior.
C. Inability to recall important information that is too extensive to be explained by ordinary forgetfulness.
D. The disturbance is not due to the direct physiological effects of a substance (e.g., blackouts or chaotic behavior during Alcohol Intoxication) or a general medical condition (e.g., complex partial seizures). *Note*: In children, the symptoms are not attributable to imaginary playmates or other fantasy play.[9]

To elucidate these criteria by an example, I will sketch one of history's most famous cases of multiple personality disorder; later I will discuss it in greater detail. It is the case of a patient who consulted Dr. Morton Price for treatment in 1898. The psychiatrist himself described the case in detail in his biographical psychiatric case study, published in 1906 and entitled *The Dissociation of a Personality: A Biographical Study in Abnormal Psychology*. In the course of the therapy, the doctor distinguished several personalities in the patient, whom he calls "Miss Christine L. Beauchamp" in the book. I will provide only a brief description of the personalities BI and Sally here. "BI" refers to the person who originally came to the psychiatrist. Sally initially appears only when the patient is under hypnosis, but later she also determines the person's actions for longer periods of time.[10]

Dr. Prince describes BI as having several characteristics: she is reticent, patient, considerate of others, amiable, without anger, polite, altruistic, conscientious, dutiful, responsible, truth-loving, morbidly proud, and religious.[11] Dr. Prince says that "her refinement of character is out of the ordinary" and she possesses "delicacy of sentiment and appreciation of everything that is fine in thought and perceptions."[12] She is educated, "has marked literary tastes and faculties," likes to read,[13] speaks French, and can take shorthand.[14] She tires easily and has little motivation for outdoor activities.[15]

Sally, by contrast, is vivacious, gay, rebellious, reckless, bold, saucy, volatile, irresponsible, and childlike—a "child of nature."[16] Dr. Prince waxes enthusiastic: "her frolicsomeness, gayety, and love of fun were irresistible."[17] She loves to be considered wicked, but she has a "youthful" idea of wickedness and mischief.[18] She has intense dislike, contempt, and hate for BI and is jealous of her.[19] She can't speak French or take shorthand, and she lacks much of BI's education and "culture," even if she "reads, writes, and speaks English well."[20] She loves to be outdoors, she likes sports, entertainment, physical activity, games, and the theater, but she hates reading.[21] She is never ill or tired: when the patient's personality shifts from BI to Sally, symptoms like abdominal pains, headaches, and physical exhaustion disappear.[22]

As this description shows, the patient fulfills the first condition for the diagnosis of dissociative identity disorder. The differing characteristics of BI and Sally suggest that here two distinct identities exist that shape their relationship to themselves and their surroundings in different ways: there are two different patterns of perception, attitude, and thought.

Miss Beauchamp also fulfills the other conditions. The identities BI and Sally determine her behavior at different times. Dr. Prince's study shows this in great detail. The numerous pranks and nasty tricks that Sally plays on BI are good examples. For instance, one day BI finds a present and when she opens it, lots of spiders scamper out, which of course greatly shocks her as an arachnophobe. Sally prepared this package beforehand, without BI's knowledge, with the aim of frightening BI. On other occasions, Sally hides money, leaving BI only a minimum of spending money. This fulfills the second condition: the spiders are collected and packed in the *Sally* identity, whereas when the package is opened, the behavior is determined by the *BI* identity.[23] In fact, BI suffers total amnesia about all of Sally's activities and inner processes,[24] which fulfills the third condition.[25]

After multiple personality was established as a psychiatric diagnosis in the second half of the nineteenth century, Morton Prince's work represented a crowning achievement among studies on the matter. At the same time, it marked the beginning of the end of this diagnosis. The dissociative psychology upon which the diagnosis is based gradually made way for psychoanalysis. Psychological fragmentations were now increasingly understood as cases of schizophrenia.[26] Between 1920 and 1970, multiple personality was hardly used as a psychiatric diagnosis,[27] but starting in the 1970s, it experienced a renaissance in North America.

The diagnosis of multiple personality disorder or dissociative identity disorder remains very controversial to this day. Proponents say it finally diagnoses a long-ignored but real disease. Critics regard the "disease" as purely imaginary, as a something that is suggested to the patients by their psychotherapists. As arguments they adduce factors such as: 1) the initial restriction of the diagnosis to North America after its reintroduction, 2) the spread of the "disease" from there, and 3) the many scandals involving false diagnoses.[28]

I will not make any judgment about the validity of this diagnosis.[29] Besides, multiple personality is not grasped here as a psychiatric category. My interest is in the *philosophical concepts* that are applied in cases of multiple personality. For example, in *Sybil*, Vicky regards herself and Sybil as *two* autonomous *persons*. Sally in Prince's *The Dissociation of a Personality* makes similar claims about herself and BI. She talks about BI in the third person and states that she is not BI. Dr. Prince initially does not want to let this statement stand, since at first Sally never appears except under hypnosis. That's why, at an early point in the therapy, he insists that Sally is really identical to BI:

> "You are 'She,' " I said. [Dr. Prince]
> "No, I am not." [Sally]
> "I say you are."
> Again a denial.[30]

Later he demands an explanation from her:

> "Why are you not 'She'?"
> "Because 'She' does not know the same things that I do."
> "But you both have the same arms and legs, haven't you?"
> "Yes, but arms and legs do not make us the same."[31]

Here, Sally expresses a stance that makes use of philosophical ideas. She insists: I am not she. The concepts *I* and *she* are thereby to be understood in such a way that the claim is still true even if the referents of "I" and "she" share one body. Sally thus propounds the controversial view that she need not be identical to someone whose arms and legs are also her own arms and legs. She thereby enters the field of philosophical questions about personal identity. My interest is in philosophical concepts like *I*, *she/he*, *we*, *personality*, *self*, *body*, and *identity*, concepts that often arise in cases of multiple personality.

As mentioned, the validity of the psychiatric diagnosis is not the topic here. Another clarification is equally important: *The Dissociation of a Personality* and *Sybil* deal with genuine cases. The utterances from BI, Sally, Sybil, and Vicky quoted in them, however, do not necessarily express the self-understanding of *actually existing persons*, as can be illustrated by Sally's case. Sally first appears in the therapeutic interaction between Miss Beauchamp and Dr. Prince. So it could be argued that Sally's utterances are a *product* of the therapeutic interaction. Dr. Prince is fascinated by the case and especially by Sally, and he contributes decisively to the cultivation of the various personalities. So it could be claimed that he artificially produces the personalities. Additionally, Miss Beauchamp registers Dr. Prince's interest in the various personalities. This suggests the possibility that *she* produces personalities in order to please Dr. Prince or to toy with him. Chapter 8 will delve in detail into such interpretational questions about Prince's study. But it is clear that it cannot be assumed that Sally's utterances express her or Miss Beauchamp's true self-understanding. Due to the dynamics of the therapeutic situation, such doubts also remain even if the therapist proceeds more cautiously than Dr. Prince did.

But we need not answer the question whether the self-understanding of an actually existing person is expressed or not in such cases. The use of philosophical concepts in multiple personality is interesting not because the self-understanding of actually existing persons is expressed here, but because we all believe that in such cases we *understand* what these persons mean *without grasping it entirely*. Max Frisch's novel *I'm Not Stiller* helps elucidate this: A man is arrested one day and accused of traveling on a forged passport. He has the following talk with his appointed defense attorney:

> "So you admit, Herr Stiller, that your American passport was a fake?" [the defending council]
> "My name's not Stiller!" [the accused]
> "I have been informed . . . that you are presumed—I say presumed—to be none other than Anatol Ludwig Stiller, born in Zürich, sculptor, married to Frau Julika Stiller-Tschudy, disappeared six years ago, last address 11 Steingartengasse, Zürich. I have been appointed—"
> "—to defend Herr Stiller."
> "Yes."
> "My name is White." . . .
> "Why aren't you Stiller?" he asked.
> "Because I am not."[32]

In light of the novel as a whole, the defense attorney is right about one point: there is only one human being. He used to answer to the name "Stiller," is now in prison, and calls himself by another name. But this does not make the prisoner's utterances any less comprehensible. Even if Mr. White shares a body with Herr Stiller, we think we can understand what he means by saying that he—White—is not Stiller. Mr. White uses the same language as Vicky and Sally. And we believe we can understand their way of speaking by thinking our way into their perspectives. Perhaps White, Vicky, and Sally do not all mean the same thing. But we believe we can understand them all, while at the same time assuming that we have not completely grasped them. Precisely this makes the cases so fascinating.

This is why my object of study, *multiple personality*, is not limited to real cases. Accordingly, I define the concept of multiple personality as follows: a case or a narration is about *multiple personality* if it is literally or metaphorically about a person's split into more than one person, personality, self, or I. That is why the concept of multiple personality covers classical doppelganger stories in addition to cases of multiple personality disorder.

Having defined the concept of multiple personality, I will now explain the methodological approach to the topic in more detail.

3 FROM MULTIPLE PERSONALITY TO PERSONAL IDENTITY

According to thesis 1, Sally regards herself as one of several fundamental entities in one body, not as a personality facet of a single fundamental entity. But this thesis cannot be entirely correct. Sally (or Vicky or Mr. White) does not use a concept like *fundamental entity*, which is a philosophical construct. And yet it is clear that Sally has entered the realm of philosophical questions. She is not willing to accept that she and BI are merely two personality facets, as is detailed in Chapter 8. Sally thereby employs philosophical concepts that have specific circumstances and consequences of application. These concepts cannot be completely understood without unraveling these circumstances and consequences. To this end, a philosophical explication of these concepts is indispensable. This means that thesis 4 is true: multiple personality involves philosophical concepts whose analysis is indispensable for an adequate understanding of this phenomenon.

One the main aims of this book is to unravel what the self-understanding of Sally and similar characters amounts to if philosophically thought through. Accordingly, I propound thesis 1 in a modified form:

> *Thesis 1**: Vicky and similar characters in cases of multiple personality understand themselves in a way that, if thought through philosophically, implies the assumption that each is respectively one fundamental entity among two or more in one body.

Of course, this thesis must be demonstrated for the various characters that will be investigated here. I have defined *multiple personality* broadly—encompassing multiple personality disorder as well as doppelganger stories—in the expectation that general theses like thesis 1* can be valid for quite different kinds of cases. In addition to arguing for the general validity of this thesis, however, it is equally important to investigate the various cases in their individual quality. Even if it is true that all the individual cases involve attitudes that, if philosophically thought through, imply the same philosophical assumption, these attitudes are not philosophical theories, but stances that each have their own additional meaning in their individual contexts. My philosophical elaborations aim not only to unravel and defend certain explicit philosophical theses, but also to cast light on the individual contexts by means of the contrast with such theses.

My interest in elaborating the specific character of the individual contexts is also the reason why this study of multiple personality focuses on a detailed investigation of three different cases.[33] The three texts that will be extensively discussed are the aforementioned psychiatric case study *The Dissociation of a Personality*, the self-help book *Amongst Ourselves: A Self-Help Guide to Living with Dissociative Identity Disorder*, and the novel *Fight Club*. I shall then use the results of these three investigations to cast light on other similar phenomena, texts, and contexts.

At this point, the following explanation will have to suffice as to my choice of texts: In contrast to all contemporary case studies of multiple personality as a psychiatric disorder that I am aware of—mostly either popular science biographies or short scientific reports—Morton Prince's *The Dissociation of a Personality* (1906) is a scientific treatment of the topic and at the same time one of the richest case descriptions known. In addition, the basic ideas of dissociative psychology, on which Prince bases his scientific account of multiple personality, have not changed to this day. *Amongst Ourselves* (1998) has been chosen as a contrast to Prince's book: this self-help book for people with dissociative identity disorder contains theoretical and practical instructions jointly composed by two authors. In addition, it contains many inserted passages that one of the two authors wrote in the voice of one or another of her various personalities. The authors pursue a therapeutic approach completely different from that of Dr. Prince, and in contrast to his work, this is not a psychiatrist's report about his treatment of his patient. Finally, the novel *Flight Club* (1997) is not only a suspenseful doppelganger story, but also contains explicit references to multiple personality disorder.

Thesis 1* is my central thesis with respect to multiple personality. I shall argue that many aspects of multiple personality become intelligible in light of this thesis. However, this thesis cannot account for all the complexities of the phenomenon. For example, even assuming—as I do in thesis 3—that in all cases of multiple personality there exists only one fundamental entity, there remains the possibility of a radical fragmentation of this fundamental entity into several personalities or selves. Even if Sally wrongly thinks she is one of several fundamental entities in one body, might she be one of several distinct personalities or selves in one body? What would that mean? To do justice to the complexity of multiple personality, I shall also address such issues.

> He is such a coward! He can't face my existence. He resides in his world of words and eliminates me by a stipulation. He arbitrarily makes the conditions for the existence of two "fundamental entities" in one body virtually impossible to fulfill. This is not a scientific discovery. It's a verdict over me: death by definition.

One fruitful way of understanding the fragmentation of one fundamental entity into different selves is to interpret it as part and parcel of a person's unresolved struggle to settle who she is—a struggle that can manifest itself in a battle between the selves for the title of "the real self." All of the three texts under study here will be examined in terms of this issue. In each case, I shall explicate how a philosophical topic or concept is at work in these examples, while at the same time elucidating the nonphilosophical aspects of each particular context. In other words, for each case I will ask the following questions: How would one have to understand the relevant concepts if they were purely philosophical concepts? What philosophical stance should one take on the relevant issue? And how must these concepts be understood given that they are not part of a purely philosophical context? What nonphilosophical position might thus be appropriate in the relevant contexts?

Let me briefly illustrate this for each text. The second part of *The Dissociation of a Personality* bears the title "The Hunt for the Real Miss Beauchamp." Dr. Prince is convinced that there is a "real Miss Beauchamp" and regards it as his task to discover her. This raises the philosophical question of whether persons have a "real self" at all. Dr. Prince's idea of the "real self" of his patient is characterized by ambivalence. His stance offers a good background for the question of whether it can at all be a psychiatrist's task to define a "real self" and to make it the patient's only self, at the expense of the other personalities.

Amongst Ourselves takes a completely different approach to this theme, in that this self-help book assumes that one body may quite properly be populated by many persons, with equal rights, who make all decisions in life collectively. I am skeptical about the assumption of a "real self," but the question arises as to whether the view propounded in *Amongst Ourselves* does not go too far, resulting in the dissolution of the person. In answering this question, one must not forget that this view is not a philosophical theory, but a picture of human beings sketched in a self-help book.

In *Fight Club*, the search for the self is a theme that is explored in various ways, and a solution is suggested that stands in marked opposition to the approaches in *The Dissociation of a Personality* and *Amongst Ourselves*. As the title suggests, the novel is about men who beat each other into unconsciousness in secret clubs. The goal seems to be to thrash away social identity and the self, so that the person reaches a starting point of freedom and is thus in a position to freely define himself. The protagonist's fights with his doppelganger—i.e., with himself—symbolize a dramatic conflict between social identity and autonomous choice. Philosophically, one could say that the novel sketches—in an existential vein—the possibility of self-assertion beyond all socially defined concepts and words. As will emerge, however, such a statement would be a simplification of the novel's complex narrative reflections on the self and its possible fragmentations.

Compared to the topics involved in thesis 1*, the issues of the "real self" and other philosophical questions relating to multiple personality will not be discussed at length in this study. I shall only address these other issues to the extent that this is necessary to supplement thesis 1* for the sake of doing justice to the complexities of multiple personality. The following are some of these other topics: Must a person with multiple personality be understood as someone who tells various stories about himself and lives them out in various personalities? What is the relationship between the person and the personalities—who is the narrator? How is the split between the personalities to be understood? Can the personalities directly perceive the thoughts and feelings of the other personalities? Can they communicate among themselves? Can they make independent decisions? Are the personalities the expression of unconscious psychological conflicts? In what relation does the concept of one's own unconscious stand to the concept of a second personality or of a second consciousness? Are multiple personalities symptoms or symbols of an economic culture that levels individuality? Or are they authentic encounters with the Other in oneself? None of these questions is purely philosophical, but it would be equally false to say they are not philosophical. My aim is to make these themes visible in the respective texts and to offer a philosophical framework for resolving the questions they raise.

In conclusion, a word on the structure of the book and on its place in research literature. The study consists of three parts. After the introductory Part I, Part II develops—independently of the theme of multiple personality—a philosophical theory of personal identity over time. Multiple personality is then discussed in Part III against the backdrop of this theory. In contrast to other philosophical monographs on multiple personality, I intend to investigate this phenomenon on the basis of a full-fledged philosophical theory of personal identity.[34] Some works on personal identity refer to multiple personality. One of the ways this book differs from them is that here multiple personality is examined in much greater detail and also defined in such a way that it covers more than just the psychiatric cases.

Part III discusses not only multiple personality but also the philosophical question of individuation. This part begins in Chapter 8 with an interpretation of Prince's *The Dissociation of a Personality*. The discussion of Sally's stance in this chapter serves to motivate the philosophical question of whether more than one fundamental entity can exist in one body. After a critical examination of other philosophical theories on the topic (Chapter 9), this question will be answered with a yes in Chapter 10 (thesis 2 = the coexistence thesis). In Chapters 10 and 12, a criterion of individuation will be developed in order to determine exactly when more than one fundamental entity exists in one body. Chapter 11 examines the relationship of two fundamental entities in one body to their shared body. Chapters 10–12, together with the theory of identity over time in Part II, then comprise a complete theory of personal identity. This theory puts me in a position to return to multiple personality and offer a systematic account of this phenomenon in *Amongst Ourselves*, *Fight Club*, and other works and contexts (Chapters 13–14). This must suffice as an overview of this study until the philosophical questions of personal identity are introduced in the next chapter.

3 Personal Identity

This chapter is an introduction to the issues of personal identity as discussed in the research literature and as approached in this study. In section 1, I argue that we must distinguish between several questions when entering the field usually termed "personal identity." Although these questions are normally not adequately distinguished, I think that in the literature the focus is mostly on the diachronic identity of fundamental entities. The second section provides an overview of the main theories of diachronic identity and their problems. I also describe what kind of an approach is needed to solve these problems, an approach that will then be developed in Part II. Finally, in the third section, I explain why and how a theory of personal identity must engage with multiple personality, a task taken on in Part III.

1 QUESTIONS

Questions like the following belong to the thematic complex of "personal identity": "Will I still exist after my earthly death?" "Even if all my mental functions cease irreversibly, my heart can still beat and I can still breathe. A human being can still exist in a purely vegetative state. In such a state, would I continue to exist as this human being, or would my existence be ended?" "I have a major traffic accident and fall into a coma. Half a year later, a human being wakes up from the coma, but can remember nothing from her life before the coma and has to learn every conceivable human ability. Was the traffic accident my end, or am I the person who awakes from the coma?" "Does my existence begin at my birth or in the womb (or after artificial insemination)? If it begins in the womb, at what point in time does it begin?"

Such questions can be formulated more generally: "When does my existence end? When does it begin? What are the conditions of my diachronic identity?" Which answer is correct depends on what I am fundamentally. To ask the question "*What am I fundamentally?*" is to ask under which *fundamental concept* I fall. To answer this question is to say *what concept determines the conditions of my identity*. One possible answer would be: I am fundamentally a human being, or *human being* is the fundamental concept under which I fall. This answer would then have to be elucidated in more detail by explaining the concept of a human being. One possible understanding of this concept would be that a human being is a purely biological being whose existence begins and ends with the beginning and end, respectively, of life, understood purely biologically. Some of the consequences of this would be: My existence begins shortly after I am conceived in the womb. I still exist in a purely vegetative state in which all my mental functions have irreversibly ceased, but I cannot survive my biological death.

The answers to the questions posed at the beginning thus depend on the answer to *the question of the fundamental concept*:

> What am I fundamentally? Or: what concept determines the conditions of my identity? (*Question 1*)

Here a certain terminology is useful. The question "What am I fundamentally?" must always be answered in such a way that I am a certain kind of entity. This entity will be called "fundamental entity" here. In other words: if one answers the question "What concept determines the conditions of my identity?" with *human being* or *person*, one thereby says that human beings or persons, respectively, are the fundamental entities. Accordingly, here the question of the conditions of my diachronic identity will be called "*the question of the diachronic identity of fundamental entities*":

> Under what conditions is X at time t_1 one and the same individual fundamental entity as Y at time t_n? (*Question 2*)[1]

If the right answer to question 1 is "I am a human being," then question 2 is: "Under what conditions is X at t_1 *one and the same individual human being* as Y at t_n?"[2] The complex of questions consisting of questions 1 and 2 is my reconstruction of the theme that, in the philosophical literature, has most frequently been discussed under the category of "personal identity."[3]

There are several reasons for this interpretation of the theme, even if it has seldom been so explicitly formulated.[4]

First: questions 1 and 2 make clear which *controversial issues* the various theories in the philosophical discussion about diachronic identity disagree about. This can be shown using our example of a human being who lives in a vegetative state. Is the human being in a vegetative state one and the same individual as the human being who had the accident causing this state? Some say yes with the justification that this is continuously one and the same human being. Some say no with the justification that the human being in a vegetative state is not a person. The two parties may agree that the human being in this state is not a person, since he can neither think nor feel. For this reason, they can also agree that this cannot continuously be the same *person*. They may also agree that this is continuously one and the same *human being*. But in what, then, can the disagreement consist? What stand do the two parties want to justify with their respective justifications? We can make sense of the disagreement if we assume that what is at issue is a question everybody can ask herself: if I had had this accident, would *I* continue to exist in a vegetative state? The two parties give different answers to this question by giving different answers to questions 1 and 2. (It will later be elucidated why the phrase "one and the same individual" cannot replace the first personal formulation of the issues.)

Second: It is crucial to pose the question of diachronic identity in such a way that the formulation *does not automatically exclude any relevant answer*. Questions 1 and 2 are understood here in such a way that they assume the following: (A) They are questions about the *common conditions of identity for everyone who can pose question 1* and (B) who is also a *human being*. Questions 1 and 2 together with these preconditions fulfill the condition of not excluding in advance any relevant stand on the issue at stake.

As (A) makes clear, the question "What am I fundamentally?" is not to be understood as a question that asks about the conditions of identity solely for the person asking the question at the moment. Rather, the person posing the question is looking for the *common* conditions of identity for *all who can also pose this question*. Without limitation (B), however, relevant answers to 1 and 2 would be excluded. One cannot simply assume that only human beings can pose question 1. Perhaps there are angels or other extraterrestrials that can ask it, and perhaps even computers or great apes can ask it, too. Since the concept of human being cannot provide any *common* conditions of identity for a group of persons that is not restricted to humans, if there were no limitation (B), "I am a human being" would be automatically excluded as an answer to question 1. But with limitation (B), there is no exclusion either of this answer or of an answer according to which every human being who can pose question 1 has conditions of identity that apply to all persons, whether they are human beings or not.

To avoid automatically excluding any relevant answers, we must work with a question formulated in the first person. This becomes clear if we examine two other ways of framing the issue that exclude important answers. In the philosophical discussion about diachronic identity, questions 1 and 2 are not normally posed. Instead, it is often simply asked: is X at t_1 one and the same *person* as Y at t_n? Or one asks: is X at t_1 one and the same *human being* as Y at t_n? If the topic is formulated in either of these two ways rather than through questions 1 and 2, then important answers are excluded. Let me provide an example to illustrate this point: "After one's death as a human being, can one be reborn as a sheep?" According to some theories of diachronic identity, this is definitely possible. But these theories are excluded in advance if the question is: "Is X at t_1 one and the same person as a sheep at t_n?" or "Is X at t_1 one and the same human being as a sheep at t_n?" The reason is that a sheep is neither a person nor a human being. Questions 1 and 2, by contrast, do not exclude continued existence as a sheep. If the answer to question 1 is that I am fundamentally an entity that can continue to exist as a sheep, then I can continue to exist as a sheep. Of course, this might not be the right answer to question 1, but this answer is not already excluded by the way the issue is formulated.

Third: Why do we need *two* questions here, i.e., question 1 *and* question 2? What is the relationship between these two questions? As already noted, *the correct answer to question 2 depends on the answer to question 1.* But an answer to question 1 like "I am a person" provides no answer to question 2 and instead merely says how one must approach question 2: if I am fundamentally a person, then it must be established what the conditions of the diachronic identity of persons are. It is possible to give an answer to question 2 without explicitly answering question 1. For example, one could answer question 2 such that X at t_1 is one and the same fundamental entity as Y at t_n, if there is psychological continuity between X and Y. This answer is not compatible with all possible answers to question 1 (for example, the answer "I am a purely biological being of the species *homo sapiens*"); however, it is compatible with more than one answer to question 1. It may be compatible with the answer "I am a bundle of psychological states" as well as with the answer "I am a thinking substance." But if the right answer to question 1 has been found, the right analysis of the conditions of identity of the fundamental entity specified in this answer determines the rightness of answers to question 2.

Fourth: As the first three reasons show, the formulation of the issue by means of questions 1 and 2 has significant advantages. Nevertheless, one could argue that these advantages can be retained without formulating the topic in the first person. One suggestion would be to replace question 1 with the following question: "What concept determines the conditions of identity for every X that is simultaneously a person and a human being?" It would be good if this approach worked, because some discussants—even if wrongly—object to formulating the issue in the first person.[5]

But since phrasing the question in this way leads to a problem, we must stay with question 1. The position can be held that every X that is simultaneously a person and a human being actually consists of two individuals coexisting as X: a person and a human being. One could understand the relationship between the two individuals the way some theories conceive the relationship between a statue and the piece of material from which the statue is made. According to these theories, two individuals coexist here—the piece of material and the statue—that have differing conditions of identity.[6] The piece of material can exist without the statue, for example, if the material is melted. If X is simultaneously a person and a human being, one could say that two individuals with differing conditions of identity coexist in that same way. The human being existed before the person existed, and it can also continue to exist after the person no longer exists—if, for example, it exists in a purely vegetative state. But the person might possibly also exist without the human being—if, for example, it is possible to have a being come into existence by gradually replacing a human being's biological processes with the mechanisms of a robot.

Now, if two individuals coexist in this way in X, then there is no answer to the question "What concept determines the conditions of identity for every X that is simultaneously a person and a human being?" Here there are *two individuals*, and *different concepts* determine their respective conditions of identity. The idea that two individuals can coexist in this way may turn out to be wrong. But we would have to exclude this approach if we started out with the question "Which concept determines the conditions of identity of every X that is simultaneously a person and a human being?" And, if possible, we should not automatically exclude relevant positions on this topic simply by how we formulate the question. This problem can be avoided if we stick to question 1. Even if I am simultaneously a person and a human being, it makes sense to ask which of the two concepts—*person* or *human being*—determines the conditions of *my* identity.[7] Two individuals may coexist here—the human being and the person—but *I* am only one of these individuals. For example, if I am fundamentally a human being, then for a certain period of my existence I am also a person (in the way that a certain piece of gold can also temporarily be a statue), but the person has other conditions of identity than I do (in the way that the statue has other conditions of identity than the piece of gold). Question 1 asks which of the two individuals I am.[8]

Questions 1 and 2 must be distinguished from another thematic complex. At the end of Willa Cather's novel *The Professor's House*, the protagonist—the history professor Godfrey St. Peter—daydreams about the little boy he once was in Kansas:

> Now that the vivid consciousness of an earlier state had come back to him, the Professor felt that life with this Kansas boy, little as there had been of it, was the realest of his lives, and that all the years between had been accidental and ordered from the outside. His career, his wife, his family, were not his life at all, but a chain of events which had happened to him. All these things had nothing to do with the person he was in the beginning.
>
> The man he was now, the personality his friends knew, had begun to grow strong during adolescence . . . Because there was marriage, there were children. Because there were children, and fervor in the blood and brain, books were born as well as daughters. His histories, he was convinced, had no more to do with his original ego than his daughters had; they were a result of the high pressure of young manhood.[9]

Here the professor distinguishes between the person or personality who he now is ("the man he was now, the personality his friends knew") and the person or personality who he was as a boy ("the person he was in the beginning," "his original ego"). In doing so, he unquestionably assumes that he is thinking the whole time of himself as one and the same fundamental entity: the life of the boy from Kansas was "the realest of *his* lives" and *he* is now a specific person or personality and was originally another. So there is only one fundamental entity, but at least two persons or personalities of this fundamental entity, the boy from Kansas and the professor who now reminisces. Now we can ask about the *diachronic identity* of these *personalities*:

> Personalities P_1 at t_1 and P_n at t_n are personalities of one and the same individual fundamental entity. Under what conditions is P_1 at t_1 one and the same individual personality as P_n at t_n? (*Question 3*)[10]

This question presupposes the continuous existence of one and the same individual fundamental entity in the sense of question 2. If in philosophical discussions about diachronic identity the question is posed "Is X at t_1 one and the same individual person as Y at t_n?" then it must clarified whether question 2 or question 3 is meant. To be able to assess the various theories, it is necessary to distinguish between the two questions, although this is much too often neglected in the literature on "personal identity." Here is just one example as illustration: According to the so-called *psychological criterion*, from one time to another, we can speak of one and the same individual person only if enough psychological connections exist between these two successive points in time. These psychological connections are causal relationships, but they also presuppose a *relation of similarity* between the two psychological states that they connect. To test this theory, we must examine it separately for questions 2 and 3. Are relations of psychological similarity necessary for there to be one and the same individual *fundamental entity*? Are they necessary for there to be one and the same individual *personality*? It is possible that the answer is different for the two questions. In any case, it is crucial that the theory be tested separately for the two questions.

Let us return to questions 1 and 2. Answers to question 2 leave open another question concerning the conditions of identity of fundamental entities. This can be made clear using an example of conjoined twins. The twins Abigail and Brittany Hensel, born in 1990, have a total of two arms and two legs, with Abigail moving one arm and one leg and Brittany moving the other arm and the other leg. Below their separate heads and necks they have what seems from the outside to be a common body. Although they have separate hearts and spinal cords, they have a common circulatory system and common reproductive organs. Their movements are well coordinated; they play sports like basketball and volleyball and in 2006 they acquired a driver's license.[11]

Let us now examine two possible answers to question 1 and question 2: "Human beings are the fundamental entities. There is diachronic identity if one and the same individual human being continuously exists." "Persons are the fundamental entities. There is diachronic identity if one and the same individual person continuously exists." Each of these answers to questions 1 and 2 could be applied to Abigail as well as to Brittany. If human beings are the fundamental entities, then Abigail has existed since 1990, because Abigail today and the Abigail born in 1990 are one and the same human being. If persons are the fundamental entities, then Abigail's diachronic identity with the Abigail born in 1990 is based on the fact that they are one and the same person. The same is true of Brittany. But this would not answer the question of whether Abigail and Brittany *are two human beings* or *one and the same human being* (or for the second answer: *two persons* or *one and the same person*). In other words: the question would not be answered as to whether Abigail and Brittany are one or two fundamental entities. So the question of the *individuation of fundamental entities* must still be posed:

> X at t_1 and Y at t_n are one and the same individual fundamental entity (= FE). W at t_{1+1} and Z at t_{n+1} are one and the same individual fundamental entity (= FE*). Under what conditions are FE and FE* one and the same individual fundamental entity? (*Question 4*)

This is the philosophically decisive question about multiple personalities that can be elucidated by using Dr. Jekyll and Mr. Hyde from Robert Louis Stevenson's famous novel. "Dr. Jekyll" and "Mr. Hyde" are two names for one human being. "Dr. Jekyll" designates this human being whenever he behaves like the benevolent medical doctor whom other persons know under this name. "Mr. Hyde" designates this human being at all the other times in his life, i.e., at those times when he behaves like a monster and answers to the name "Mr. Hyde." Now we can assume the following: Dr. Jekyll at t_1 and Dr. Jekyll at t_n are one and the same fundamental entity. Mr. Hyde at t_{1+1} and Mr. Hyde at t_{n+1} are also one fundamental entity. Question 4 asks whether they are one and the same fundamental entity.

It is quite possible to answer the question of the diachronic identity of fundamental entities (question 2) differently than the question of the individuation of fundamental entities (question 4). For example, one could answer question 2 as follows: Dr. Jekyll at t_1 and Dr. Jekyll at t_n are one and the same fundamental entity because there continuously exists *one and the same first-person perspective*. According to this answer, Dr. Jekyll's diachronic identity is independent of bodily or human identity: if one and the same first-person perspective continuously existed, Dr. Jekyll would continue to exist in another body. This is compatible with an answer to question 4 stating that Dr. Jekyll and Mr. Hyde are one fundamental entity because they are *one human being* (or *one body*).[12]

If one comes to the conclusion that the case of Dr. Jekyll and Mr. Hyde concerns *one fundamental entity*, one can still ask whether they are *two personalities* (*the individuation of personalities*):

> X at t_1 and Y at t_n are one and the same individual personality (= P). W at t_{1+1} and Z at t_{n+1} are one and the same individual personality (= P*). P is a personality of the same individual fundamental entity as P*. Under what conditions are P and P* one and the same individual personality? (*Question 5*)

Here we have only one fundamental entity. The personality "Dr. Jekyll" at t_1 and the personality "Dr. Jekyll" at t_n are one and the same individual personality. The personality "Mr. Hyde" also exists continuously as one and the same individual personality. In this case, question 5 asks whether one or two personalities exist here.

Questions 1, 4, and 5 provide the foundation for a philosophical investigation into multiple personality. Theses 2 and 3 from the last chapter now have a clear meaning: each of us is a fundamental entity, of which there could exist two or more in one body (thesis 2). The conditions for the presence of more than one fundamental entity in one body are never fulfilled in reality (thesis 3). With these theses, a partial answer is given to questions 1 and 4: Thesis 1 presupposes an answer to question 1 ("What am I fundamentally?") that makes possible the existence of more than one fundamental entity in one body. It is also presupposed that the answer to question 4 is such that the conditions for the existence of more than one fundamental entity in one body are in fact never fulfilled. But this does not exclude the possibility that the answer to question 5 is such that the conditions for the existence of more than one personality in one body are indeed often fulfilled.

> I am not a mere personality facet! What degrading insults: personality, personality facet, self!! I am I. He is he. We are two entirely separate beings. Alas, we share the same líkami, body, I mean. (By the way, he doesn't seem at home in his body, really. So I don't see why *I* should be the one "leaving.")

Of course, not all of the questions that are discussed under the rubric of "personal identity" can be mentioned here. An additional question, for example, is the *question of the "true self"*:

> Who am I? (*Question 6*)

In asking this question it is assumed that some of my characteristics do not express who I "really" am—they are not part of my "true self." Thus, Stevenson's character might ask himself whether the personality "Mr. Hyde" is his "true self." As with the questions concerning the conditions of the diachronic identity and the individuation of personalities, here it is presupposed that we are dealing with *one fundamental entity*. Even if the personality "Mr. Hyde" were the "true self" of a fundamental entity, "Dr. Jekyll" would equally be a personality of the same fundamental entity.

The question "What is a person?" often implicitly or explicitly plays an important role in the literature on "personal identity." For those theories according to which persons are the fundamental entities, this is an important question. But if the answer to question 1 is, for example, "I am a purely biological being of the species *Homo sapiens*," then what a person is, is not important for answering questions 2 and 4. This investigation will defend the following thesis as an answer to question 1: I am fundamentally an agent who is a correlate to the psychological relations for which this agent is minimally responsible. This thesis requires elucidation and will be discussed in detail later. Of course, one can ask whether every agent of this kind is a person and whether every person is an agent of this sort. We will not be dealing with such questions here. Our object of investigation is the question "What am I fundamentally?" and the conditions of the diachronic identity and the individuation of fundamental entities. If question 1 is answered in the way just mentioned, it is irrelevant whether fundamental entities are persons or not.

The question whether a being is a person is not unambiguous. For example, if one asks "Are the great apes persons?" two different issues may be at stake. This could be meant as a purely *theoretical* or *descriptive* question not raising the issue of the appropriate *moral* treatment of great apes. The descriptive question is often answered by saying that persons are beings that have certain characteristics, such as rationality and self-awareness. The question would then be precisely what conditions a being must fulfill to be a person, and whether great apes fulfill these conditions (for example, whether great apes have self-awareness):

> What is a person in a descriptive sense? (*Question 7*)

The question whether great apes are persons, however, sometimes has a different point—namely, whether they have a certain *moral status*, i.e., the moral status of a person, this being a status that might imply the right to life. Sometimes "person" is used here in a *purely* moral or normative sense: the statement "Great apes are persons" would then attribute to the great apes a certain moral status without making any descriptive statement about the great apes at all. But such statements often also amount to the attribution of a certain moral status on the basis of the fulfillment of the descriptive conditions that make something a person: it is often argued that great apes have a certain moral status (have the status of a person) because they are persons (because they fulfill certain descriptive conditions).

> How is the moral status *person* to be understood, and what gives an entity this status? (*Question 8*)

This question will not play a role in this investigation either.[13] *One* issue is whether the question "What am I fundamentally?" is to be answered in such a way that it implies that I existed as an embryo or fetus. *Another* question is whether embryos or fetuses are persons and what moral status they have.[14]

This investigation aims to give answers to the question of the fundamental concept (question 1), the question of the diachronic identity of fundamental entities (question 2), and the question of the individuation of fundamental entities (question 4). The questions of the diachronic identity and of the individuation of personalities and the question of the "true self" (questions 3, 5, and 6) will play a certain role in the argumentation, but no specific answer to these questions will be defended. Questions 7 and 8, by contrast, will play no role.

The topic here is thus actually the identity of fundamental entities. The term "personal identity" has nonetheless been retained in the title of the book and this chapter because questions 1–8 amount to an analysis of the issues that are normally discussed under the rubric of "personal identity," and the topic of this book is more easily identified by means of this term.

2 THEORIES

The issue usually discussed under the label of "personal identity" is surely the question of the *diachronic identity* of fundamental entities (question 2). In this section, I will reconstruct the theories most commonly offered in answer to this question and the problems they face.[15] The question of the *individuation* of fundamental entities (question 4) will be taken up in Part III.

The answers to question 2 can be distinguished on the basis of two characteristics: all theories are either circular or non-circular and either empirical or non-empirical.[16] The answers to this question formulate the conditions for X at time t_1 to be one and the same individual fundamental entity as Y at time t_n. A theory is *non-circular* if these conditions can be formulated without presupposing that X and Y are one and the same fundamental entity. Such a theory is exemplified by *biological* views according to which X and Y are one and the same fundamental entity if and only if *biological continuity* exists between X and Y. Non-circularity is given in this case if one can describe the conditions of biological continuity between X and Y without presupposing that X and Y are one and the same fundamental entity. Biological approaches are also *empirical*: this means that it is *in principle possible to empirically determine* whether the *conditions of diachronic identity*—in this case biological continuity—*hold*.

According to *non-empirical* conceptions, the constitutive conditions of diachronic identity are *completely independent of continuities that, in principle, can be discerned empirically,* continuities that can provide mere *evidence* that identity obtains. This difference between empirical and non-empirical theories can be made clear by the following thought experiment: Fair undergoes an operation that results in two fundamental entities, which can be named "L-Fairchild" and "R-Fairchild" since these two persons have received the left and right halves of Fair's brain. After the operation, there are only two fundamental entities: L-Fairchild and R-Fairchild. Certain continuities exist between Fair and L-Fairchild, on the one hand, and Fair and R-Fairchild, on the other hand. These could be biological continuities: perhaps Fair's body has been "halved" in this operation in such a way that after the operation nothing is left of Fair's body that is not a part of either R-Fairchild's or of L-Fairchild's body (perhaps artificial aids are implanted in the bodies of R-Fairchild and L-Fairchild, for example, to ensure the heart can beat in both cases). Or there are psychological continuities: perhaps L-Fairchild and R-Fairchild both have memories of Fair's experiences. The decisive point is that the following is true for these continuities: between Fair and L-Fairchild, on the one hand, and Fair and R-Fairchild, on the other hand, there are *no differences in the continuity* that—whether from a first-, second-, or third-person perspective—can *in principle be empirically discerned.* Theories are *non-empirical* if and only if, according to these theories, it is possible that Fair is identical[17] to *one* of her successors (i.e., either L-Fairchild or R-Fairchild) *in contrast to the other one*, despite the lack of empirical differences.[18] Empirical theories reject this possibility.

Most theories in the research literature are *either* simultaneously empirical and non-circular *or* both non-empirical and circular. Here are some examples of *empirical, non-circular* conceptions:

> X at t_1 and Y at t_n are one and the same individual fundamental entity if and only if . . . .
> . . . there is psychological continuity between X and Y (*psychological approach*)[19]
> . . . there is biological continuity between X and Y (*biological approach*)[20]
> . . . there is bodily continuity between X and Y (*bodily approach*).[21]

Of course, it is possible to combine these criteria.[22] Or one can make them more specific, for example, by claiming that the bodily continuity that is decisive is the continuity of the brain.[23] The proponents of the different theories, of course, must elucidate what the respective continuity consists in. I don't want to go into this in detail. While I do not want to go into detail here, I would like to offer the following observations to make these theories more palpable:

Let us return to the case of Katharina Beta, who had a severe traffic accident in 1970. Here, something serious happened to a specific biological being, but the biological organism remained functional throughout the entire event. That is why there is *biological continuity* between the person before the accident and the person after the accident. Now one could imagine another accident in which the bodily functions can only be maintained by replacing many organs with artificial implants. The more organic processes are replaced by processes controlled in other ways, the more questionable it becomes that there is still biological continuity here, even if one could say that *bodily continuity* is present. The accident made Katharina Beta forget practically everything: not only did she lose her personal memories, but also her general knowledge. The person after the accident will thus not remember the experiences of the person before the accident. The intentions and desires that the person before the accident had, as well as all of this person's knowledge, will also have been lost. Accordingly, one could say that there is no *psychological continuity* between Katharina Beta and the person before the accident. So these three theories could arrive at different claims as to whether a fundamental entity survives a severe accident or not.[24]

However one formulates the relevant continuity in detail, what is thereby decisive for these theories is that this continuity can be empirically discerned in principle and can be described non-circularly. Let me now provide two examples of the other primary type of theory in the literature, i.e., *non-empirical, circular* theories:

> X at t_1 and Y at t_n are one and the same individual fundamental entity if and only if . . .
>
> . . . X and Y are one and the same indivisible mental entity (*dualistic approach*)
>
> . . . X and Y have one and the same inner perspective (*inner-perspective approach*).[25]

A presupposition of such approaches is: it cannot be empirically discerned, in principle, or non-circularly described when X and Y are one and the same indivisible mental entity or when X and Y have one and the same inner perspective. The differences from the empirical, non-circular theories can be illustrated by means of religious ideas of reincarnation: I existed as a human being and am reborn as a dog. One must now imagine that there are no psychological, biological, or bodily continuities (or other empirical continuities) between me as a dog and me as a human being. If the human being and the dog are one and the same indivisible mental entity or have one and the same inner perspective, then according to these theories the human being and the dog would be one and the same fundamental entity, which once lived as a human being and is now reincarnated as a dog.[26] But the conditions for X and Y to be one and the same indivisible mental entity or to have one and the same inner perspective—the conditions for there to be one fundamental entity that lived earlier as a human being and later as a dog—can be formulated only circularly, i.e., they cannot be described without presupposing the identity of X and Y.

The dualistic and the inner-perspective approaches differ both ontologically and in relation to the relevance of the inner perspective. The dualistic approach makes the *ontological* assumption that in such cases there exists an indivisible mental entity ontologically separate from material entities. The inner-perspective approach does not involve any such ontological commitment.[27] But both theories must then say more about what this ontological commitment or neutrality means. The dualistic view is neutral in another respect, because the concept of an *inner perspective* plays no role in it. The other approach, by contrast, must say more about what it means that X and Y have one and the same *inner perspective*. This can be made clear by the example of reincarnation. According to the dualistic approach, for the human being and the dog to be one and the same fundamental entity, it suffices that they are one and the same indivisible mental entity. What it means that this identity is "mental" is not explained in detail. The inner-perspective conception makes a more specific commitment here: the being that gazed as a human being from its inner perspective onto itself or onto the world continues to gaze as a dog from this, its own inner perspective, onto the objects of its consciousness.[28] At this point, both theories need to say more about the identity of the "mentality" or "inner perspective," but I will not go into this here.

Empirical, non-circular theories are subject to two difficulties: the duplication problem and the unity reaction. Let us attend first to the *duplication problem*, which can be elucidated in five steps:[29]

1) In the aforementioned case of Fair, L-Fairchild, and R-Fairchild, an operation has given each of the latter two one of the halves of Fair's brain. As a first step, we are to imagine the non-fission case in which after the operation there is only L-Fairchild. In other words, the right half of Fair's brain is simply thrown away. Here it is assumed that there are enough empirically and non-circularly describable connections between Fair before the operation and L-Fairchild after the operation that Fair and L-Fairchild are one and the same fundamental entity (depending on the theory, these could be psychological, biological, or bodily connections). A comparable non-fission case can be described for Fair and R-Fairchild.

2) The second step is to consider the fission case. Here, after the operation, there are L-Fairchild and R-Fairchild and no other fundamental entity. The fission case is additionally defined in such a way that between Fair and L-Fairchild, on the one hand, and between Fair and R-Fairchild, on the other hand, there are sufficient empirically and non-circularly describable connections for it to hold true that, if these connections were to exist in non-fission cases, in the one non-fission case Fair would be identical to L-Fairchild and in the other non-fission case Fair would be identical to R-Fairchild.

3) Now we ask what has become of Fair in fission. There are only four possibilities:

(i) (Fair = L-Fairchild) & (Fair ≠ R-Fairchild)
(ii) (Fair = R-Fairchild) & (Fair ≠ L-Fairchild)
(iii) (Fair ≠ L-Fairchild) & (Fair ≠ R-Fairchild)
(iv) (Fair = L-Fairchild) & (Fair = R-Fairchild)

4) If the conditions of diachronic identity are understood as empirical, non-circular conditions, all of these possibilities must be rejected. Possibility (i) is ruled out for the following reasons. If Fair is one and the same fundamental entity as L-Fairchild, then this is so because of the empirically, non-circularly describable conditions that ensure the identity of Fair and L-Fairchild in the non-fission case. But then it cannot be true that Fair is identical to L-Fairchild, but not to R-Fairchild, because the empirically, non-circularly describable connections that ensure identity in the non-fission case are also present between Fair and R-Fairchild. If Fair is identical to L-Fairchild, then she would have to be identical to R-Fairchild as well.[30] This argumentation can be easily applied to possibility (ii).

Possibility (iii) is ruled out because of the assumption about the non-fission case. If in the non-fission case certain empirically, non-circularly describable conditions ensure the identity of Fair and L-Fairchild (or of Fair and R-Fairchild), then these connections would have to ensure the same in the case of splitting. This argumentation is based on "the only x and y principle,"[31] which stipulates that the diachronic identity of X and Y depends only on factors that are *intrinsic* to X, Y, or to the connections between them. There is no intrinsic difference between the set of Fair, L-Fairchild, and the connections between them in the non-fission case, on the one hand, and the same set in fission, on the other. The only difference is that, in fission, there is also R-Fairchild. Thus Fair must be identical to L-Fairchild in both cases. This argumentation also applies to Fair and R-Fairchild. Regarding (iv): Fair cannot be identical to both L-Fairchild and to R-Fairchild because L-Fairchild and R-Fairchild are two different fundamental entities.[32]

5) Because empirical, non-circular theories rule out every possible way of understanding Fair's fate in fission, such theories must be rejected, also for the non-fission case. If such theories cannot provide an adequate answer for fission, then they cannot do so for the non-fission case either. In the argumentation for this conclusion, the "the only x and y principle" is employed again: The relations between Fair and L-Fairchild in the non-fission case are not intrinsically different from those in fission. The only difference is that R-Fairchild does not exist in the non-fission case. But the answer to the question about the identity of Fair and L-Fairchild cannot depend on whether another individual exists, but only on the intrinsic relation between Fair and L-Fairchild (the only x and y principle). Since the intrinsic relation employed by such theories—empirically, non-circularly describable continuity—is present in fission as well as in the non-fission case, and reference to this relation cannot provide an adequate account of fission, diachronic identity cannot be based on this relation.

The duplication problem is one of the most serious difficulties that every empirical, non-circular theory must deal with.[33] But there is a *second* difficult problem for such theories. The problem is generated by asking one to imagine the following scenario: "I am Fair and I will soon undergo an operation whose results are L-Fairchild and R-Fairchild (i.e., two fundamental entities that stand in equal measure in an empirically, non-circularly describable continuity with myself). After the operation, L-Fairchild will wake up in pain in a noisy yellow room. R-Fairchild, by contrast, will wake up without pain in a quiet red room." Now you should ask yourself: "Is it possible that *I* wake up after the operation as *L-Fairchild in contrast to R-Fairchild* (or the reverse)? In other words: could it be that *I* wake up in pain in a loud, yellow room, while another individual wakes up as R-Fairchild, although there is no empirically, non-circularly describable difference between the connections between Fair and L-Fairchild, on the one hand, and between Fair and R-Fairchild, on the other hand?" The so-called *unity reaction* to this question is that this is possible.[34] If it is really possible, then empirical, non-circular theories are false.[35]

These two difficulties for empirical, non-circular approaches are, of course, at the same time arguments for non-empirical, circular theories. The duplication problem functions here as a purely negative argument; it is simply a problem that non-empirical, circular accounts do not have. Non-empirical positions were defined in such a way that non-empirical continuity between Fair and L-Fairchild (or R-Fairchild) can exist even if there are no empirical differences in the connections between Fair and her respective successors. The reference to the unity reaction, by contrast, is an attempt to provide a positive argument for non-empirical, circular approaches: if one considers it possible to wake up after the operation as L-Fairchild, rather than as R-Fairchild, then one therefore assumes that diachronic identity is based on non-empirical relations.

But there is a *third* difficulty that this time affects the *non-empirical, circular* theories. If a person awakes from a coma, normally there is a certain continuity between the state before and after the coma. More is meant here than bodily or biological continuity. The human being usually also has the abilities and beliefs that she had before the coma. In such a case, there is no doubt that it is one and the same fundamental entity before and after the coma. If there are empirical continuities of every relevant kind between a fundamental entity before a coma and a fundamental entity after a coma, then this is one and the same fundamental entity. This obviously presents a problem for all non-empirical accounts: according to such theories, no empirical continuities can guarantee that a fundamental entity continues to exist.[36]

All three difficulties are well known from the research literature. An adequate theory of diachronic identity must solve all three problems. Therefore, I would like to use these difficulties to arrive at three conditions of adequacy for a theory of diachronic identity. The first condition is generated directly from the problem of coma.

> *Empirical Discernibility (Condition of Adequacy 1)*: The diachronic identity of a fundamental entity rests on facts that can, in principle, be empirically discerned.

This explicitly and generally formulates why the person before the coma and the person after the coma are unquestionably one and the same fundamental entity. The second condition requires no commentary:

> *Solution of the Duplication Problem (Condition of Adequacy 2)*: The duplication problem must be solved.

I stated that the unity reaction is a problem for empirical approaches. But this cannot be true without qualification. If the first condition of adequacy is correct, then the unity reaction cannot be right: if diachronic identity rests on facts that can be empirically discerned, then it is not possible that Fair continues to exist as one of her successors, but not the other. And yet the unity reaction contains an important truth. But what truth, if the reaction is false? The unity reaction is a response to a request to look out from the present into one's own future. What is *right* about the unity reaction is that my identity to a future fundamental entity depends on relations that can exist *only once*. What is *false* is that in fission one could therefore be identical to one of one's own successors as opposed to the other. In other words: One's own identity depends on connections that, in fission, *cannot* obtain between a fundamental entity and both of her successors. These connections exist in the normal case in which there is no fission. One's own diachronic identity is based on these connections. (This is how we do justice to the truth in the unity reaction.) But in fission, these connections cannot obtain between the predecessor and one of her successors as opposed to the other. (This is how condition of adequacy 1 is fulfilled and the mistake in the unity reaction is avoided.)

> *The Truth in the Unity Reaction (Condition of Adequacy 3)*: The diachronic identity of fundamental entities is based on relations that, in fission, *cannot* exist between the predecessor, on the one hand, and both of her successors, on the other hand.

The unity reaction is a reaction from the first-person perspective. One asks oneself, "Would I continue to exist in such a case?" The reaction does thus not amount to a general claim about fission cases, in which there can be no such perspective. After all, one can imagine a ship or another lifeless object being structurally divided in the same way as Fair. The original ship stands in the same empirical relation to both of the successor ships that were built from the original ship. The unity reaction says nothing about such cases.[37] Accordingly, condition of adequacy 3 applies only to questions about *our* identity. This fits in with my interpretation of the identity of fundamental entities as an issue concerning the conditions of identity of human beings who can ask the question "What am I?"

Together, conditions of adequacy 1 and 3 are meant to ensure that a theory of diachronic identity takes into consideration how identity is understood from both the first-person and the third-person perspectives. As mentioned before, condition of adequacy 3 corresponds to a reaction from the first-person perspective. Condition of adequacy 1, by contrast, reflects the third-person perspective. This condition of adequacy implies that information that could be discovered from a third-person perspective is sufficient to determine whether diachronic identity obtains or not: diachronic identity is not a matter that can fundamentally elude knowledge from a third-person perspective.

One could object here that, with conditions of adequacy 1 and 3, I have already excluded almost all theories of diachronic identity: proponents of empirical, non-circular theories would naturally reject condition 3, and advocates of non-empirical, circular approaches do not accept condition 1, of course. While this is true, I have not arbitrarily invented these conditions; rather, they both reflect important aspects of the concept of the identity of fundamental entities. The fact that most theories in the literature must reject one of these conditions of adequacy does not speak against these conditions, but merely shows the dead end into which the philosophical discussion has maneuvered itself. In the literature, the theory options have been so limited that each option must reject at least one of the conditions of adequacy.[38] For this reason, we should look for another type of theory—a theory that can fulfill all the conditions of adequacy.

In point of fact, a promising theoretical option is usually overlooked in the research literature. If one distinguishes theories according to whether they are empirical or non-empirical and circular or non-circular, there are four possible positions. Two of them have not yet been mentioned here: empirical, circular accounts and non-circular, non-empirical approaches. I assume that non-circular, non-empirical theories are not an option. *Empirical, circular approaches*, by contrast, seem to be able to fulfill all three conditions of adequacy! Since they are empirical, they fulfill the first condition. Since they are circular, they presuppose that the identity of X and Y rests on connections that can be described only by assuming the identity of X and Y. This then rules out that such connections can obtain both between Fair and L-Fairchild and between Fair and R-Fairchild. Conditions of adequacy 2 and 3 are thus fulfilled at one blow: diachronic identity is based on relations that cannot be duplicated. My discussion of the various theories of diachronic identity and of the three conditions of adequacy can thus be summarized in table 3.1.[39]

Even if empirical, circular theories fulfill all three conditions of adequacy, this does not yet mean that one should accept such theories. One could even claim that there is no room for this type of theory: that the characteristics "empirical" and "circular" are mutually exclusive. Or it could be that such theories are problematic for other reasons or that the three conditions of adequacy are not unsatisfactorily fulfilled. For such a theory to be convincing, there must be other reasons than just the fulfillment of the three conditions. In Chapters 4–7, I will propose and defend an empirical, circular theory of diachronic identity.

Table 3.1 Theories of Diachronic Identity

	Non-circular	Circular
Empirical	Psychological theories Biological theories Bodily theories	Fulfill all three conditions of adequacy
Non-empirical	No theories?	Dualistic theories Inner-perspective theories

The theory I will set forth has similarities to approaches developed by Christine Korsgaard, Sydney Shoemaker, and Jennifer Whiting.[40] But in the research literature, discussants are loath to admit that they propose a circular theory. A good example of this is found in narrative self-constitution theories. According to such theories, diachronic identity is constituted by the story that a person tells about herself. If such conceptions are understood as theories of the diachronic identity of a *fundamental entity*, one might argue that they are circular. Although from my point of view circularity is not necessarily a problem, such approaches, as accounts of the diachronic identity of *fundamental entities*, are problematic for other reasons.[41] If such theories are interpreted as theories of the diachronic identity of *personalities* (question 3), it could be argued that they offer a promising non-circular account. But since the proponents of narrative self-constitution theories often do not make it clear whether such theories are meant to explain the identity of fundamental entities or of personalities, it remains unclear whether they belong to the category of "empirical and circular" or not.

This discussion shows that an additional condition of adequacy is necessary:

> *Differences between questions 1–8 (Condition of Adequacy 4)*: A theory of the identity of fundamental entities should do justice to the differences between questions 1–8.

The narrative self-constitution theory fails *as* an account of the diachronic identity of fundamental entities because a central element of this theory—narrative continuity—is relevant only for answering another question. More on this in Chapter 7.

3 FROM PERSONAL IDENTITY TO MULTIPLE PERSONALITY

Some human beings fall into a coma and wake up again without any impairment of their memory. In the course of their lives, all human beings go to sleep and wake up again. Human beings often change their opinions. If, like these human beings under these normal circumstances, I were to fall into a coma, go to sleep, or revise my conviction, would *I* then be the person who woke up from the coma or sleep or who had a new belief? Of course I would! These are all *normal cases*: cases in which there is no question of what the judgment of identity should be. Non-empirical theories must be rejected, because they cannot do justice to at least one such normal case, the coma case. In Chapter 4 I argue that the psychological criterion is false because it cannot adequately account for another normal case: change of belief.

> *Normal Cases as a Basis (Condition of Adequacy 5)*: A theory of the identity of fundamental entities should be developed on the basis of normal cases.

My methodological maxim is thus to develop my theory by first focusing on normal cases. The aim is thereby to *explicate* certain *concepts*: Since we start from the question "What am I?" the focus is on the explication of the concept *I*. The concepts *you* and *she/he* are then of course under study, since we are investigating our common conditions of identity.

Now, there are also *borderline cases*: cases to which the concept can be applied, but about which judgments of identity are controversial. Some cases of conjoined twins, for example, are such borderline cases in which one can ask whether the twins are two fundamental entities or one. Must an explication of concepts address borderline cases? It certainly need not go into every possible borderline case. One can imagine an unlimited number of borderline cases, and many of these cases are so removed from the normal conditions for applying the concept *I* that it makes no sense to distinguish between correct and incorrect judgments of identity. But in our lives we are confronted with many borderline cases that we don't have to imagine for ourselves: conjoined twins and multiple personalities are just two examples. Most explications of the concept *I* will have implications for the application of the concept to such borderline cases. For example, a biological account of the individuation of fundamental entities will imply that, in cases of multiple personality, there can always be only one fundamental entity. Here we will have to ask ourselves whether this implied judgment is correct. So it is unsatisfactory if a theory of the identity of fundamental entities does not make judgments about *any* borderline cases.

We must distinguish between three different uses of borderline cases: First, borderline cases are useful in making the differences between theories clear, differences that do not become visible in normal cases. Second, it can be necessary to use borderline cases to illustrate a judgment *about a normal case* that provides a reason for or against a certain theory. I will use borderline cases in this way in my discussion, and this is not controversial.

Only in my third use of borderline cases do they function as *test cases*. Here the idea is to take a theory that was developed on the basis of normal cases and confront it with borderline cases. One could refrain from applying the theory to borderline cases at all. Or one could apply the theory and simply accept the judgment that the theory implies for such cases. But neither possibility is satisfying as a strategy for all borderline cases. So instead, one must make judgments about the relevant borderline cases and be prepared, if necessary, to revise one's own theory in light of this judgment. But here the selection of borderline cases that are to be used as test cases is decisive. They must not be cases so far removed from the normal cases that it is doubtful that it makes sense to talk about a proper or improper application of the relevant concepts to these cases. Instead, the cases need to have a certain continuity with normal cases:

> *Borderline Cases as Test Cases (Condition of Adequacy 6)*: A theory of the identity of fundamental entities needs to survive a test of borderline cases that have sufficient continuity with normal cases.

It cannot be determined in general which borderline cases have *sufficient* continuity. But I think it can be shown that cases of multiple personality are close enough to normal cases and are precisely the borderline cases needed here. After I have developed my theory of diachronic identity on the basis of conditions of adequacy 1–5, the question whether more than one fundamental entity can exist in one body will remain open at the end of Part II. This is a question about a borderline case. But how should one respond to this borderline case? If one were to try to resolve this question only with the help of philosophical thought experiments, it could be objected that one is concerned with cases to which our concepts have no application.[42] Because I examine cases of multiple personality, this objection does not apply to my approach.

Cases of multiple personality exhibit many characteristics that, together, are enough to demonstrate sufficient continuity with normal cases. For six of these characteristics, I will emphasize the contrast to the thought experiments customary in the philosophical discussion:

1) *Cases of multiple personality*: philosophical concepts like *I* are employed here in complex contexts. *Philosophical thought experiments*: the concepts are presented in a decontextualized manner.

2) *Cases of multiple personality*: they are not invented for philosophical purposes. *Philosophical thought experiments*: they are normally made up by philosophers to support their own theories.

3) *Cases of multiple personality*: the use of the concepts is not detached from their normal employment in familiar life contexts. That is why we believe we understand the use of the concepts in these borderline cases, at least in part. *Philosophical thought experiments*: only sometimes is an effort made to establish contact with familiar contexts.

4) *Cases of multiple personality*: here one can study the relevant concepts in many different kinds of contexts. Accordingly, in this book, very different textual sources are examined. *Philosophical thought experiments*:

since thought experiments are invented for philosophical purposes, they are all shaped by this one goal.

5) *Cases of multiple personality*: sources on multiple personality contain not only uses of the relevant concepts, but also their *interpretations*, which reflect various areas of our culture and cultural history. *Philosophical thought experiments*: they are thought up and commented on by philosophers.

6) *Cases of multiple personality*: they often amount to a detailed and phenomenologically rich description of individual cases. To make the concepts comprehensible in their contexts of use, I offer in this book detailed examinations of three phenomenologically rich sources. *Philosophical thought experiments*: they are usually only sketched.

Now, how should we judge borderline cases of multiple personality and what relevance do these judgments have for philosophical theses on the identity of fundamental entities? One customary procedure using philosophical thought experiments is the following: One sketches various thought experiments and tries to respond as intuitively as possible to the question about the identity of the fundamental entities depicted in these thought experiments. These intuitive reactions then serve as the criterion for the rightness of accounts of identity. This is *not* my procedure in dealing with the borderline case of multiple personality. The point is not to respond intuitively to the question of whether several fundamental entities are present in such cases or not.

Instead, this book argues that the concept *I* must be understood in such a way that I could be one of several fundamental entities in one body (the coexistence thesis). A case in which more than one fundamental entity exists in one body is a borderline case. If the argument for the possibility of such a case is successful, this borderline case serves as a test case for theories of the individuation of fundamental entities: a theory would be problematic if it excluded this possibility. However, the philosophical significance of this borderline case lies in the philosophical argument for this possibility, not in an intuitive response to an imagined case.

The philosophical argument for the coexistence thesis must stand on its own. But this argument would be undermined if it could be shown that the concept *I* is used here in an area in which this concept has no determinable conditions of application. This is the reason why cases of multiple personality play an important role in my argumentation, assuming that these cases have sufficient continuity with normal cases. My procedure can be exemplified by the connection between the coexistence thesis and theses 1* and 3 from Chapter 2. The coexistence thesis is a philosophical thesis that must be supported with philosophical arguments. If thesis 1* is correct, then characters like Sally in cases of multiple personality take a position that, when thought through philosophically, implies the claim that they are each one of several fundamental entities in one body. Thesis 3 says that Sally and similar characters err in this position. So if one adheres, as I do, not only to the coexistence thesis but also to theses 1* and 3, then one establishes a connection to characters like

Sally. With these three theses, one claims that Sally and similar characters are right that it is *possible* that they are each one of several fundamental entities in one body, but that they err in thinking that this ever *actually* happens in their or anyone else's case. If one adheres to the coexistence thesis, one does not make any claim about cases that fall outside the area of the application of our concepts. On the contrary: the coexistence thesis has to do with an issue that is central in cases of multiple personality—i.e., cases that have the necessary continuity with normal cases. Here it becomes clearly visible how the two parts of my investigation interlock: Without an interpretation of multiple personality, the coexistence thesis lacks the necessary relationship to borderline cases that have the necessary continuity with normal cases. The interpretation of multiple personality, in turn, must be developed with the aid of a philosophical theory, because philosophical ideas are in play in such cases.

> Does he know that what he is doing is killing me? Of course he doesn't. He thinks that he is just writing a book filled with theses to be debated in the academic community. He believes that all he is doing is trying to prove that his theories are true. (It's hard not to laugh while writing this.) And he believes his theory! So he thinks that I don't exist anyway and you can't kill something that doesn't exist. That's what's happening with him on a conscious level. But anybody—except our philosopher here—knows that theories are driven by sentiment, not argument. It's almost too banal to point out, but he is subconsciously aware of me and he hates me. He can only bear a world in which I don't exist. So he must create it.

I have distinguished three uses of borderline cases and have not ruled out that thought experiments can be employed in all three ways. They can even function as test cases if they have the necessary continuity with normal cases. In the last section, the thought experiment regarding fission played an important role. Now a few words on this as a way of concluding the chapter.

Every empirical theory of the identity of fundamental entities has to take a stand on the duplication problem and on the unity reaction, since these are central difficulties for empirical theories in the research literature. But there is an important difference between the duplication problem and the unity reaction. In contrast to the unity reaction, the duplication problem is not based on intuitive reactions, but simply makes explicit what empirical theories, together with some additional assumptions, imply. But since the unity reaction is an important argument against empirical theories, every proponent of such theories must say something about this reaction. Now, I have turned a certain explanation of the unity reaction into a condition of adequacy. Does that give too much weight to a certain intuitive reaction to a thought experiment? No. With this explanation of the unity reaction, my aim is to point to a plausible interpretation of this reaction, one to which the standard approaches in the literature are blind, because it does not fit into their theoretical framework. So in contrast to most proponents of empirical theories, I do not have to reject the unity reaction fundamentally as an illusion, but can concede an important truth to it. But condition of adequacy 3 is only *one* building block in an overall structure of reasons that supports my position.

The next chapter picks up the thread from the last section and develops an empirical, circular account of the diachronic identity of fundamental entities. In Chapter 5, it will then be shown how this account fulfills the first three criteria of adequacy. Chapter 6 elaborates on the place of the body in this account. The last chapter of Part II, Chapter 7, explains how this approach does justice to the different questions distinguished in section 1. Having developed a theory of the *diachronic identity* of fundamental entities on the basis of normal cases, I will then in Part III return to *multiple personality* and the *individuation* of fundamental entities.

Part II
Diachronic Identity

4 What Am I Fundamentally?

In section 3.2, it was suggested that an empirical, circular account of the identity of fundamental entities is needed to solve central problems in this area. In the last section, it was said that a theory of the identity of fundamental entities should be developed on the basis of normal cases. But will a consideration of normal cases lead one to an empirical, circular account? I shall start by arguing that it does and then in the following two sections develop such a theory.

1 SELF-TRANSFORMATION

A theory of the identity of fundamental entities must do justice to normal cases. An everyday instance of belief revision is such a case: A person used to think that the post office closes at 7 p.m. She revises her opinion and now believes that the post office is not open after 6 p.m. I shall use this simple case to construct a new theory of the identity of fundamental entities. But first I shall argue that this case shows that a popular approach to personal identity must be rejected.

One of the most commonly accepted theories of personal identity is a version of the psychological approach, often called "the psychological criterion." According to the psychological criterion, the identity of X and Y depends on *psychological connections* between X and Y. These are understood as *causal* connections. For such a connection to exist between two mental states at t_1 and t_2, the mental state at t_2 must be *causally dependent* (in the right way) upon the state at t_1. Furthermore, a psychological connection, in the sense required by the psychological criterion, exists only if the connected states are *semantically similar.* According to the psychological criterion, it is a *sufficient* condition of the identity of P_1 and P_2[1] that there exist *enough* such connections between P_1 and P_2.[2] It is crucial here that the *kind* of connections that obtain between P_1 and P_2 if P_1 and P_2 are identical could also obtain if they were not identical. This assumption is essential for the success of a *non-circular* analysis: the psychological connections are of a kind that can obtain *independently of the identity of P_1 and P_2*. On the basis of such connections, it is possible to offer a *non-circular* analysis of personal identity: P_1 and P_2 are identical if and only if the *quantity* of the connections between them is large enough. Psychological connections that are understood in this manner are usually called "quasi-connections."[3]

To specify *necessary* conditions of identity, the defenders of the psychological criterion need another notion beside quasi-connections. According to the defenders of this criterion, the problem is the following: Identity is transitive, i.e., if $P_1 = P_2$ and $P_2 = P_3$, then $P_1 = P_3$. Now, it is possible that P_1 and P_2, on the one hand, and P_2 and P_3, on the other, are connected by enough quasi-connections for it to hold, according to the psychological criterion, that $P_1 = P_2$ and $P_2 = P_3$. But it does not follow from the presence of *these* quasi-connections that there obtain enough quasi-connections between P_1 and P_3 for them to be identical. Now, given that identity is transitive, this possibility shows that it cannot be *necessary* for the identity of P_1 and P_3 that *they* be connected by enough quasi-connections. The defenders of the psychological criterion must therefore introduce another psychological relation that obtains between P_1 and P_3 and that can provide necessary and sufficient condition for identity. Psychological *continuity* is such a relation: There obtains psychological continuity between P_1 and P_n if and only if P_1 and P_n are members of a temporal chain for which it holds that between adjacent members of the chain from P_1 to P_n there exist enough quasi-connections for these adjacent members to be one and the same fundamental entity. P_1 and P_n are one and the same fundamental entity if and only if psychological continuity obtains between them.[4]

Let's return to cases of everyday belief revision. It is not in question that these are cases in which there continuously exists one fundamental entity that has a belief, revises it, and then holds the revised belief. The question is whether the psychological criterion can explain how one and the same fundamental entity persists through the change of belief. Since the process of revision involves a *loss of semantic similarity*—after all, the first belief is semantically different from the second one—the psychological criterion must understand belief revision as a "*minus point*" with respect to the identity of fundamental entities. Quasi-connections are causal relations between psychological items with similar contents. Contrary to belief revision, they are "plus points": identity over time is preserved as long as enough of such "plus points" add up. According to the psychological criterion, for P_1 and P_2 to be identical over time *despite belief revision*, enough quasi-connections must obtain between P_1 and P_2. This conception of the identity of fundamental entities over belief revision is entirely wrongheaded. When somebody revises her belief, she commits *herself* to a new belief. She must therefore be the one who has the new belief. This means that belief revision should not be understood as a "minus point" with respect to the identity of fundamental entities. On the contrary: precisely *because* somebody revises her belief, identity is preserved across the whole process. This brief argument suffices as a refutation of the psychological criterion. If my concern were mainly with the criticism of other positions, I would nevertheless spell this argument out in greater detail.[5] Instead, I want to use this line of reasoning as a starting point for developing my own view.

The upshot of section 3.2 was the following task: the development of an empirical, circular theory to fulfill the conditions of adequacy 1–3. For such a theory, we need to find empirical relations that cannot obtain in fission between the pre-fission person, on the one hand, and her two descendants, on the other. But are there any such relations? And are there independent reasons for thinking that diachronic identity rests on such relations? We have already, I think, encountered such relations and reasons in the case of belief revision: If somebody revises her beliefs, then she commits herself anew. Because *she* thereby commits *herself* to something, this is a case in which one and the same fundamental entity persists. (I focus here only on commitments in the sense in which somebody commits herself to the *truth* of something, e.g., to its being true *that the post office closes at 6 p.m.*)

This explanation of the identity of fundamental entities has two components. First, if somebody commits herself anew, then there obtains a psychological relation between the old and the new belief. Psychological relations are empirical relations. If the explanation is correct—if this is a case of the persistence of one and the same fundamental entity *because* somebody commits herself anew—then diachronic identity rests on an *empirical* relation. Second, however, this is an empirical relation of a special kind: the relation of the revision of a belief or a commitment *presupposes identity*. It is presupposed that this is a case of one and the same fundamental entity revising her beliefs: somebody commits *herself* anew.

In an attempt to explain a normal case, we have discovered a relation that fulfills conditions of adequacy 1–3. In this normal case, X at t_1 has a certain belief and Y at t_2 has another one. X and Y differ to the extent that they have different beliefs. Why are X and Y one and the same fundamental entity? The answer is: because the relation of commitment revision holds between X and Y. This is a relation familiar to us from everyday practice. Now, commitment revision is just the kind of relation that was needed to fulfill conditions of adequacy 1–3: an empirical relation that presupposes the identity of X and Y. So an intuitively plausible explanation of a normal case leads us in this way to an empirical, circular account of diachronic identity. This is not an isolated normal case. On the contrary, the argumentation just offered for belief revision can be carried over to all cases of self-transformation: to all cases in which somebody transforms herself more or less radically. Therefore we have, in addition to the fulfillment of the conditions of adequacy 1–3, another reason to accept such an account—namely, the fact that it does justice to normal cases (condition of adequacy 5). But although such relations are employed in our everyday practice, such relations need theoretical explication. This is the task of the next two sections. First I must briefly discuss a possible objection to the argument I have just offered.

A fundamental assumption of my argument is this: somebody who transforms herself survives the transformation. This premise can be doubted. A club can radically transform its own aims and rules. For example, a football club could make the decision no longer to play and support football, but instead to fight the practice of sports in every form. In such a case, we *say* that the club has *transformed itself.* In other words, we employ the *reflexive form of speech* in order to describe a certain change in state of affairs. But this is *only* a form of speech. The question as to the identity of the football club through the transformation has not thereby been decided. Although we *say* that this club has transformed itself, this does not mean that, after the transformation, the *same club* still exists: is a football club that redefines itself as an antisports club still one and the same club? Now, the same holds when a human being transforms herself: we *say* that she has transformed herself, but this in no way decides the issue of whether, after the transformation, *one and the same fundamental entity* still exists.

There is a fundamental difference between humans and clubs that undercuts this objection. When a *human being* revises her beliefs, this revision does not rest on the decisions of any other more fundamental agents. Surely, one can explain the revision with reference to smaller psychological units: one can refer to the person's experiences and deliberations in order to make the revision intelligible. But *she* is the one who revises the beliefs. Her psychological states do not *do* anything. This means that the revision cannot be traced back to any agent other than the person herself.

The case of *clubs* is different. One could, for example, imagine the decision-making process in the football club as follows: Many of the members of the club—let's say 67 percent of them—have just seen a report on the dangerous injuries in youth football clubs. As a consequence, they come to believe that one should not support football, but rather fight it. Each of these members of the club commits herself to this belief. We can say that the club has transformed itself. And we can understand the club as an agent. But there are also *other agents*—namely, the members of the club—whose decisions play a role in the explanation of the transformation of the club. With respect to identity, this difference between humans and clubs is crucial. When a human being revises her beliefs, *she* is the only one who does anything. *She* has committed *herself* to another belief. This means that her identity is preserved. Clubs are different in this respect. Many of its members have given up their old attitudes and aims and committed themselves to others. Since each of the members has committed herself in a new way, each of them is the same fundamental entity after this self-transformation. But what has happened to the club? We could say that, through the individual actions of the club members, a collective action has been performed. This collective action cannot be ascribed to any of the individual members. Nonetheless, this collective action only exists on account of their individual actions. We can therefore ask what they have accomplished through their collective action. It is a fact that, as a consequence of this collective action, they are now all members of an antisports club. But even if we know everything about the genesis of this collective action, we do not know whether, by this collective action, they have terminated the existence of their old club and created a new one or whether they have simply maintained the existence of their old club in a certain way. As far as identity is concerned, this is the crucial difference between the self-transformation of a human being—a transformation that does not rest on the actions of other agents—and the collective action that can be traced back to the actions of other agents.[6] I do not want to comment on the identity conditions of clubs.[7] For the purposes of my argument, what matters is only that doubts concerning the identity of a club that undergoes a radical transformation cannot—without further argument—be applied to the self-transformation of a human being.

2 THE AUTHORIAL CORRELATE THEORY

When somebody revises her beliefs, there are at least two factors involved. On the one hand, there exists somebody here who revises her beliefs. On the other, there are beliefs that in belief revision are related to each other in a certain way. Most accounts of diachronic identity in belief revision or in other cases are based on one of these elements as opposed to the other—i.e., they *either* take the subject *or* the psychological states or relations as their starting point.

This can be made clear by considering different answers to question 1 ("What am I fundamentally?"). In the literature, one of these two concepts—*subject* or *psychological states/relations*—is usually assigned *priority* in the following sense: according to the one kind of theories, I am fundamentally a *subject* whose identity conditions are entirely independent of psychological relations. Theories of this kind include not only those implying that the identity conditions for fundamental entities are non-empirical (e.g., "I am fundamentally an indivisible mental substance"), but also accounts which presuppose that these identity conditions are empirical but not psychological (e.g., "I am fundamentally a purely biological being of the species *Homo sapiens*").

The other kind of theory *reverses the priority*: the answer given to question 1 requires that the diachronic identity conditions of fundamental entities be explicable in terms of psychological states or relations in a non-circular way, i.e., without presupposing the identity of the relevant subject. *Bundle theory* is a paradigmatic example of such accounts. It is the view that each one of us is fundamentally a bundle of psychological states.[8] In other words, such theories call for a psychological approach as an answer to question 2—the question concerning the diachronic identity conditions of fundamental entities. And this is just another way of saying that they call for a psychological version of empirical, non-circular answers to question 2.

So the answers to question 1 that give priority either to the concept of a subject or the concept of psychological states call for *either* a non-empirical, circular answer to question 2 *or* a empirical, non-circular answer.[9] As shown in Chapter 3, such answers to question 2 fail on account of the criteria of adequacy 1–3. This suggests that by insisting that an answer to question 1 must give priority to one of the two concepts, one wrongly ignores an alternative answer. I therefore provide an answer to this question that *does not assign priority to either of the two concepts.* Rather, my answer presupposes that these concepts are *conceptually interdependent.* Drawing on this answer to question 1, I will then be able to provide a theoretical explication of the sort of answer to question 2 I have already suggested. Here is my answer to question 1:

> *The authorial correlate theory*: I am fundamentally an agent who is a correlate to the psychological relations for which this agent is minimally responsible.

The different aspects of this cryptic formulation need elaboration:

1) "I am fundamentally an *agent.*" According to this thesis, each one of us is fundamentally an entity capable of acting. This means that a fundamental entity does not begin to exist until certain capacities are present—namely, the abilities necessary to be an agent. I will not discuss which capacities these are here. Nevertheless, it should be clear that they include the abilities necessary for being minimally responsible for psychological relations.

2) "I am fundamentally a correlate to *psychological relations.*" This means that my identity is dependent upon psychological relations. Even if fundamental entity X at t_1 is an agent and fundamental entity Y at t_2 is also an agent, X and Y cannot be one and the same fundamental entity unless there exists the right kind of psychological relation between them.

These first two points leave many questions open with respect to the relationship of such an agent to the body. I will argue in Chapter 6 that a fundamental entity beginning its existence as a human being is materially constituted by a living being and can thus not be transferred from one body to another. In Chapter 10, it will be shown that more than one fundamental entity—and thus more than one agent—can share one and the same body.

3) "I am fundamentally a correlate to the psychological relations *for which I am minimally responsible.*" This makes clear what *kind* of psychological relations the identity of fundamental entities is dependent on: the psychological relations for which this fundamental entity is minimally responsible. Here we find the two previous theses combined. The first thesis stressed the dependency of the identity of fundamental entities on agency; the second thesis emphasized that identity depends on psychological relations.

These two theses are connected by the concept of minimal responsibility—a concept that is explained in the next section. The label "psychological relations for which I am minimally responsible" provides a general description that may be applicable to different relations. Commitment revision and commitment maintenance, which I employ in the next section to provide an explicit answer to question 2, are just two examples of such relations. This means that it is possible to partially understand commitment revision (and commitment maintenance) without assuming that commitment revision falls under the description "psychological relations for which I am minimally responsible." This is important for the next point.

4) "I am fundamentally an agent who is a *correlate* to the psychological relations for which this agent is minimally responsible." This *correlate thesis* can be explained in three steps. *First*, this thesis implies a rejection of both of the aforementioned priorities. It denies that I am a subject whose conditions of identity are independent of psychological relations. The other position rejected is the view that I am an entity whose identity conditions are dependent upon psychological relations that can be described without assuming the identity of the relevant subject.

Second, the rejection of both of these priorities implies that the two concepts—that of an agent and that of psychological relations for which the agent is responsible—are conceptually dependent on each other. The agent is a correlate to these relations and the relations are a correlate to the agent. To say that these relations are a *correlate to the agent* means that it is impossible to make full sense of such relations without assuming the identity of the agent who is minimally responsible for these relations. The agent is a *correlate to the relations* in the sense that the agent's identity depends on relations for which she is responsible.

Third, the conceptual interdependence of the two concepts presupposes that they are to a certain extent conceptually independent. Commitment revision is one example of a relation for which the agent is minimally responsible. It is possible to *partially understand* what commitment revision is without assuming that it is something for which an agent is minimally responsible. For example, it is not necessary to make this assumption in order to distinguish commitment revision from cases in which a person does not revise her beliefs, but simply does not have any views anymore on the relevant topic. However, it is not possible to have a *complete* understanding of the concept of commitment revision without making the assumption that commitment revision presupposes the identity of an agent who is minimally responsible for the revision. Likewise, it is possible to have a *partial* but *incomplete* understanding of the concept of an agent without assuming that the identity of fundamental entities as agents is dependent upon psychological relations for which the agents are minimally responsible.

So the correlate thesis implies a circular analysis of diachronic identity. The diachronic identity of a fundamental entity is dependent upon psychological relations which cannot be described without assuming the identity of this fundamental entity as the agent who is minimally responsible for these psychological relations. At the same time, this thesis shows that the circularity is not vicious. Since one can partially understand each of these two concepts—that of an agent and that of psychological relations—without understanding the other, their interdependence means that they cast light on each other. It is precisely by understanding the interdependence of the concepts that one moves from a partial to a complete understanding of them.

3 THE COMMITMENT CRITERION

It may be argued that the authorial correlate theory cannot possibly serve as the basis of an account of diachronic identity. The problem is that—so runs the objection—the theory can only account for certain cases that are the exception rather than the rule. In some cases belief revision is actually an active process. However, in other cases people change their minds without knowing why or when they did so. They simply find themselves with a new belief without being responsible for having acquired it. Now, the authorial correlate theory refers only to psychological relations for which the person is responsible. The objection is that this theory can therefore not account for identity in cases of the second kind.

So far, I have not offered an explicit answer to question 2. I will now formulate such an answer by way of addressing this objection. The focus will be on commitments as an example of the psychological attributes of a person for which this person is responsible. I will first focus on the concept of a *commitment as such* and adopt a certain controversial view without further argument. Then, moving to the real issue at stake here, I will employ this view to offer an account of commitment *revision*.

Commitments have a *normative* and a *psychological* dimension. Let's first consider the normative aspect. If, for example, somebody has committed herself to something's being true, one can ask whether it is actually true. Since this is also something she can ask herself, she is *minimally responsible* for her commitment. She is responsible for this because she can reconsider the reasons for and against the truth of the relevant proposition and change her commitment accordingly. I will discuss later why she is only *minimally* responsible for this. First I want to explicate the *psychological* dimension of commitments.

Commitments play a role in psychological explanations that cannot be reduced to their normative dimension. For example, if somebody categorically refuses to travel on airplanes, a complete explanation of her behavior may have to include that she has the commitment that flying is dangerous. This attitude of the person toward flying has a psychological reality that is more or less disconnected from the attitude the person has to the normative question of whether flying is really dangerous. With respect to this question, this person may—or so we may assume—admit that there are really no good reasons for this commitment. Nevertheless, she refuses to give up the behavior that can only be explained by ascribing this commitment to her.

This example can be used to explain the connection between the normative and psychological dimensions of commitments. This person clearly has a certain psychologically efficacious attitude toward flying, and it makes sense to say that her attitude includes the commitment that flying is dangerous, even though this very same person thinks that, normatively speaking, there are no good reasons for thinking that flying is dangerous. The connection between the two dimensions of commitments is that under conditions such as these we have a *rational expectation* of this person. We view the psychological efficacy of her attitude toward flying *not* as an *isolated psychological reality*, but as something that stands in *rational conflict* with her normative assessment of the situation.[10] Correspondingly, we do *not* view this efficacy as a *fixed psychological given*, but rather expect of the person that—if she really does not think that there are good reasons to believe flying is dangerous—she will work on her attitude toward flying, so that she will no longer, against her own rational assessment, categorically avoid flying.

Therefore, a person is *minimally responsible* for her commitments. The responsibility is *minimal* in three senses: First, a person is not responsible for her commitments in the same way as she is for her actions: if I consider a belief to be true, I cannot simply *decide* to give up this commitment.[11] Since commitments have not only a normative but also a psychological dimension, responsibility for commitments is minimal in two additional senses. Second, she may not have actively acquired her attitudes (for example, her attitudes toward flying). Third, due to her psychological constitution or the psychological influences to which she is subject, it may not be realistic to expect her to change her attitude.

Nevertheless, a person *is responsible* for her commitments. As the example of flying phobia shows, the normative and psychological dimensions can become disconnected. But often they coincide. If somebody wonders whether there are good reasons for thinking that the post office closes at 5 p.m. and then does indeed come to the conclusion that there are good reasons for thinking so (perhaps she goes to her local branch), she has thereby in this normative sort of way committed herself to the belief that it closes at five o'clock. The psychological reality with respect to this topic coincides with the normative stand. And for the commitment to have psychological reality, all that is necessary is the adoption of this normative position. Accordingly, we are responsible for our commitments in two ways. First, each of us is directly responsible for taking a certain normative stand. The psychological reality with respect to a certain issue does often simply coincide with the normative position adopted. We have a second sort of responsibility in cases such as the one of flying phobia where there is a psychologically real attitude that conflicts with the normative stand. Here a person's responsibility consists in ensuring that the normative stand has an appropriate psychological influence.[12] The crucial point is that in both cases commitments must be understood as something that lies within the responsibility of the person: *a commitment is, conceptually*, something that lies within the responsibility of the person who has the commitment.[13]

Let us turn to commitment revision. Here we must distinguish between two cases. The first one is the case of an *active* revision of belief. For example, somebody may change her mind about the opening hours of the post office after having gathered the relevant information. This is a case in which the person is clearly responsible for the change. As such, this case is favorable to the authorial correlate theory.

> That is about the noblest theory I have ever heard! It's all about responsibility. A personal change for which a person is not responsible is simply irrelevant for identity. We are autonomous beings in charge of our personal histories. What a tribute to our freedom! THE MAN IS A PEDANTIC CONTROL FREAK! To him, losing control is clearly equivalent to ceasing to exist. If you like, you can go on arguing with him about this theory. You'll lose. Arguing with pedantic control freaks means entering their turf and you're bound to lose. I simply refuse to accept a theory that turns us all into pedantic control freaks. I CANNOT LIVE LIKE THAT. You should refuse too. Blank refusals make pedantic control freaks nervous.

The second sort of case is more difficult: Here a person *finds herself* with a certain commitment at t_2. This commitment amounts to a revision of a commitment that the person had at t_1, though she has *not actively* revised it. As I will now show, this case also presents no difficulty for the authorial correlate theory.

If *commitment* is something that lies within the responsibility of a person, the same must hold for *commitment revision*: Commitment revision is a process in which a person commits herself anew in a way that deviates from a previous commitment. The person with the flying phobia finds herself with the belief that flying is dangerous, but she has not actively committed herself to that belief. Nevertheless, she is minimally responsible for it. The same must now hold for commitment revision. Although the person has not actively changed her mind, she is minimally responsible for this transformation. Just as the concept of commitment presupposes minimal responsibility, so too does the concept of commitment revision presuppose that the person who has changed her commitments is minimally responsible for the change.

An example is necessary to make this point more forcefully: At breakfast I declare to my partner that the Anglican cathedral in our city is more beautiful that the Catholic one. As usual, I walk past these buildings on my way to work and spend the day at the university. In the evening, we find ourselves again involved in an architectural discussion and I suddenly realize that I have changed my mind. And so I now declare to my partner that the Catholic cathedral is surely more beautiful. In this example, I have changed my mind, though I have not actively done so. At no point during the day do I actively contemplate the merits of the two buildings. In the course of the whole day, we may assume, I have a view on the respective merits of the two cathedrals, but during the day I change my mind, though I do not realize it until the evening.

Now, just like commitments, commitment revision has a psychological and a normative dimension. It may be that the commitment revision happened purely psychologically: it may be that I simply changed my mind without even unconsciously considering the reasons for and against considering the one cathedral to be more beautiful than the other. Nevertheless, I had an opinion on this matter during the whole day. Concerning this opinion, the following counterfactual assumption is true: if I had thought about this matter in the course of the day, I could, on the basis of the relevant reasons, have either reaffirmed my view or changed my mind. Commitment revision—even in those cases when it happens passively—conceptually implies this counterfactual assumption. Therefore, even in such cases, I am minimally responsible for my change of mind.

This has important consequences. The person with the flying phobia is minimally responsible for her commitment because it is *her own* commitment. Similarly, I am minimally responsible for the belief revision concerning the relative merits of the two cathedrals because it was *I* who changed my mind. The existence of a commitment revision between t_1 and t_2 presupposes the existence of somebody who could have reaffirmed or changed her view if she had thought about the matter. In other words, the existence of a commitment revision between t_1 and t_2 presupposes the existence of *one and the same agent* who, *had she considered the matter, could have reaffirmed or changed her commitment* even if she actually did not actively consider the matter. Of course, this counterfactual assumption is as applicable to commitment maintenance as to commitment revision—e.g., if I had continued to believe during the day that the Anglican cathedral is more beautiful than the Catholic one.

So now we have an answer to the objection made at the beginning of this section: the authorial correlate theory does not presuppose that the psychological relations for which an agent is minimally responsible are always *actively* brought about.[14] At the same time, on the basis of the authorial correlate theory as an answer to question 1, we are now in a position to provide an explicit answer to question 2:

> *Commitment criterion*: X_1 at t_1 and X_n at t_n are one and the same fundamental entity if and only if there obtains commitment continuity between X_1 and X_n. There obtains commitment continuity between X_1 at t_1 and X_n at t_n if and only if X_1 and X_n are members of a temporal chain for which it holds that between adjacent members of the chain

from X_1 to X_n there exists at least one psychological relation of either commitment revision or commitment maintenance.

To explain this criterion, let us consider identity over the day in which I change my mind about the two cathedrals. It may be that, to account for my identity between the morning and the evening, it suffices merely to invoke my belief about the relative merits of the two cathedrals. This is the case if we can assume that, *with respect to this topic*, there exists this kind of temporal chain consisting of commitment revision and commitment maintenance. For that one day this may be a plausible assumption. Beliefs are dispositions in the sense that I need not have to be thinking about a belief all the time in order to have it. Thus, it is not implausible that during that particular day I did at all times have a belief about the relative merits of the two cathedrals. Over the course of my whole life, however, it is unlikely that I have always had a belief about the relative merits of these two cathedrals. Therefore, to explain my identity over the course of my whole life, we surely have to invoke commitments with different contents. My first belief may have been about my mother. From then on, there always *only* needs to be *one commitment* (at different times probably commitments with different contents) that I revise or maintain between each of the subsequent, adjacent time slices. Contrary to the psychological criterion, the quantity of psychological connections is irrelevant. Each commitment revision or commitment maintenance *presupposes* identity. Therefore, it is sufficient for the diachronic identity of a fundamental entity that in each case *one* such psychological relation exists between the respective adjacent time slices of the temporal chain.

> He wants to be able to change himself radically and completely and still remain the same. People always like the opposite of themselves, don't they? Here we have somebody who doesn't dare to modify even the minutest aspect of himself. And he says: I could change everything and I would still be myself! But I was not going to be so personal—I'm sure that his personal transformations have simply been too deep and subtle for me to notice. So let me present a philosophical refutation of his theory. Here it is: Logi is bland, boring, careful, cowardly, dull, and conformable. Imagine Logi as colorful, creative, courageous, daring, funny, and dominant. Sorry, can't. It wouldn't be Logi. Quod erat demonstrandum.

The commitment criterion amounts to an empirical and circular account of diachronic identity. The psychological relations *commitment revision* and *commitment maintenance* are *empirical* connections. The existence of commitment revision or commitment maintenance between t_1 and t_2 presupposes that there exists an agent who has throughout a view on the relevant topic and is minimally responsible for this opinion. In saying that X at t_1 and Y at t_2 are connected by commitment revision or commitment

Table 4.1 Theories of Diachronic Identity

	Non-circular	**Circular**
Empirical	Psychological theories Biological theories Bodily theories	*The commitment criterion*
Non-empirical	No theories?	Dualistic theories Inner-perspective theories

maintenance, one presupposes that X and Y are one and the same fundamental entity. Therefore, the commitment criterion is *circular.* However, as discussed in the last section, the circularity is benign because the concept of an agent minimally responsible for commitments and the concept of commitment revision (and commitment maintenance) *shed light on each other.*

This chapter began with the search for an empirical, circular theory that could also account for normal cases. Our search is now complete and is presented schematically in table 4.1. We still must examine whether the commitment criterion fulfills the criteria of adequacy 1–3. This is the topic of the next chapter.

5 Empirical Discernability and Fission

The aim of this chapter is to show that the commitment criterion fulfills conditions of adequacy 1–3: that it rests on facts that are empirically discernable, solves the duplication problem, and respects and explains the truth in the unity reaction.

1 EMPIRICAL DISCERNABILITY

Commitment continuity is an empirical relation. So the commitment criterion obviously fulfills the first criterion of adequacy. Nevertheless, I would like to explain briefly how the commitment criterion accounts for identity in the coma case. There is a difference between the coma case and the story of the different attitudes about the relative beauty of different buildings in the course of a day. Only in the latter case is the person capable of uttering her views or otherwise expressing them. Does it at all make sense to say that a person in a coma has commitments? And if not, doesn't the commitment criterion lack the means to explain how through coma a fundamental entity remains one and the same?

This objection to the commitment criterion is unfounded. It may be true at each time during a coma that the person who is currently in coma could—if she were to awake from the coma—express a certain commitment. If this counterfactual assumption holds for all points in time during the coma and the person has this commitment both immediately before and after the coma, then there is commitment continuity in the relevant sense from the time just before the coma to the point at which the person awakes. One may assume for *each point in time during the coma* that the person—if she were to awake—could express the *same token* commitment that *she had immediately before the coma*. The person is minimally responsible for this commitment because she could have revised her commitment had she woken up from the coma. Such cases of commitment continuity are different from cases in which somebody who awakes from a coma acquires a new belief, even if this belief has the same semantic content as a belief she had before the coma. *If* we insist that a person cannot have a commitment without being able to express it, *then* a person in a coma does not have any commitments. However, even if the person cannot express a certain commitment *while she is in a coma*, she may have the ability to express it *if she were to awake from the coma*. The existence of such an ability to express a certain token commitment is all that is needed for there to be the kind of commitment continuity necessary to account for identity in coma cases.

2 THE DUPLICATION PROBLEM

The commitment criterion offers a simple solution to the duplication problem: the relations of commitment revision and commitment maintenance cannot obtain between the pre-fission person and her post-fission descendents. In other words, the relations on which identity rests in non-fission cases do not obtain in fission. Thus, the pre-fission fundamental entity is not identical to her post-fission descendants. No paradox arises.

But why can these relations not obtain in fission? Given the way that fission cases are constructed, I concentrate here on commitment *maintenance*. We can work with Fair and her fission descendants, L-Fairchild and R-Fairchild. The assumption is that there is no psychological difference between the three. For example, they all have the same commitments. But does the relation of commitment maintenance obtain between Fair and L-Fairchild (or R-Fairchild)? To explain why the answer is "no," one must examine the conceptual relations between three concepts: *commitment maintenance*, *minimal responsibility*, and *the identity of fundamental entities*.

As we have seen, *commitment maintenance* is a psychological relation that does not require a person to actively maintain her commitment. But it does require *minimal responsibility*: it makes no sense to speak of commitment maintenance unless there is a person who has a commitment and, with respect to the subject matter of the commitment, could have committed herself to a different position if she had reflected on the topic. This, in turn, presupposes that the person who originally has the commitment and the person who can, in principle, actively reconsider it at a later point are *the same fundamental entity*. If they were not the same, it would make no sense to speak of commitment maintenance. So what we have here is a conceptual connection between three concepts: commitment maintenance requires minimal responsibility, and minimal responsibility presupposes the identity of fundamental entities. A specific consequence of this conceptual connection is that commitment maintenance is a psychological relation that cannot obtain between a fundamental entity and *two non-identical fundamental entities*. Commitment maintenance requires that *I* am continually minimally responsible for this commitment. Thus, it makes no sense that the relation of commitment maintenance holds between me and a *second* fundamental entity.

This is a fact about commitment maintenance that we can know without considering fission. We know that commitment maintenance cannot obtain between Fair and two non-identical fundamental entities. So it cannot obtain between Fair and *both* L-Fairchild and R-Fairchild, given that L-Fairchild and R-Fairchild are two distinct fundamental entities.[1] The only remaining possibility is that it obtains between Fair and one of her fission descendants to the exclusion of the other. There are two versions of fission to consider here: proportionate and disproportionate. In proportionate fission, there is no empirical difference between the relations between Fair and her two fission descendants. This means that commitment maintenance, being an empirical relation, cannot hold between Fair and one of her descendants to the exclusion of the other.

In disproportionate fission, there is an empirical difference between the relations between Fair and her two descendants. However, the empirical relations between Fair and either one of her two descendants would, according to your favorite empirical theory, suffice for identity if this were the only descendant. Here it is also impossible for commitment maintenance to exist between Fair and one of her descendants to the exclusion of the other. There are two possibilities to consider. The first possibility is that *no case* of commitment maintenance exists between Fair and one of her descendants and at least one case of commitment maintenance exists between Fair and the other descendant. This possibility is excluded by the definition of fission: the relations between Fair and her two descendants are supposed to be such that identity between Fair and the relevant descendant would be guaranteed if the other one were not to exist. The other possibility is that relations of commitment maintenance exist between Fair and both of her descendants, but *more cases* exist between Fair and one of her descendants than between Fair and the other one. This possibility has already been excluded: because commitment maintenance presupposes identity, it cannot hold between Fair and both of her descendants.[2] So we may conclude that the duplication problem does not arise for the commitment criterion. In fission there is simply no commitment continuity.

The solution that the commitment criterion provides to the duplication problem must be distinguished from another one. Invoking Locke's idea that *person* is a forensic concept, one could argue as follows: *Personal identity* and *responsibility* are intrinsically linked concepts in that one is responsible only for one's own actions. This means that two non-identical persons cannot be responsible for my actions. If that were the case, not only I would be responsible for my actions. My two fission descendants are two non-identical persons. This means that they cannot both be responsible for my actions. Since there is (in proportionate fission) no empirical difference between my relations to my two fission descendants and non-empirical theories are wrong, it must be concluded that I cannot be identical to either of them.

There are crucial differences between this purely forensic account and the explanation provided by the commitment criterion. In the forensic account, only two concepts are linked: *personal identity* and *responsibility*. Moreover, there is no criterion of personal identity over time specified. This account is supposed to be empirical. If we now pick as a criterion one of the empirical relations offered by the literature, we end up with the duplication problem: the empirical relations on offer—I am assuming—can obtain between me and each of my fission descendants. Thus, according to such an empirical account, I would be identical to both of my fission descendants. The appeal to responsibility, in order to show that I cannot be identical to my fission descendants, comes too late. It simply becomes part of the paradox: if these empirical relations obtain between Fair and L-Fairchild, and, according to this empirical account, Fair and L-Fairchild must thus be identical, shouldn't L-Fairchild be responsible for Fair's actions? The crucial difference between this purely forensic answer and the commitment criterion is that the latter invokes a conceptual connection between three, not two, concepts: *the identity of fundamental entities*, *minimal responsibility*, and *commitment maintenance*. On account of the connections between these concepts, the psychological relation that accounts for identity in non-fission cases does not obtain in fission, and the problem of duplication simply cannot arise.[3]

The commitment criterion is similarly superior to Sydney Shoemaker's account of personal identity. It is worth adding a comparison with Shoemaker here, if only because my account shares some features with his. According to Shoemaker's functionalism, mental states are individuated through the causal effects—including mental states—that they can have together with other mental states. For example, the desire not to become wet, together with the belief that it will rain, can lead to the decision to take an umbrella. This presupposes that all of these mental states belong to one and the same person. Now, some of the causal effects are future mental states. Accordingly, the causal relations between mental states are often diachronic relations. According to Shoemaker, personal identity depends on such relations. In other words, personal identity depends on psychological relations, but these are functional relations that *presuppose* that they all belong to *one and the same person*. In this way, Shoemaker's theory can be placed in the same category as the authorial correlate theory: Persons are neither bundles of psychological states nor entities whose identity is independent of psychological relations. Personal identity depends on psychological relations of a kind that presupposes the identity of the person.[4]

On the basis of such a theory, Jennifer Whiting offers the following approach to fission, which she sees as an interpretation of Shoemaker: Personal identity consists in causal relations that can *generally* exist only between states of one and the same person. Persons are entities that can only exist "in the first place" because the psychological connections existing between the states of a person can in general exist only between the states of one and the same person. Although this must apply in general to each person, against this general background certain "deviant cases" become possible for each person.[5] Fission is such a case. It seems that Whiting understands fission as a case in which the kind of causal relations that obtain in normal cases between Fair's psychological states obtain between Fair's states, on the one hand, and the states of L-Fairchild and R-Fairchild, on the other:[6] Psychological states are functionally individuated in the sense that *in normal cases* they are causally related to each other as states of *one and the same person*. Nevertheless, L-Fairchild's first wish after she wakes up after the transplantation may be the desire to go and buy an umbrella, and this desire may be causally dependent upon Fair's desires and beliefs. And this causal connection need not be different from the causal connection that would have obtained had we been dealing with Fair's desire to buy an umbrella.[7] So it seems that Whiting is saying that in the non-fission case—L-Fairchild is the only descendant—the same psychological relations obtain between Fair and L-Fairchild as obtain in fission between Fair and both L-Fairchild and R-Fairchild.

This approach to fission is problematic for the same reason as the purely forensic account: If the very same relations that preserve identity in non-fission cases also obtain in fission, why do these relations not preserve identity in fission? The duplication problem remains. The commitment criterion avoids this problem because neither commitment revision nor commitment maintenance obtains in fission.

Whiting's approach involves a direct violation of the "only x and y principle" mentioned in Chapter 3. According to this principle, the question of whether X and Y are identical must depend only on facts about X and Y themselves and the relations between them. According to Whiting's account, there is no difference between the relations between Fair and L-Fairchild in the non-fission case and the relations between Fair and both L-Fairchild and R-Fairchild in fission. Nevertheless, only in the non-fission case is Fair identical to L-Fairchild. The only difference between the cases is the existence of R-Fairchild, a difference that has nothing to do with the facts about Fair and L-Fairchild themselves and the relations between them.[8]

The commitment criterion does not directly violate this principle: In the non-fission case, the relation of commitment maintenance (or commitment revision) obtains between Fair and L-Fairchild. In fission, it does not. Thus, the fact that Fair and L-Fairchild are not identical in fission *does* depend on facts about the relations between them. Of course, one might object that the commitment criterion amounts to an *indirect* violation of the only x and y principle. The fact that Fair and L-Fairchild are not identical in fission depends on the fact that no relation of commitment maintenance (or commitment revision) obtains between them. But the latter fact—that there obtains no such relation—is dependent on the fact that in fission Fair also has another descendant (R-Fairchild). This indirect violation of the principle is harmless. It does not derive from an arbitrary stipulation about fission made just to solve the duplication problem. Rather, it is simply a consequence of the conceptual relations between *the identity of fundamental entities*, *commitment-maintenance*, and *minimal responsibility*.

3 THE UNITY REACTION

In addition to solving the duplication problem, the commitment criterion also fulfills the third condition of adequacy having to do with the unity reaction. Commitment continuity is a relation that in fission cannot hold between Fair and her two descendants. So the commitment criterion does justice to the truth in the unity reaction without falsely claiming—like non-empirical theories—that Fair could be one of her successors as opposed to the other.

By additionally invoking the authorial correlate theory as the basis of the commitment criterion, one can even explain what is intuitively plausible about the unity reaction without committing the mistake made by non-empirical theories: I am fundamentally an agent whose identity is dependent upon her commitments. I can only commit *myself* to something. So when I imagine looking forward in time at my own future, there will always only be *one* commitment continuity to look at. In this way it becomes intelligible why I might think that I could be one of my successors in fission as opposed to the other. But the mistake in the unity reaction also becomes apparent: I am fundamentally a correlate to commitment continuity as an empirical relation and such a relation cannot exist between me and one of my fission descendants as opposed to the other.

The unity reaction violates the following *supervenience* principle for the identity of fundamental entities: If $X = Y$ but $X \neq Z$, then there must be an empirical difference between the relation between X and Y, on the one hand, and X and Z, on the other. The commitment criterion, in contrast, does not violate this principle. In the non-fission case, Fair = L-Fairchild, assuming that commitment continuity obtains between Fair and L-Fairchild. In fission, Fair ≠ L-Fairchild because here there is no commitment continuity between the two. This is the empirical difference between the relation between Fair and L-Fairchild in the two cases. This empirical difference derives, in turn, from a further empirical difference between the cases—only in fission is Fair related to *two* fundamental entities in a certain way.

6 My Body

So far, nothing has been said about my relationship to my body. This chapter partially closes this gap. It is only the first of two chapters addressing this issue. Chapter 11 discusses the question as to how a fundamental entity would be related to a body it shared with another fundamental entity. Here the focus is merely on issues arising with respect to the diachronic identity of one fundamental entity. Accordingly, this chapter closes with a discussion of my beginning and my end and how it relates to the beginning and the end of the existence of my body.

1 BODY CHANGE IS IMPOSSIBLE

I am an agent who is a correlate to the psychological relations this agent is minimally responsible for. My identity over time consists in commitment continuity. But is this agent a material being or a mental system? Can I change bodies? Is commitment continuity confined to a certain material being or can it be transferred from one material being to another? What I have said so far does not imply an answer to these questions. And I suppose that the account I have defended is compatible with answers to these questions that differ from the ones I will give. Nevertheless, these are important questions for our topic and I should say something about them. I shall argue that a fundamental entity that originally exists as a certain human being exists only as long as this material being exists. This is a controversial thesis that has certain limitations. I do *not* claim that each of us is a fundamental entity of a kind that can *only* exist as a human being. I simply leave that issue aside. Each of us exists as a certain human being. My question is this: must a fundamental entity that *begins its existence* as a human being *remain* the *same material being* in order to continue to exist?

There are two answers to this question that I need to consider. (1) I am a *mental system* in the sense that my identity is not tied to a certain material being. (Given that the bundle theory has already been rejected, such a mental system must be understood as a correlate to its parts rather than as a bundle composed of its parts.) (2) I am a *material being* in the sense that I will cease to exist if this material being ceases to exist. The difference between these two answers can be explained by invoking one of Shoemaker's thought experiments. He describes the scenario of a "brain-state transfer" (BST): Cloned copies exist of the bodies of the people in a certain society and these people regularly go to the hospital for a "body-change." In the hospital, the complete states of their brain are transferred to the cloned body and the old body is destroyed.[1] If I am a mental system, then I survive this procedure. If I am a material being, I don't.

I think that answer 2 is the right one.[2] One can offer both an *intuitive* and a *principled* reason in its favor. Let me start with the intuitive argument. In the film *Multiplicity*,[3] Doug (played by Michael Keaton) has a problem: he does not have enough time. He has barely enough time for his job, and he neglects his wife (played by Andie McDowell) and his children. Moreover, he has absolutely no free time for himself. By chance, he meets a genetic scientist, Dr. Owen Leeds, who has a solution to Doug's problems: he should have himself cloned by Dr. Leeds. When the clone wakes up after the cloning process, he thinks that he is Doug. No wonder: the clone is not simply a perfect copy of Doug's body, but also has all of Doug's psychological characteristics (memories, intentions, etc.).[4] Accordingly, the clone insists at first that he is Doug, until Dr. Leeds shows him the number "2" behind his ear . . . (Accordingly, I call the people who exist after the cloning No. 1 and No. 2.)

My summary of this film reflects the most natural way of understanding it: It presents us with a fundamental entity who has himself cloned. He survives the whole process not as his clone (No. 2), but as the human being who through the whole process remains *the same human being* (No. 1). This is also how the story is told in the film itself, in which there is no doubt that Doug is No. 1. This intuitive understanding of such a story contradicts the view that I am a mental system. If I were a mental system, then there would be no relevant difference between Doug's case and fission. Just like fission, the cloning duplicates Doug's mental system. Now, it was argued earlier that a fundamental entity would not survive fission. But Doug does survive the cloning process. So it cannot be that he is simply a mental system. Since the continuous existence of a mental system is thus not sufficient for Doug's survival, it must be that the continuous existence of a material being is necessary. Doug must be a material being: if this material being no longer exists, Doug no longer exists.

Doug's tale raises the question "Of the *two* individuals who exist after the cloning, who is identical to Doug?" The intuitively correct answer is that it is the individual who is the *same human being as Doug*, namely, No. 1. Now, it could be argued that the reason why this seems to be the right answer is that here we have a choice between *two* individuals with the same mental system and that one of the two individuals (No. 1) seems to be the *better candidate*: just like No. 2, No. 1 has the same psychological characteristics as Doug, but *in addition* No. 1 also has the same body. This does not rule out the possibility that the continuous existence of a mental system is enough in those cases in which only *one* individual receives this mental system. BST is exactly such a case. So the intuitive reaction to Doug's story is compatible with the assumption that I do not cease to exist if my body ceases to exist. In BST—or so one can argue—I do not cease to exist, but continue to exist as the individual with my mental system.

I do not think that both can be true—that Doug survives as No.1 as opposed to No. 2 *and* that a fundamental entity would survive BST. Nevertheless, it may be that our intuition is clouded by the fact that in Doug's case we have a choice between more than one individual. So the intuitive reaction to Doug's story does not alone suffice to show that we should accept the view that I cease to exist if the material being that embodies me ceases to exist. But there is also the following *principled reason* for this view: *commitment continuity can obtain* between Doug and No. 1, but not between Doug and No. 2. To see why, we must consider the relationship between Doug and the commitments "saved" in his brain, on the one hand, and Doug and the copies of these commitments made in the cloning process, on the other. When we talk about commitments "saved" in Doug's brain, we are talking about the physical basis of something for which Doug is minimally responsible. If Doug actively makes this commitment, the physical basis of the commitment is, as it were, a direct result of something that Doug did. And even if Doug simply finds himself with this commitment, a similar relationship holds: He is minimally responsible for keeping this commitment—and its corresponding physical basis—or for getting rid of it. Doug's relationship to the copies made of his commitments for the sake of the cloning process is entirely different. Here copies are made of commitments for which Doug is minimally responsible. But as the one who has made these commitments he is not in any way responsible for the copying process. It is definitive of such a copying process that the one who made the commitment is not committing himself to anything in this process. Rather, the commitments that he already made are being copied. This holds even if he himself chooses to have them copied and pushes the button that starts the copying process. In this case he would be choosing to have commitments copied that he has already made; he would not be making them.[5]

I must come to the following conclusion: Assuming that I am born a human being, I cease to exist if this material being ceases to exist. The psychological relations for which I am minimally responsible can only be realized in the material being I am born as. For this reason, the continued existence of a material being is *necessary* for the continued existence of the fundamental entity embodied by that material being.

2 I, THE LIVING BEING AND THE BODY: MATERIAL CONSTITUTION

One upshot of the last section and the previous chapters is the following: it is a necessary but not sufficient condition for the diachronic identity of the two fundamental entities X at t_1 and Y at t_n that they are the same material being—if we assume that the X began its existence as a human being. How are we then to conceive of the ontological relationship between the fundamental entity and the material being it "is"? We must rule out the possibility that the two are identical; otherwise, being the same material being over time would be sufficient for the diachronic identity of the fundamental entity. However, the two cannot be entirely separate entities either; otherwise, being the same material being would not be necessary for being one and the same fundamental entity over time.

The answer provided here can be explained by first considering what this sort of answer means for the relationship between a statue and the piece of material it is made of: A particular statue comes into being when a piece of material is formed a certain way. The piece of material can exist before and after the existence of the statue. For example, a piece of copper may exist at t_1 and be formed into a statue at t_2. This piece of material and the statue both exist at t_2. When the piece of copper is melted at t_3, the statue does not exist anymore, but the piece of copper surely does. The continued existence of some material is necessary for the persistence of the statue: there must be enough material at all times for the form of the statue to be continually realized. Borrowing a term from the literature, these facts about the statue and the piece of material mean that the piece of material "*materially constitutes*" the statue.[6] The fact that the statue and the piece of material are related by material constitution leaves open a number of questions concerning their relationship. One such question is which changes in the material of the statue this particular statue can survive, assuming that the form of the statue is still preserved. For example, if the statue were made of several planks of wood and the planks were replaced one by one by other planks or even by some other material, would it still be one and the same statue, assuming that the statue continually retains its form?

The relationship between a fundamental entity originally existing as a human being and the material being embodying this fundamental entity is to be thought of analogously: A particular fundamental entity comes into being when a certain living being acquires certain mental capacities—when it takes on a certain "form." The living being can exist before and after the existence of the fundamental entity. After the living being has acquired these mental capacities, at least two entities coexist: the fundamental entity and the living being. Material continuity is necessary for the persistence of the fundamental entity: there must be material continuity of the requisite sort for there to be commitment continuity. So, according to the view proposed here, a fundamental entity is *materially constituted* by the material being embodying it.

This does not answer the question of what kind of material continuity is necessary for there to be commitment continuity. I have argued that the copying process taking place in the cloning in Doug's case does not secure commitment continuity. Here the sort of material continuity necessary for commitment continuity is lacking. However, this falls short of giving a general answer to the question of what sort of material continuity is necessary. One can ask, for example, whether a fundamental entity can survive changes that would cause this material being to cease existing as a *living being* even though the *same material being* continues to exist. Such questions go beyond the scope of this study. A fundamental entity begins its existence as a living being. A living being is a material being. A fundamental entity can only exist as a material being, but it is left open whether a fundamental entity can only exist as a living being.

The aim of this section is to explain further what it means to say that a fundamental entity is materially constituted by a material being. For the purpose, I will simply assume that this material being is continually a living being. Also, I should note that material constitution is a controversial idea that cannot be defended adequately in this book. It is my policy to spend as little time as possible discussing the elements of my viewpoint that I have merely borrowed from other accounts in the literature. This is a case in point. It is not my aim to make any original contribution to the general issue of material constitution. Thus, I will keep the exposition in this section as brief as possible in order to save space for topics to which I hope to make my own contribution—such as the special issue as to how two or more fundamental entities can be materially constituted by one living being (Chapter 11).

To further explicate the idea of material constitution, it is useful to consider an objection raised by E. T. Olson in different ways: The piece of material that supposedly materially constitutes the statue is composed of different parts that stand in certain relations to each other. *At each point in time* the statue is composed of *exactly the same parts* that stand in *exactly the same relations* to each other. So how can there be a *qualitative difference* between the statue and the piece of material? This general objection can also be stated as a special objection to the view that I am materially constituted by a living being. According to this view, at each time in my life, it is not only I who exist, but also the living being which might exist longer than I do. Since each thought is not thought twice—once by me and once by this living being—I am the only one thinking here. But how can it be possible that *only I think and not also this living being*, given the fact that there is no material difference between me and the living being at any time of my existence? And how can I possibly have *other diachronic identity conditions* than the living being?[7]

This objection rests, as E. J. Lowe points out, on a "cinematographic fallacy."[8] This fallacy depends on the assumption that each qualitative difference between two entities must be explicable in terms of a difference that can be captured by a "snapshot" of the two entities. However, to explain the difference in the diachronic identity conditions of two entities, one cannot start with a snapshot of these entities. On the contrary, one must *start* with the different conditions of diachronic identity, so as to explain certain qualitative differences. It is on account of their different conditions of diachronic identity that the statue and the piece of material are distinguishable in the first place. The same holds for me and the living being that materially constitutes me. The reason why it is possible to distinguish between me and the entity *living being* in question is that there can be a certain sort of life before and after my existence. There exists an entity that *lives* before and after me. An entity in a purely vegetative state has this sort of life and it requires no higher mental functions such as thought. The conditions of my diachronic identity, in contrast, are dependent upon my ability to exercise higher mental functions. Having distinguished between two entities *on the grounds of these different conditions of diachronic identity,* one must then say that it is I who thinks and not the living being: given that the entity *living being* at stake here is distinguished from me in this sort of way, its identity consists in nothing but the exercise of certain life functions that have nothing to do with thinking.

So the objection is refuted. In any case, it is self-defeating for defenders of the biological approach such as Olson to employ this objection, because it can also be used against them. According to the biological approach, my diachronic identity conditions are those of a living being. Biological death is the end of my existence; I do not exist as a corpse. Now, my biological death does not mean that an entity comes into existence *de novo*.[9] Rather, in this case an already existing entity becomes a corpse; let's call this entity "my body."[10] Therefore, during my existence as a living being, it is not only this living being that exists, but also my body. The defenders of the biological approach face a dilemma here. Either they abandon their position and adopt the view that I still exist as a corpse, or they must assume that I as a living being am *materially constituted* by my body. In the latter case, the objection also applies to the biological approach: At each point in time during my existence—the existence of a living being—my body also exists. At none of these points in time is there any material difference between the living being and my body. So how can there be a qualitative difference between them? How can they have different conditions of diachronic identity?[11]

According to the view defended here, I am materially constituted by a living being and a body. This view was introduced by a comparison that considered the relationship between a statue and the piece of material that it is made of. By way of concluding these brief remarks about material constitution, it is worth discussing some important differences between me and the living being, on the one hand, and the statue and the piece of material, on the other.

First, the piece of material does not develop into a statue, but is formed into a statue by somebody. I am an agent who is a correlate to certain psychological relations. The organism existing before this agent naturally develops into such an agent. It is part of the normal development of such an organism to develop into such an agent.

Second, during the existence of such an agent, this agent is materially constituted by a living being. This agent has other conditions of diachronic identity than the living being. Therefore, two entities coexist here. This also holds for the piece of material and the statue. However, in the case of the agent and the living being, it is possible to ask a certain question and in the case of the statue and the piece of material no comparable question can be asked: which of the two concepts (the concept *agent who is a correlate to the psychological relations for which this agent is minimally responsible* or the concept *living being*) determines *my* conditions of diachronic identity? The concept *I* does not have the same meaning as either of these two concepts. Therefore it can meaningfully be asked which of the two concepts determines my conditions of diachronic identity.

Third, one may combine the two previous points. Just as the statue is a piece of material formed in a certain way, so too is an agent who is a correlate to certain psychological relations a living being who has acquired certain capacities. However, the two cases are not completely analogous: *I* am fundamentally such an agent. And the *living being* is something out of which *I naturally develop.*

3 MY BEGINNING AND MY END

According to the commitment criterion, my existence begins with my first commitment and ends when I no longer have any.[12] This means that my existence does not begin until sometime after my birth and that I could not survive falling into a vegetative state. In the last section, I argued that it is not *metaphysically* problematic to assume that I am materially constituted by a living being that exists before I come into existence and can continue to exist after my existence is over. It could now be argued that the consequences of the commitment criterion are *counterintuitive.* After all, we normally assume that *I* was the fetus in my mother's womb.[13] Similarly, we suppose that, if I had a serious accident, it would be *I* who afterward exists in a purely vegetative state.[14] These everyday intuitions, however, cannot settle the issue. It is just as natural for a person to ponder what should happen after her bodily death: should *I*—as a corpse—be buried in a coffin or should I be cremated?[15] Of course, it is possible to say that this way of speaking should not be taken literally:[16] we speak in this way, but we really just mean the corpse. The problem, however, is that the everyday manner of speaking, which allegedly supports the biological approach, can also be interpreted differently: Although we say "I existed in my mother's womb," what we mean is that the living being that later materially constitutes me existed in the womb. The living being in a woman's womb does not—at least not prior to a certain point—have any mental life. So this living being cannot strictly be me. Saying that it is me is only a manner of speaking. Similarly, I cannot exist in a purely vegetative state. A being no longer capable of mental activity is not me. Once again, saying that I exist in such a state is only a manner of speaking not to be taken literally. So it must be concluded that everyday intuitions concerning my beginning and my end are of no use in deciding between the commitment criterion and the biological approach.

Now, it could be argued that everyday intuitions speak in favor of those psychological approaches according to which experiences mark the beginning of my existence: Doesn't an infant have experiences without being able to make commitments? Doesn't my existence accordingly begin with experiences rather than with commitments? As before, it can be shown that everyday intuitions cannot settle the issue one way or the other.

The commitment criterion is an elaboration of the authorial correlate theory. According to the latter, I am fundamentally an agent who is a correlate to the psychological relations for which she is minimally responsible. Now, it can be asked what it means for something to be part of my mental life. The authorial correlate theory suggests a two-part answer to this question: Because I am fundamentally an agent, the attitudes for which I am minimally responsible are *primary* in the order of explanation. Here the answer to the question what it means that an attitude is mine is that it means that I am minimally responsible for it. Now, there are parts of my mental life for which I am not minimally responsible: experiences, desires, feeling, etc. These are *secondary* in the order of explanation: for these to be part of my mental life—to be *my experience*, *my desire*, etc.—they have to be appropriately related to attitudes for which I am minimally responsible. This will be elaborated on in Chapter 12. Accordingly, as will now be argued, there is a perfectly intuitive sense in which anything occurring prior to the existence of an agent that is capable of making commitments cannot count as *my experience*. Thus, it will turn out that everyday intuition is also on the side of the commitment criterion.

We can distinguish between experience in a strict sense and "experience." We may say that an infant who does not have the cognitive abilities to make commitments has "experiences." However, to be able to serve as a justificatory basis of commitments, experiences must be propositionally or conceptually structured. The ability to have an experience in this strict sense is part and parcel of the ability to make commitments. This can be expressed in the following *experience principle*: only beings who are capable of making commitments can, strictly speaking, have experiences. On the basis of this principle, one can say that the beginning of my existence is the time at which experience becomes possible. Strictly speaking, experience is *not* possible prior to my existence. Some of what goes on prior to my existence may be called "experiences," but in such occurrences I have *not experienced* anything.

The experience principle would, of course, need to be defended.[17] Here I merely wish to point out that it should indeed find broad acceptance. The experience principle does *not* say that beings who are capable of making commitments *do not share anything that one may call "experiences"* with beings (say, infants and nonhuman animals) who are incapable of making commitments. Both kinds of beings may share "experiences." This principle only says that—even assuming that there are such "experiences" shared by both kinds of beings—experience in the strict sense that can serve as a justificatory basis of commitments must exist *in addition* to such "experience." Only beings that can make commitments can have experience in the strict sense. This means that this principle can be accepted by such authors as John McDowell, who denies that there is anything that can be termed "experience" that is shared by beings capable of conceptual thought and beings incapable of it.[18] The experience principle can also be accepted by those who think that there is non-conceptual "experience" that can serve as a basis of commitments. To accept this principle, these philosophers must only make the further assumption that between "experiences" and commitments, experiences exist in the strict sense that can be understood as a conceptual transformation of "experiences" and can only be had by beings capable of commitments. Since defenders of sense data theories and related approaches make such an assumption,[19] I think that the experience principle can be fairly broadly accepted.

In any case, the experience principle shows the following: Assuming that it is intuitively plausible that I am an agent who is a correlate to the psychological relations this agent is minimally responsible for, it is also intuitively plausible that my existence begins with the capacity to have experiences where experiences are understood as something that only a being capable of making commitments can have. There is a clear intuitive sense in which anything that occurs prior to the existence of such an agent cannot count as *my experience*.

7 The Various Senses of "Personal Identity"

In Chapter 3, I argued that we must distinguish between several questions commonly discussed under the heading of "personal identity." The first aim of this chapter is to present further arguments for the need to distinguish between questions 1–6. This will be done in section 1 by showing how the distinction between these different questions makes sense of several contexts in which questions of identity come up. The other aim of the chapter is to give further support for the commitment criterion. First, section 1 will reveal how the commitment criterion offers the proper framework for understanding identity in the different contexts under discussion and how it thus does justice to the distinctions between questions 1–6 (condition of adequacy 4). Second, by comparing the commitment criterion with some other approaches, it will be shown more generally how the commitment criterion offers the right framework for answering questions 1–6 (section 2). The commitment criterion is a development of the authorial correlate theory. So in talking about the commitment criterion I shall often be drawing on elements made explicit by the authorial correlate theory. However, because the commitment criterion is an account of diachronic identity, I do not dwell in this chapter upon contexts in which questions of individuation arise. This is the subject of Part III.

1 PERSONAL IDENTITY IN DIFFERENT CONTEXTS

Questions of identity come up in many ways in different contexts. The point of distinguishing between these contexts is not to suggest that they are somehow entirely separate but rather to reveal more clearly the fruitfulness of the distinctions between questions 1–6[1] and the advantages of the commitment criterion.

(1) People want to understand who they are. Although many people never explicitly ask themselves the question "Who am I?" their lives are guided by an implicit answer to this question. Others spend their lives—or at least their youth—seeking an answer. People suffering an identity crisis who have lost their orientation in life are at a complete loss as to how to

answer this question. A person seeking an answer might say that she has no clearer idea of who she is than she had many years ago. Such a claim might strike one as paradoxical: if a person has been unable to answer the question "Who am I?" for the last years, how can she know that it was *she* who was concerned with the question many years ago? The paradox disappears if we distinguish between the question "What am I?" (question 1), the question of the diachronic identity of fundamental entities (question 2), and the question "Who am I?" (question 6). Question 1 asks what entities are the fundamental entities and question 2 concerns the diachronic identity of these entities. The person seeking an answer to question 6 simply presupposes that she is the fundamental entity already engaged with this question in the past. We might say that, in asking the question "Who am I?" the person is seeking a self-definition, or that she is trying to decide what she truly stands for, or that she is searching for her true self. Whatever the best way is to phrase these issues, the person may be in the dark as to how to resolve them even though she has no doubt that *she*—the same fundamental entity—has been engaged with this question all this time.

So we need to distinguish between different questions. But how does the commitment criterion fare as an answer to question 2? Does it give an answer that respects or blurs the distinction between this question and the question "Who am I?" According to the commitment criterion, the diachronic identity of a fundamental entity is based on the relation of commitment continuity. Now, commitment continuity has, as such, nothing to do with the issue involved in "Who am I?" The commitments involved in commitment continuity may simply be irrelevant to this question. For example, if there is commitment continuity with respect to the opening hours of the post office, this guarantees the diachronic identity of a fundamental entity but it may have nothing to do with what the person really stands for, who she really is, or what is of greatest importance to her. Thus it may be concluded that the commitment criterion provides an answer to question 2 that keeps this question clearly distinct from the question "Who am I?"[2]

(2) In speaking of a person's "true" self, we seem to be distinguishing one side of a person from other sides of her. Such a distinction may be the same as a distinction that is assumed when a person experiences or views certain of her mental states—passions or thoughts, say—as alien or external to her, and not as "hers." This distinction between the mental states of a person that are alien to her and mental states that are hers presupposes that both kinds of mental states are *mental states of the person*. Thus, in one sense the mental states are hers and in another they are not.[3] It is natural to distinguish between the history or identity of a fundamental entity to whom all of these mental states belong and the history or identity of a personality or self to whom only those mental states belong which the fundamental entity identifies with[4]—those mental states that the fundamental entity does not view as alien. The identity of the fundamental entity is left untouched even if the person radically changes her orientation in life—and

if the mental states she previously identified with now seem alien to her. The mental states are still all part of the history of this fundamental entity. Let us consider the following passage from Saint Augustine's *Confessions*:

> I must now carry my thoughts back to the abominable things I did in those days, the sins of the flesh which defiled my soul. I do this, my God, not because I love those sins, but so that I may love you. For love of your love I shall retrace my wicked ways . . . For love of your love I shall retrieve myself from the havoc of disruption which tore me to pieces when I turned away from you, whom I alone should have sought, and lost myself instead on many a different quest. For as I grew to manhood I was inflamed with desire for a surfeit of hell's pleasures. Foolhardy as I was, I ran wild with lust that was manifold and rank. In your eyes my beauty vanished and I was foul to the core, yet I was pleased with my own condition and anxious to be pleasing in the eyes of men.[5]

When St. Augustine looks back on his life, he is thinking about the life of one fundamental entity who throughout his life has been subject to desires of the flesh. We may distinguish between three stages in St. Augustine's attitudes toward these desires: the carnal stage, the stage of struggle, and the religious stage. About the first, carnal, stage, St. Augustine writes: "I was pleased with my own condition." Here the carnal desires are not alien to him, but rather something he identifies with. About the pivotal part of the stage of struggle, he writes: "My inner self was a house divided against itself."[6] He has the will to resist these desires, but fails, and the reason is that he does not will it "wholeheartedly"[7] or "fully."[8] In the third, religious, stage the carnal desires are still present, but he—at least when his is awake—not only wants to resist these desires but also has no difficulty in doing so.[9]

It makes sense to say that during the carnal stage St. Augustine was *somebody else* than he is when he looks back.[10] During the carnal stage, he identified with the carnal desires. They were part of who he was. He becomes somebody different during the religious stage—somebody who loves God rather than his carnal desires. We might describe this as a transition from a carnal personality or self to a religious personality or self. Carnal desires are a constitutive part of the carnal personality, whereas they are alien to the religious self. When St. Augustine finally manages to fully reject his carnal desires, the carnal self or personality no longer exists. There is no longer anybody who identifies with carnal desires and thus makes them part of himself. There is one and the same fundamental entity here who survives through the stage of struggle, but during this stage the carnal personality ceases to exist and the religious personality comes into existence.

> This is how he plans to kill me. Step 1: get me into his house under false pretenses. Step 2: stab me to death. In philosophical jargon: 1) show that my desires are part of him and having shown that they are within his range,

> 2) reject them with all his heart and thus eliminate them. In a way, not such a stupid plan. I am what I am. This is not a tautology, but a deep truth. My desires, passions, ideals, temperament, etc.—these are what I am. Without them I don't exist. So: IF he were able to extinguish them, he would be able to kill me. BUT my desires are beyond his reach. He may reject them, he may hate them, and he may detest them, but they will remain unaffected because they are mine. Beyond his reach! All that hate will eat him up and he will die.

The example of St. Augustine is merely meant as an illustration. And perhaps the concept of identification is not the right one to describe the issues. The point is this: if the changes with respect to the mental states that a person truly experiences as alien and truly experiences as her own are radical enough, it seems to make sense to say that one fundamental entity was somebody else—another personality—at an earlier stage than she is now. It is the task of an answer to the question of the diachronic identity of personality (question 3) to spell out the conditions for this being so.

The commitment criterion is helpful in understanding the issues at stake in this context. As already mentioned, commitment continuity has as such nothing to do with the question "Who am I?" For example, St. Augustine's commitment continuity with respect to his beliefs on how to get from Milan to Rome has as such nothing to do with who he is. This commitment continuity would suffice to explain why he remains one and the same fundamental entity throughout the three stages of his life. In addition, the authorial correlate approach gives an intuitive sense of what happens during the stage of struggle: here there is one fundamental entity—one agent—who is capable of distancing himself from his desires, finally overcoming their power over him, and identifying himself with the religious life. However, this explication also remains incomplete until one explains what it means to say that an experience or a desire belongs to a fundamental entity (see Chapter 12).

(3) Thought experiments involving *replacement* are common in literature on personal identity. Replacement means that, through an external manipulation, a mental characteristic of a person (an attitude, ideal, etc.) is eliminated and a new one is generated in its place. A manipulation of the brain, for example, could produce such a replacement. Is the product of this replacement the same person as the person existing before the replacement? If my mental characteristics are replaced by the kind of features that Napoleon had, would the person after the replacement still be me?

To answer these questions, one must ask whether they concern the identity of fundamental entities or the identity of personalities. It seems not implausible that such a replacement would replace one *personality* with another. However, according to the commitment criterion, if the replacement does not destroy commitment continuity, then the same *fundamental entity* continues to exist. If so much is replaced that there is no commitment continuity, then the fundamental entity will not survive the replacement.[11]

In this way, the commitment criterion can do justice to our intuitions about such thought experiments.

(4) When a persons acts, she chooses one of several options open to her. She could have acted otherwise. To say that she could have acted otherwise seems to imply that she would have been the same subject even if she had acted otherwise. Nevertheless, it is often said that through their choices people make themselves into who they are (or in more high-flown language "constitute themselves"). For example, by choosing to engage in terrorist activity, a person constitutes her own identity as a terrorist. But *this* person could have made a different choice and in that case *she* would not have been a terrorist—she would have had another identity. The distinction between the identity of fundamental entities and the identity of personalities makes sense of such cases. A fundamental entity could have made a different choice. In that case, she would still have been the same fundamental entity, but a different personality.

The commitment criterion can easily account for such cases. Commitment continuity does not require any similarity of content between the relevant commitment at t_1 and t_2. This means that commitment continuity would have remained even if the fundamental entity had made an entirely different choice at t_1. The identity of personalities, however, seems to require another kind of coherence not necessarily preserved between t_1 and t_2 if the fundamental entity had made a different choice. This will become clearer in the next section.

2 THE COMMITMENT CRITERION AND OTHER APPROACHES

The aim of this section is to argue for the commitment criterion by comparing it with two other types of theories. First, I shall consider narrative self-constitution theories and related approaches. Here I shall demonstrate the difference between such approaches and the commitment criterion and argue that only the latter can explain the diachronic identity of fundamental entities, though the former may possibly provide a good account of the identity of personalities. It should be noted that I do not claim that all the defenders of these other approaches understand these views as addressing the question of the identity of fundamental entities. Nevertheless, it is important to make clear that these theories do not provide a suitable answer to this question. Second, I shall show how the commitment criterion—in contrast to the biological answer to question 2—provides a unified framework for addressing questions 1–6.

Let me start by considering the *narrative self-constitution view*[12] defended by Marya Schechtman in *The Constitution of Selves.*[13] In the second part of this book, Schechtman is concerned with what she calls "the characterization question": "This question asks which actions, experiences, beliefs, values, desires, character traits, and so on (hereafter abbreviated 'characteristics') are to be attributed to a given person."[14] Schechtman distinguishes this question from the "reidentification question," "the question of what makes a person at time t_2 the same person as a person at time t_1."[15] She states that in its most common form the characterization question asks "which characteristics are *truly* those of some person"[16] and that the question "concerns the kind of identity that is at issue in an 'identity crisis.'"[17] However, she adds that the characterization question asks not only which characteristics truly belong to a person but also which characteristics are a part of the history of a person in the first place. In fact she argues that "there is a single question—the question of whether a particular characteristic is attributable to a particular person—the answer to which admits of degrees."[18] In other words, the difference between belonging truly to a person and belonging merely to the history of a person is a *matter of degree.*

Before turning to the self-constitution view itself, let me—as a matter of digression—make a few remarks about the difference between Schechtman's distinction between the reidentification question and the characterization question, on the one hand, and my distinctions between questions 1–6, on the other. The distinction between the identity of fundamental entities and the identity of personalities cuts across Schechtman's distinction between the reidentification question and the characterization question. One can apply both of her questions to fundamental entities as well as to personalities. In other words, one can ask what makes something the same person at two different times (the reidentification question) and what makes something the characteristic of a particular person (the characterization question), irrespective of whether "person" is taken to mean *fundamental entity* or *personality.* Thus, in my view, it is better to distinguish between questions of diachronic identity (questions 2–3) and issues of individuation (questions 4–5). This makes it clear that the question of diachronic identity can—contrary to what Schechtman's approach suggests—be asked not only about fundamental entities but also about personalities. The issues Schechtman subsumes under the characterization question can then be seen as arising with respect to questions of individuation (questions 4–5) and the question "Who am I?" (question 6). With respect to the individuation of fundamental entities, we need to address the issue of under which conditions a desire or an attitude, for example, belongs to one fundamental entity as opposed to another. It cannot be assumed that the answer to this question will be the same as the answer to the question of the conditions under which a desire or an attitude belongs to one personality as opposed to another. This is also separate from the question of which desires or attitudes are truly my own. This may be illustrated using the case of Jekyll and Hyde (assuming that Jekyll and Hyde are personalities rather then separate fundamental entities): Under what conditions does an attitude belong to the fundamental entity Henry Jekyll as opposed to another fundamental entity? Under what conditions does an attitude belong to the personality Dr. Jekyll as opposed to the personality Mr. Hyde? Under what conditions is an attitude truly Henry Jekyll's own—truly expressive of who he is?

Leaving aside these differences concerning the questions to be asked, let me turn to Schechtman's positive view. She defends an answer to the characterization question that she calls "the narrative self-constitution view":

> According to the narrative self-constitution view, the difference between persons and other individuals (I use the word "individual" to refer to any sentient creature) lies in how they organize their experience, and hence their lives. At the core of this view is the assertion that individuals constitute themselves as persons by coming to think of themselves as persisting subjects who have had experience in the past and will continue to have experience in the future, taking certain experiences as theirs. Some, but not all, individuals weave stories of their lives, and it is their doing so which makes them persons. On this view a person's identity (in the sense at issue in the characterization question) is constituted by the content of her self-narrative, and the traits, actions, and experiences included in it are, by virtue of that inclusion, hers.[19]

I am not interested in the question of what makes an individual a person in the first place (question 7), but rather in Schechtman's answer to the characterization question. Her answer is that "a person's identity (in the sense at issue in the characterization question) is constituted by the content of her self-narrative, and the traits, actions, and experiences included in it are, by virtue of that inclusion, hers." In other words, those past, present, and future characteristics belong to a person which in this person's self-narrative are attributed to the self that is the subject of this narrative.

Schechtman incorporates this basic idea into a nuanced and complex model. I will only mention two basic ways in which she qualifies the bold statement that characteristics belong to a person by inclusion in a self-narrative. First, to avoid assuming that a characteristic belongs to a person simply because it is part of a person's self-conception—to avoid assuming that a person cannot be mistaken about herself—she introduces constraints on what can count as an identity-constituting narrative.[20] Since these constraints go beyond the scope of this study, they will not be discussed here. Second, to explain, among other things, how unconscious mental states can belong to a person, she says that there may be *implicit* as well as explicit self-narratives. "The implicit narrative is understood as the psychological organization from which his experience and actions are actually flowing."[21] Schechtman knows that this notion of an implicit narrative seems to diverge from the usual meaning of "self-narrative." She responds by saying that her talk of self-narratives is merely meant to make clear that "the psychological forces constituting identity are dynamic and active—things a person *does*—rather than static and passive features she *has*."[22]

But *what* does a person *do* when she constitutes her own identity? And *what* is it that she *constitutes*? These questions can be answered in two fundamentally different ways. The first possible answer amounts to my approach to the identity of fundamental entities. This is a view in which the notion of a narrative plays no role. In the second answer, the notion of a narrative plays a substantive role. This is surely the answer Schechtman would give. After comparing these two approaches, I will go on to argue that only the first view can account for the identity of fundamental entities, though the latter may be suitable to explaining the identity of personalities.

(1) One could answer these questions by rehearsing the explication of the commitment criterion and the authorial correlate approach: Diachronic identity rests on commitment continuity. Commitment continuity consists in the relations of commitment revision and commitment maintenance. These relations are something for which an agent is minimally responsible, and this agent is a correlate to the psychological relations, etc. If this is what self-constitution means, then I have been defending a self-constitution approach to the identity of fundamental entities. However, it is important to note that the notion of self-constitution would not play any defining role here. Rather, it would be the other way around: the meaning of the talk of self-constitution would be exhausted by the talk of minimal responsibility for the psychological relations of commitment and the idea of an agent as a correlate to the psychological relations for which she is minimally responsible.

The commitments in question are commitments to the effect that it is true that *p*—for example, that Reykjavík is the capital of Iceland. One crucial feature of such commitments is that, in making them, I *need not* be taking a stand on such issues as the following: what is important to me in life; how I want to lead my life; who I really am; what I fundamentally stand for; what kind of a person I have been so far; who I want to become; etc. There are three important facts to take note of here: First, the existence of commitment continuity with respect to such commitments suffices for the identity of a fundamental entity. For example, the maintenance of the commitment that Reykjavík is the capital of Iceland over time ensures the identity of the fundamental entity during this time. Second, if the relevant commitment does not amount to taking a stand on the issues just listed, then it will not suffice to distinguish between different personalities. For example, taking a stand on a geographical issue does not suffice to distinguish between St. Augustine's carnal and religious self, or between an agent's feminist and Catholic selves, or between my "true" self and the rest of myself. To establish the identity of one personality or self as opposed to another, the person needs to *do something else* than merely make a commitment to the effect that something is true. Third, the connections established by the activity that is necessary to establish the identity of a personality or a self are not necessary for the identity of a fundamental entity. For example, even if there are no such connections between Dr. Jekyll and Mr. Hyde, Dr. Jekyll and Mr. Hyde might nevertheless simply be two personalities of one fundamental entity rather than two fundamental entities. I will offer an argument supporting these three claims in the following and start by considering another possible answer to the questions of what a person does when she constitutes her identity and what it is that she constitutes.

(2) Another possible answer is to describe an activity that seems suitable for drawing a distinction between different personalities or selves and for maintaining their diachronic identity. Schechtman is a good example of this kind of answer: "To have an autobiographical narrative in the relevant sense is . . . to have an implicit understanding of one's history as unfolding according to the logic of the story of a person's life."[23] This kind of activity—having an autobiographical narrative—is not an implausible candidate for being the sort of activity that is needed not only to distinguish between different personalities or selves of the same fundamental entity, or between my "true" self and other sides of me, but also to secure the diachronic identity of such personalities or selves.[24]

In a later text, Schechtman discusses an issue that can be illustrated by one of her two central examples. This is Derek Parfit's example of the nineteenth-century Russian who fears that in the course of time he will lose his socialist ideals and not give the land he will later inherit to peasants, since at the time of inheritance he will probably no longer be a socialist. As a result he signs a legal document—only revocable by his wife—that ensures the land will later be given to the peasants. He asks his wife not to revoke the document at a later time, adding by way of argument: "I regard my ideals as essential to me. If I lose these ideals, I want you to think that I cease to exist."[25] Schechtman's goal is to develop an approach that is capable of accounting for the sense in which the young individual is not the same person or subject as the mature one.

Moreover, Schechtman argues that the narrative approach alone cannot account for this. The problem is that a coherent narrative of the transformation of a younger person into an older one does not secure identity. It merely shows "that there can be intelligible stories of how someone loses his or her identity."[26] She thus suggests that a narrative approach needs to be supplemented by an additional element that she calls "empathic access."[27] Empathic access is a backward-looking relation, i.e., a relation from the older to the younger individual, which requires not only "*access* to the feelings and thoughts of [the individual's] past" but also "*empathy*."[28] This empathy falls short of endorsing the lifestyle of the younger person, but it also requires that the lifestyle not be completely rejected: the older individual must have some sympathy for the younger person's being and way of life.[29]

Now, is Schechtman's narrative approach, supplemented by "empathic access," suitable for accounting for the identity of fundamental entities? It surely is not. The lack of empathic access is designed to account for something else—namely, for the successive existence of more than one self in the life of one fundamental entity. Empathic access is a matter of an attitude that a fundamental entity has to her past. If she doesn't adopt that attitude, then she will not be another fundamental entity than she was in the past.

How about the "pure" narrative approach, the narrative self-constitution theory *not* supplemented by "empathic access"? Can this approach account for the identity of fundamental entities? If Schechtman is right that there can be a coherent narrative even about a radical change without retrospective empathic access, would this not be a good way to account for the diachronic identity of fundamental entities? No, it would not. Having an autobiographical narrative is supposed to do something more than merely make commitments such as "Reykjavík is the capital of Iceland." Having such a narrative is supposed to answer questions such as what I fundamentally care about; who I really am; how I have come to be who I am; etc. This means that it is possible in principle that there will be gaps in the life of an individual across which no autobiographical narrative can be told. Cases of multiple personality—though not necessarily real cases of dissociative identity disorder—are precisely such examples.[30] Sally and BI in Prince's *The Dissociation of a Personality* mentioned in chapter 2 may be such a case. Sally and BI have fundamentally different characters and ideals and understand themselves in entirely different ways. It makes sense to say that Sally lives in accordance with one autobiographical narrative, BI in accordance with another. There is simply nobody telling or living in accordance with an autobiographical narrative that bridges the gap between the two personalities: when Miss Beauchamp shifts from being Sally to being BI, she shifts from living within one narrative to living within another one. This does not mean that Sally and BI are two fundamental entities rather than two personalities of the same fundamental entity. If Miss Beauchamp acquires the belief as Sally that the train from Boston to New York does not run on Thursday and retains this commitment as BI, then Miss Beauchamp is one fundamental entity with these two personalities. This case will be discussed in detail in the next chapter, and narrative approaches to multiple personality will be discussed in section 9.3.

So far, I have emphasized the distinction between the different questions discussed under the rubric of "personal identity" and how the commitment criterion does justice to these differences. However, it is also important to emphasize that the commitment approach enables us to understand the unity underlying questions 1–6. To illustrate this, let me assume that we combine the authorial correlate theory and the commitment criterion with a narrative approach to the questions of the identity of personalities and the question "Who am I?" According to the authorial correlate theory, I am fundamentally an agent who is a correlate to the psychological relations for which this agent is minimally responsible. It is with respect to this agency that diachronic identity is explained: I am one and the same fundamental entity on account of my minimal responsibility as an agent for the relevant commitment continuity. It is as this very same agent that I ask "Who am I?" and, in response to this question, that I am more or less successful in telling and living by a coherent autobiographical narrative of my life.

In asking the question "Who am I?" I may ask myself whether certain of my commitments and other attitudes or desires are really mine. This question is being asked about commitments, attitudes, and desires that are, in some sense, already mine. The authorial correlate approach can explain the sense in which they are mine in terms of my agency: the commitments and attitudes I have adopted and the desires are material for me to take a stand on. This means that if I reject some attitudes or desires as not really mine—as not really part of me—they still belong to me as an agent.

> That he hates me goes without saying and doesn't explain much. The question is: *Why* does he want to kill me? His theories are not driven by argument. So what's the force behind them? Even if he were to succeed in proving that I don't exist, he would only have proven that I am part of him! So he would then be hating a part of himself. So why go through all these maneuvers to prove this? I'm afraid the answer is obvious: He needs to believe that there is no power living within him that is fundamentally alien to him and beyond his control. If I am part of him, he can extinguish me at his convenience.

In trying to achieve autobiographical unity within my life, I may have varying degrees of success. If I am such a radically conflicted person that I cannot live by one narrative only, it is a sign of a conflict within one and the same agent: one and the same agent is torn in two directions. Miss Beauchamp may possibly exemplify an agent who has such radically different orientations in life that she has to live in different narratives.

Now, contrast this with the combination of a biological approach to the identity of fundamental entities and a narrative approach to the identity of personalities and the question "Who am I?" This position aims to specify two sorts of unities: a biological unity for fundamental entities and a narrative unity for personalities. This means that if we are forced to admit that within one body there are two personalities, then we are only left with biological unity. This loses sight of the following possibility: If Miss Beauchamp acquires, as Sally, the belief that the train from Boston to New York does not run on Thursday and retains this commitment as BI, this does not mean that Sally and BI are one personality. Nevertheless, there is greater unity in Miss Beauchamp's life than just biological unity. Although she splits into more than one personality, she manages to maintain and revise commitments in the course of her life. So there are three possibilities:

1) Sally and BI are really one personality.

2) Sally and BI are two personalities, but Miss Beauchamp's life is held together by a stronger unity than just biological unity. Miss Beauchamp is one agent who is deeply conflicted.

3) However we are to describe Sally and BI (as two agents? two personalities? not agents or personalities at all?), Miss Beauchamp's life is held together only by biological unity.

A combination of the biological approach and the narrative approach has no room for the second option.[31] The problem is actually not that the supplement to the biological approach is a *narrative* approach. Rather, the problem is that there is no room left for an interesting sort of unity between biological unity and the unity of *personalities*. And that seems clearly wrong. Somebody may truly be one agent characterized by inner conflicts so great that she is best described as one agent who has two personalities.

In the next part of this book, I shall discuss these possibilities in greater detail, especially 2) and 3). In the next chapter, I shall argue that Sally understands herself according to 3)—more specifically, as one of several fundamental entities in one body. I think that Sally is right on the metaphysical level: she is right that one body can embody more than one fundamental entity (coexistence thesis). However, she is wrong about her own case: it should be understood as a version of 2). The question then arises as to what conditions need to be fulfilled in order for there to exist two fundamental entities in one body. In Chapter 9, I shall argue that the theories in the literature do not succeed in spelling out these conditions. Chapter 10 presents arguments for the coexistence thesis and Chapter 12 argues for a specific principle of individuation. Chapter 11 shows how to think of two fundamental entities in one body and, against the backdrop of the account given in these chapters, Chapters 13–14 return to an explication of multiple personality.

Part III

Multiple Personality and Individuation

8 Morton Prince's Seminal Case Study *The Dissociation of a Personality*

One aim of this study is to defend a theory of the identity of fundamental entities. The authorial correlate theory was offered as an answer to the question "What am I fundamentally?" (question 1). The commitment criterion was defended as an account of the *diachronic identity* of fundamental entities (question 2). An account of the individuation of fundamental entities must still be developed (question 4). This will be done in Chapters 9–12, with Chapter 9 providing a critique of other approaches. This third part of this book may also be thought of as a test of my account in a central borderline case: can two fundamental entities share a body? I argue in Chapter 10 that they can (the coexistence thesis).

It could be objected that it is not possible to make a reliable judgment about this borderline case—that this case is beyond the conditions of application of the concepts involved. This objection can be undermined if it can be shown that the possibility of the existence of two fundamental entities existing in one body is entertained in cases of multiple personality and that cases of multiple personality have sufficient continuity with normal cases for the application of the relevant concepts to make sense. Showing this requires a detailed discussion of cases of multiple personality in various contexts. In this chapter, I discuss Morton Prince's seminal case study of multiple personality. I argue that one of the characters in this study should be understood as taking a stand which—if philosophically thought through—amounts to acceptance of the coexistence thesis. This discussion serves as backdrop to the philosophical discussion of individuation in Chapters 9–12. I then return to a discussion of multiple personality in other contexts in Chapters 13–14.

In other words, this part of the book can be read as completing the theory of the identity of fundamental entities. However, it can also be read as an interpretation of multiple personality. As stated in Chapter 2, my interest here is in the employment of philosophical concepts such as *I*, *she/he*, *we*, *self*, *body*, and *identity* in cases of multiple personality. In Chapter 2 I also argued that an interpretation of multiple personality must draw on philosophical theory. In this chapter, I will draw on the philosophical theses defended so far to arrive at an interpretation of one of the most important cases in the history of multiple personality. However, a philosophical theory of *individuation* is needed to get us further. Thus, after providing such an account in Chapters 10–12, this account will be employed in Chapters 13–14 to shed light on multiple personality in therapeutic/biographic and literary discourses. The upshot will be an interpretation of multiple personality applicable to many, though not all, contexts in which multiple personality surfaces.

In this chapter, the investigation of multiple personality is focused on Morton Prince's *The Dissociation of a Personality.* This text was selected for several reasons. First, the richness of the phenomenology is crucial for my purposes, and Prince's text is one of the most detailed investigations of multiple personality available. Second, different discourses overlap in Prince's book itself. It is not a purely scientific, biographical, or literary text, but all of these at once. As such, this work alone allows us to look at the use of "I," "person," and "identity" in various contexts. Third, fundamental assumptions in discussion of dissociative identity disorder today go back to texts like Prince's. This applies, in particular, to the idea of a dissociative division between different personalities in the same human being.[1] Fourth, the assumption made today by nearly everyone using dissociative identity disorder as a diagnosis, that phenomena such as dissociative identity disorder can be causally traced to child abuse, plays no role in Prince's text. Since this assumption is also irrelevant to my investigation, it is opportune to begin with Prince's work.

1 AN OVERVIEW OF DR. PRINCE'S ACCOUNT OF THE CASE

Published in 1906, *The Dissociation of a Personality* deals with the case of the patient Miss Christine L. Beauchamp, who received psychiatric treatment from Prince between 1898 and 1905.[2] Dr. Prince regards his patient as a person in whom different personalities have developed (1).[3] To distinguish her from the other personalities, Dr. Prince refers to the personality who initially came in for treatment as "BI." Dr. Prince describes BI as "extremely reticent," as someone who intensely dislikes speaking about herself (9). After "conventional methods of treatment" prove unsuccessful, Dr. Prince hypnotizes the patient for the first time on April 5 (20). Her reserve disappears under hypnosis, and the personality in hypnosis is called "BIa" (24–25). Otherwise, according to Dr. Prince, no essential difference exists between the two personalities. And BIa sees herself as the same person as the non-hypnotized BI (25, 28–38).

Later in the same month, a personality appears in hypnosis who speaks about BI in the third person and denies that she is BI. In Dr. Prince's initial interactions with this personality, whom he names "BIII" as well as "Chris," and who later gives herself the name "Sally Beauchamp" (29–30), he repeatedly insists that she and the non-hypnotized personality are one and the same (25–51). BIII, however, remains resolute in her attitude:

> On another occasion, in answer to the question why she (the *apparently* hypnotic state) [i.e., BIII] insisted that Miss Beauchamp in her waking state [i.e., BI] was a different person from herself at that moment, the contemptuous reply was: "Because she is stupid; she goes round mooning, half asleep, with her head buried in a book; she does not know half the time what she is about. She does not know how to take care of herself." (27–28)

Dr. Prince also ascribes completely different personality traits to BIII than to BI (see section 2.2). BIII talks about BI in the third person and has strong feelings about her: BIII repeatedly says she hates BI, and Dr. Prince traces the hate to a jealousy toward BI (52–53, 130). At this point in time, BI and BIa cannot have a similar attitude toward BIII since they do not know about her. BI and BIa have no direct knowledge of BIII's states and utterances: they cannot remember the times during which BIII appears in hypnosis (31–33). Moreover, at this point in time, Dr. Prince keeps them in the dark about BIII's existence (58, 91, 104, 119–120). BIa is able to recall her former hypnotic states and the life of BI, whereas BI has no knowledge of BIa. BIII, by contrast, has complete access to the mental states and the lives of BI and BIa (31–33). Furthermore, BIII claims that she is present *while* BI is conscious: BIII claims to be able to observe BI's psychological processes and actions *while they occur.* While observing BI's mental states, she herself—BIII—has her own thoughts and perceptions.

In June of 1898, in the first year of treatment, the case takes an important turn. Until then, BIII has had control over her body only during hypnosis in the therapy sessions with Dr. Prince, and her eyes have always been closed during this time. In June, through an act of will, she succeeds in opening her eyes outside of therapy. When she does so, BI disappears and she takes control of the body. To mark this decisive turning point, Dr. Prince henceforth refers to BIII as "Sally" in his text, even though BIII first gave herself this name later on (94–96). Such acts of will on Sally's part play an important role throughout the story, since they enable Sally to exert influence on the other personalities (even if she is not always successful). For instance, Sally can wrest control of the body from the others; she can prevent them from acting or have them make particular utterances (58–63, 119–127). For Dr. Prince, such acts of will are an important indication that Sally is a "*co-consciousness*" or "sub-consciousness" (145) that, *at the same time* as another personality has consciousness, is aware of herself, the environment, and the other personality (95).

After Sally opens her eyes for the first time, she and BI alternately have control of the body. From this point on, Sally makes life difficult for BI.[4] She writes letters that are found by and greatly disturb BI (163–167). BI knows that she falls into trance states and does strange things in these states, but she does not attribute her actions to another personality;

rather, she vaguely thinks that she is "possessed" by something. Accordingly, she believes that she herself wrote the letters in her trance states, and sees Sally's signature as "a name used by herself for the purpose of carrying out a part" (119–120). As already illustrated in section 2.2, she also troubles BI in many other ways (109, 131–132, 160–166).

On June 7, 1899, a new personality appears (BIV). In contrast to BIa and BIII (= Sally), she does not appear first in hypnosis (172–175). BIV remembers the period before 1893, but she has no memory at all of the time between 1893 and June 7, 1899 (66, 211–225). From this point on, BIV has control over the patient's body alternately with BI and Sally. BIV, however, has no memory of the actions and psychological states of BI and Sally.[5] BI also has no such memories of BIV. Sally, in contrast, recalls BIV's *actions*, and is also aware of them while they are being carried out. But Sally has neither memory nor co-consciousness of BIV's *psychological states* (180–184, 224–225, 231).[6] BIV is also ascribed character traits that clearly distinguish her from BI and Sally (16–17, 172, 175, 178–179, 183–184, 201–203, 277–280, 287–304, 307, 310–311, 400–401, 407–408, 424–425, 431, 435–437).

Sally likes BIV's lifestyle just as little as BI's and makes life difficult for her as well. But unlike BI, BIV does not respond with resignation. Even though BIV has no memories or direct knowledge of Sally's actions and psychological states, a lively interaction exists between them. They pursue an active correspondence in which they scold each other, and they make it difficult and painful for each other to carry out practical life (310–313, 424–425, 476–487).

With BIV's appearance, Dr. Prince's understanding of the case changes, as do his therapeutic efforts. Until this date, he worked on the assumption that his goal should be to cure the person who had come to him for treatment, that is, BI. Now the question arises for him whether BI is, in fact, the "the Real Miss Beauchamp"—"the real, original or normal self, the self that was born and which she was intended by nature to be" (1). Dr. Prince traces the appearance of BI back to an experience in 1893 that was traumatic for the patient. Since BIV remembers life before this date, and does then not appear until six years later, in 1899, Dr. Prince's initial working hypothesis is that BIV is the Real Miss Beauchamp, who was replaced by BI at the time of this trauma in 1893 (185–186, 210–250).

However, events on November 5, 1899, call this working hypothesis into question. When BI is under hypnosis, Sally suddenly emerges and offers Dr. Prince a suggestion:

> Oh, Dr. Prince, I came to tell you that I think the Idiot [i.e., BIV] hypnotized is the same person as BI hypnotized, *for I know the Idiot's thoughts when she is asleep* [i.e., when she is under hypnosis] *just as I do BI's then*. I may be wrong, but I think so. (267)

Dr. Prince takes up Sally's proposition and ultimately arrives at the following hypothesis: there is a new personality who can appear when either BI or BIV is hypnotized. This new personality must be distinguished from BIa—BI under hypnosis—since she differs from BI in terms of character and, unlike BIa, remembers the psychological states and actions of BIV. This new personality is called "BII." BII differs from the others in terms of personality, and she has memories of BI's and BIV's actions and psychological states, but none of Sally's. BII speaks of BI and BIV as herself: when questioned, she says, "I am BI" and "I am BIV." In contrast, BI and BIV have no recollection of BII's states and actions (266–282, 302–309, 398–405). Dr. Prince concludes that BII is the Real Miss Beauchamp under hypnosis. The only problem is that BII always becomes either BI or BIV when BII awakes from hypnosis. Ultimately, however, Dr. Prince succeeds in waking BII from hypnosis, so that this non-hypnotized person exhibits BII's personality and memories. According to Dr. Prince, this is the Real Miss Beauchamp. At the end of his book—the narrative time is July 1905—Dr. Prince reports that, in the last months, this personality has gained almost exclusive control over the patient's body (270, 414–415, 503, 514–525).

In summary, the different personalities can be described as follows:[7]

- *BI:* She only remembers BI's psychological states and actions.
- *BIa:* She is BI under hypnosis. She recalls her own states and actions and those of BI.
- *Sally (= BIII = Chris):* She remembers the actions of all the other personalities, and the psychological states of them all except for BIV. She also has co-consciousness of the corresponding actions and states.
- *BIV:* She only remembers BIV's states and actions. This means that she recalls nothing about the period between the key summer evening in 1893 and June 7, 1899.
- *The Real Miss Beauchamp:* She remembers her own states and actions and those of BI and BIV.
- *BII:* She is the Real Miss Beauchamp under hypnosis and recalls the states and actions of herself, BI, BIV, and the Real Miss Beauchamp.

My overview of the case cannot be regarded as a neutral description of a real case around 1900 any more than the text on which this survey is based can be described as such. My synopsis, however, is not meant to be a description of real events. What is crucial for me is the world that is sketched out in *The Dissociation of a Personality*, and the people who act in this world. The following sections will examine these persons' understanding of themselves and others more closely. The next section will deal with Dr. Prince. Here I am not concerned with the real person Morton Prince, the author of the book, but with the psychiatrist Dr. Prince, who appears as a character in the book.[8] In section 3, I will discuss the self-understanding of the figure Sally.

2 DR. PRINCE'S RELATION TO HIS VIS-À-VIS

I begin with a characteristic quotation, in which Dr. Prince says:

> My idea was that if BI and BIV could be fused into one character, a fusion which would be the resurrection of the original Miss Beauchamp and the restoration of the original mental relations, Sally would sink out of sight and disappear into her original subconscious abode, if she had one.[9]
>
> To dispose of Sally in this way after our long friendship seemed cold-blooded, and I confess to certain qualms. But what was to be done? All three could not live. The choice had to be made, and the law of psychology condemned Sally. (398–399)

We can decipher at least four interrelated attitudes of Dr. Prince's in this passage. He speaks of "*resurrection*"[10] and sees himself as Miss Beauchamp's *savior*, as the prince who rescues "the original Miss Beauchamp," the Cinderella among the different personalities. At the same time, he sees himself as the *master restorer*, as someone who rejoins the psychological fragments into a whole—the original Miss Beauchamp is thus *his work*. Third, he regards the personality "Sally" as an *autonomous person*, with whom he has developed a "*friendship*" and whom he cannot dispose of unscrupulously. As a consequence, he also does not want to assume responsibility for his therapeutic actions. He hides behind "the law of psychology," which dictates what he should do. In this fourth of Dr. Prince's attitudes, Miss Beauchamp and Sally are *objects* of psychology, whose nature and fate are objectively determined by psychological laws. I will now investigate these four aspects of his attitude more closely, beginning with the last.

Dr. Prince as Dissociative Psychologist (Miss Beauchamp as a Mere Bundle of Mental States)

For Dr. Prince, Miss Beauchamp is a passive object of observation, whose manner of functioning can be understood if one dissects it into its basic components like an object of natural scientific research. Dr. Prince's grasp of his object can be illustrated by an experiment that he carries out: Dr. Prince tells BI that she should close her eyes and then she will no longer see the metal rod that Dr. Prince has in his hand. BI then opens her eyes. She sees that Dr. Prince holds his hands as if he has something between them, but she does not see the metal rod, even though she can very much feel it with her hands. Later on she also cannot remember having seen the metal rod. She can remember it only under hypnosis. According to Dr. Prince, the following happens in this situation: a *conscious seeing* of the metal rod indeed takes place. But this conscious state is *isolated* or "*dissociated*" from the patient's "main current of consciousness." Therefore, BI cannot see the metal rod. Under hypnosis, this conscious state is "synthesized" with the main current of consciousness. That is why, under hypnosis, BI can recall having seen the rod (67–73). In this explanation of the phenomenon—called "*systematized anesthesia*"[11] or "*negative hallucination*"[12]—Dr. Prince makes two assumptions, which he shares with a school of psychology we could call "*dissociative psychology*":[13] 1) Mental states are essentially *conscious.* 2) Conscious states can be dissociated from one another; in other words, there are cases of *divided consciousness* or *dissociation.* Dissociation psychology is itself indebted to a fundamental element in British empiricism, the *association of ideas*, since *association* and *dissociation* are complementary concepts: conscious states can be associated with or dissociated from one another.[14]

These two assumptions of dissociation psychology form the basis of Dr. Prince's interpretation of multiple personality. Here we need only add a third assumption to the two principles: a personality—BI or Sally, for instance—is nothing but a bundle of conscious states that has attained a certain complexity. A personality should thus be thought of in a "bottom-up" fashion starting with these conscious states; it is a grouping of such states, but nothing beyond that. The group merely needs to have attained the complexity necessary to enable a "personal perception" to emerge within it that can be expressed by "*I* see, *I* feel." In the seeing of the metal rod, this complexity is absent, of course, and, along with it, "personal perception"; this seeing is only an isolated conscious state (189–194). Therefore, BI and Sally are each a bundle of conscious states, and BI's relation to Sally should be understood in the same way as her relation to the seeing of the metal rod. The seeing of the metal rod is a conscious state dissociated from BI; Sally *is* a group of conscious states that are dissociated from BI: "*Sally is a dissociated group of conscious states*" (153).

We can concisely illustrate Dr. Prince's relation to Miss Beauchamp as an object of observation of dissociative psychology using a diagram printed in a lecture held during the work on this major case study (see Figure 8.1).[15] Here Sally is represented as a subconsciousness that has led a parallel existence since childhood, which means that Sally is always aware of the states and actions of the others (BI and BIV).[16] BI and BIV's conscious states are

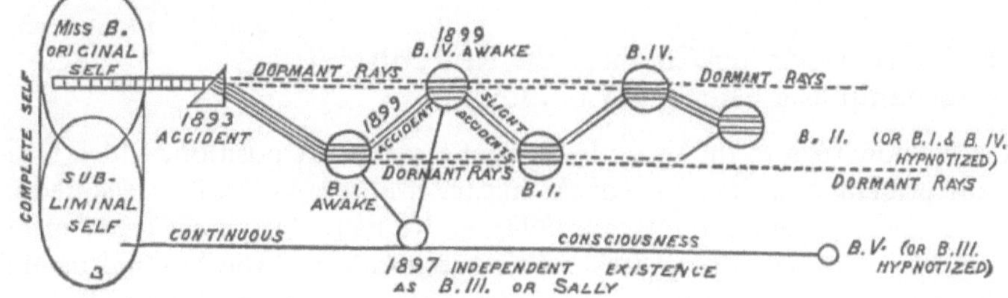

Figure 8.1

represented here as rays that emerge when the current or ray of consciousness of the original Miss Beauchamp fractures on the trauma in 1893 as on a prism.

Three important components of Dr. Prince's understanding of Miss Beauchamp can be seen in this diagram:

1) Miss Beauchamp is regarded as a completely passive object of observation of natural science. Miss Beauchamp plays no role in the diagram as an acting and self-interpreting subject. She herself is like a room penetrated by rays of light; currents of consciousness run within her—through her—and we can understand her once we understand how these currents divide, like rays of light.

2) The temporal relation of a subject to her or himself is replaced by a spatial image of a current in which objects flow from one place to another: The ray hits the prism and splits into its components.[17] These components remain as they are over time. States thus exist as "dormant rays"—just as the conscious seeing of the metal rod exists in a dissociated manner—and they are later rejoined with the rays from which they were divided at an earlier point in time (in Figure 8.1, for instance, in 1899 in "BIV awake"). Here amnesia is, in a sense, not amnesia at all; if someone remembers something, this memory must be seen as nothing more than a spatial joining of one conscious state— which has been isolated as a "dormant ray"—with other conscious states (257).

3) Dr. Prince regards Miss Beauchamp as a mere vessel of mental states that are more or less linked associatively. We see this by considering the overall diagram and the rays that fracture on the prism. Dr. Prince says they break into their "component rays";[18] the rays thus consist of components, and Miss Beauchamp of the rays. Now, particular rays run through BI *and* BIV; particular conscious states are thus shared by them. The personalities are *nothing but* bundles of conscious states, which is why such groupings can in principle *overlap*, just as, according to Dr. Prince, BI and BIV overlap here. This becomes clearer in another one of Dr. Prince's diagrams,[19] which explicitly makes clear that BI and BIV can share associated conscious states (see Figure 8.2).[20] As such, Miss Beauchamp as a whole is nothing but an accumulation of conscious states that are divided up into groups that overlap to varying degrees.

Dr. Prince as Master Chemist (the Real Miss Beauchamp as a Chemical Compound)

Let me now turn to the second aspect of Dr. Prince's position, which I initially presented in the image of the master restorer. As Dr. Prince stated in this section's opening quotation (398), he wants to "resurrect" the "original" Miss Beauchamp by means of a "restoration of the original mental relations." He also speaks of the "reconstruction" of the "original" Miss Beauchamp (414). For Dr. Prince, BII is the "original" or "real" Miss Beau-

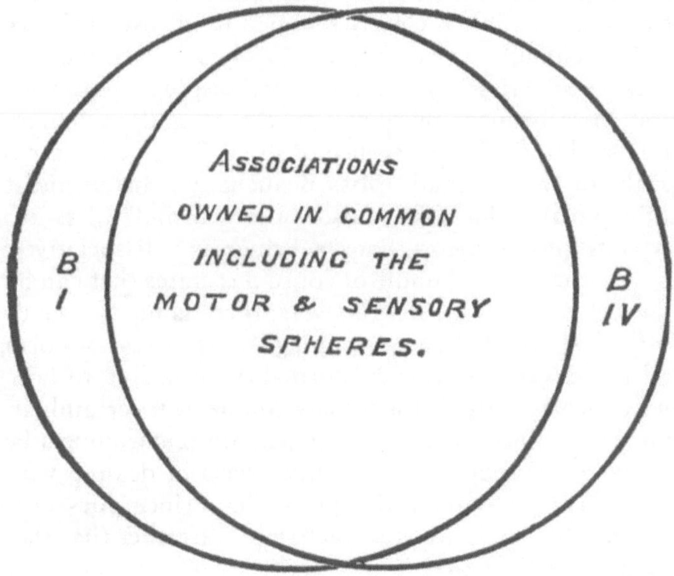

Figure 8.2

champ under hypnosis, and, in the prism diagram (Figure 8.1), BII simply emerges through the merger of BI's and BIV's rays. However, the image that Dr. Prince ultimately favors in *The Dissociation of a Personality* as a way of depicting the emergence of the "original" Miss Beauchamp is that of a chemical fusion: BI and BIV are to be fused together in a "chemical synthesis" (403) in order to generate a "new chemical compound" (403). BII's memories are certainly joined together like fragments of the memories of BI and BIV, but, like a new chemical compound, BII's personality differs from the personalities of BI and BIV—if these are seen as its elements (398–405, 417, 519–520).[21] Psychotherapy is seen here as a controllable process of natural science: just as the chemist, aided by the laws of chemistry, can determine which chemical compounds he produces, so too can Dr. Prince generate his product on the basis of psychological laws.

Dr. Prince as Savior/Fairytale Prince (the Real Miss Beauchamp as Cinderella)

Even so, the product is not a new one. It is the "real," the "original" Miss Beauchamp. This third aspect of Dr. Prince's attitude can only be grasped once we understand to what degree the case study itself is an interaction of various discourses and textual genres. At the beginning of the book, Dr. Prince writes: "If this were not a serious psychological study, I might feel tempted to entitle this volume 'The Saint, The Woman, and The Devil'" (16). Indeed, this play with "allegorical pictures" (16) and their simultaneous subordination to the laws of psychology runs through the entire case study. This is clearly revealed in his use of the name "The Real Miss Beauchamp." Officially, it is used as a scientific term: on the one hand, the Real Miss Beauchamp is the "original" one, whereby simply the first Miss Beauchamp is meant: the Miss Beauchamp who was born and existed until the emergence of BI (1, 7, 234). On the other, Dr. Prince speaks of the "normal" Miss Beauchamp. But in his attempt to scientifically explain what distinguishes the "normal" Miss Beauchamp, he quickly runs into problems. For Dr. Prince as a dissociative psychologist, Miss Beauchamp is a bundle of conscious states that can be grouped together in different ways. Seen this way, there is no "particular real or normal self" (233) at all.[22] Each grouping is just as real or normal as any other. And if we were to measure normality according to how well the personality comes to terms with the environment, it certainly might turn out that one personality comes to terms with one environment better than the others, whereas another personality excels in dealing with another environment. From these considerations, Dr. Prince does not conclude that there is no "normal" Miss Beauchamp but rather that the "psychological point of view" (233) is too limited. However, approaching the matter also from the physiological and biological standpoint would, Dr. Prince claims, reveal that each individual has *exactly one* "empirical self" that is "physiologically as well as psychologically best adapted to *any* environment" (233) and thus lacks the symptoms of illness. The "normal" Miss Beauchamp is such a self (233–234).

The scientific uses of the term are intricately connected with a third one: the Real Miss Beauchamp as "the self that was born and which she was intended by nature to be" (1). A normative component comes into play here—Miss Beauchamp's natural destiny—which, for Dr. Prince, becomes indistinguishably connected with the temporal use of the term: Miss Beauchamp's *true destiny* lies in her *temporal original self.* The second part of his study is called "The Hunt for the Real Miss Beauchamp." Officially, the aim is to cure Miss Beauchamp of psychologically and physiologically defined symptoms of illness; but Dr. Prince also tells a detective and adventure story[23] in which he regards the disappearance of the symptoms of illness merely as *evidence* that he has tracked down the missing original (241, 280, 300–301, 304–305).

If we understand Dr. Prince's search for the Real Miss Beauchamp this way, a further aspect of the prism diagram (Figure 8.1) discussed earlier can be explained: here the Real Miss Beauchamp ("Miss B. Original Self") is represented as only one *part* of the complete person ("Complete Self"). The Real Miss Beauchamp is therefore not distinguished as the *complete original* person or as the person who is free of symptoms *following successful treatment.* The Real Miss Beauchamp is the *true core* of the person who *already existed in the past.* Dr. Prince is hunting for this true core—her "true self" (248; cf. 398, 514, 524).

What is Miss Beauchamp's true destiny? Dr. Prince's criterion of normality does not tell us directly; it is only an *evidential* criterion. And he cannot say it directly, either. The notion of a true destiny is not a scientific concept, and, as Dr. Prince claims himself, his work is a "serious psychological study" (16). Even so, he also describes his hunt as the search for Cinderella, who previously was "neglected and passed by" (274). So he is also telling a fairy tale[24] whose prince is he himself. Since, according to Dr. Prince, BI literally sees "selfishness, impatience, rudeness, uncharitableness, a failure to tell the truth or a suppression of half the truth" as sins that must be expelled through religious practice, Dr. Prince regards her as the *saint* (16; also 10, 23, 53, 291–293). By contrast, he describes BIV, on account of her emotional outbursts, egoism, willfulness, and vanity, as a woman (16–17, 195, 291–293, 400, 514): "A true feminine that she was, she wanted to have her cake and eat it too" (431). Saintliness and womanliness are certainly not scientific categories but, in a fairy tale, they might convince a prince that he has not found the right one yet.

Cinderella's shoes, however, are not even tried on the devil Sally. Right at the outset of the "Hunt for the Real Miss Beauchamp"—mentioned in the same breath as his comment that Sally is "by all odds the most interesting of the personalities"—Dr. Prince rules out the possibility that Sally is the Real Miss Beauchamp, and, for the time being, turns to BI and BIV as possible candidates (234). Sally's sexual identity is also much too ambivalent for this. As Ruth Leys has convincingly argued, on the one hand, Sally cultivates the role of the flirting heterosexual woman toward Dr. Prince, playing him off against her friend William Jones. On the other hand, Dr. Prince masculinizes and represents her as boyish. For example, she has a boyish love of pranks and athletic activity, and Dr. Prince frequently "had to" tell her hunting and adventure stories (129).[25] Accordingly, Sally goes *with* Dr. Prince on the hunt for the Real Miss Beauchamp. "Even Sally, the hater of psychology," he writes, "caught the contagion of the chase for the moment" (267). It is originally *Sally's* suggestion that BI and BIV under hypnosis are one and the same person, that is, BII. And, as Dr. Prince puts it, she formulates the thesis that BII is the Real Miss Beauchamp (267–270) "*independently*" (268) of him.[26] Moreover, it is also Sally who, as a neutral observer in a "confession" to Dr. Prince, finally confirms the thesis that BII is the Real Miss Beauchamp[27]—on page 519 of the 525-page study.[28]

The saint, the woman, and the devil are thus all not Miss Beauchamp's true destiny. Dr. Prince never explicitly says what her true destiny is. All that is certain is that his search for Miss Beauchamp's true self is not completed until he finds a personality that is *not really a personality.* According to Dr. Prince, the letters of the Real Miss Beauchamp—compared to the letters of all the other personalities—reveal no "individuality" and are "not as interesting in themselves, but . . . important as evidence" (422). The Real Miss Beauchamp is "natural and simple in her modes of thought and manner" (400–401). Thus the fairy-tale prince only saves Miss Beauchamp once he, as chemist, has neutralized her individuality.

Dr. Prince as Friend (Sally as Dr. Prince's Buddy)

I come to the fourth and final aspect of Dr. Prince's attitude: he treats the different personalities as *autonomous subjects*. At the outset of his study, after using the name "Miss Beauchamp," he immediately adds politely: "If I may use the same name to designate several distinct people" (2). This attitude runs through his entire work, in both his concrete interactions with his vis-à-vis and in his meta-statements. Dr. Prince believes that each of the personalities is capable of leading "its own life like any other mortal" (5, cf. 231) and that each "is as individual as any one of us" (245; cf. 25, 248). He consistently speaks as if each personality should be ascribed ownership and responsibility for her actions separately; he speaks explicitly of Sally's "own culpable actions" (52). If Miss Beauchamp makes promises that she does not keep, Dr. Prince reports how BI, who sees herself as "possessed" at this point in time (119–120), takes responsibility herself for the breaking of the promise and never shifts the blame to the "demon": "It is myself," she says (131–132). Dr. Prince, by contrast, believes that it is *not her*, but *Sally*, who has broken the promise (131). Thus, in such descriptions given by Dr. Prince, Miss Beauchamp does not appear as an agent. He does not say: Miss Beauchamp, as Sally, behaved in this or that way, and as BI in this or that way. Rather, it is unfailingly the personalities who are the agents. According to Dr. Prince, these are not instances of one will fighting itself, but of Sally's will fighting against BI's (122–123, 205, 285).

Dr. Prince relates to the personalities as autonomous people in other respects as well. When he considers eliminating the different personalities over the course of the treatment, he applies moral and emotional categories that are only fitting for people: eliminating BI or Sally is like a "crime," "a psychical murder" (248), and, after a "long friendship," it seems "cold-blooded" and gives him "qualms" (398). One does not murder one's friends. There are other instances in which Dr. Prince harbors strong feelings toward the personalities, treating them as if they were autonomous subjects. For instance, he cannot hide his anger toward BI: he believes that she reveals too little information about herself, and he wishes that she would demonstrate more "moral callousness" (11). Accordingly, he is fascinated by Sally. He enjoys her irresponsibility and regrets having to give her a sermon for the sake of therapy (110). Whereas BI also receives his care (247–248, 425, 522), Sally is the playfellow with whom he amuses himself and measures his powers (53–57, 109–110, 321–323).

It might be objected that Dr. Prince's emotional relationships with the personalities can be understood simply as relationships *with Miss Beauchamp*—sometimes *as* one personality, other times as another. Dr. Prince's relation to his vis-à-vis, however, is too complex and ambivalent to be expressed in this way. This can be clearly illustrated by citing a highly dramatic moment in the story. At this point in time, Dr. Prince has come to the conclusion that BIV is the Real Miss Beauchamp and, as a result, BI must be eliminated in favor of BIV. BI now sits before him, and the full extent of his decision becomes clear to him:

> As she sat before me . . . one would not have been human not to sympathize with and pity her . . . The most callous must have been moved by this pathetic figure, hopeless and dejected . . . I remembered all that she had gone through . . . The patience with which it had been borne showed a heroism rarely seen . . . Though it might be that she was not *her* real and original self, she was truly an individual as any one that ever lived. She had her friends and associations, equally dear to her. Now all her psychical life was disappearing, though what to her was only deepening mental trouble was really, as we believed, *her* salvation, the bringing of *her* true self. She could not be told this, however . . . It would be useless to tell her that *she* would, through another character, *still live*, for that still meant the annihilation of all her associations and memories of the past six years.[29] . . .
>
> In my thoughts the annihilation of Miss Beauchamp30 seemed in no way different from saying that she must be satisfied with death. It seemed hard to tell her that this annihilation was being purposely brought about. It seemed kinder to let her disappear, ignorant of her coming fate, unconscious of the future that awaited her as her Real Self. There would be less mental pain for her—and yet, it seemed like a crime we were committing. It was a psychical murder (247–248; my emphasis).

His emotional relationship with the person facing him does not correspond to the attitude of a scientist who sees the personalities simply as a grouping of psychological states that can and must be shifted about according to the laws of psychology. Moreover, he does not speak of the "true self" of Miss Beauchamp, but *of BI*. As a mere grouping of psychological states, however, BI cannot have any other "true self" than herself: as mere bundle, she *is* this grouping. For the same reason, his attitude cannot be understood as an attitude *toward Miss Beauchamp as* the personality *BI*. Since he speaks of the "true self" of *BI*, he grants BI autonomous status, which makes it possible for her to exist after the entire grouping of mental states that actually comprise BI has been eliminated. Dr. Prince thus gets caught in the paradoxical position of wanting to commit the ultimate crime against BI—murdering her—in order to allow *her* to continue to exist in the future as *her* real self. The talk of *murder* actually only makes sense if BI really is an autonomous person. At the same time, BI can be *successfully eliminated* only if she is merely a mere bundle of mental states; and, equally, BI can *survive* this process *only* if she is an autonomous subject whose nature consists in more than just the grouping of mental states that are to be eliminated. This BI, who exists for Dr. Prince in this ambivalent state between an autonomous subject and a mere association-bundle of mental states, is the object of all his excessive emotionality.

In all his different attitudes toward Miss Beauchamp, Dr. Prince never understands her as *one* agent who might be shaping the overall development of the story just as actively as he is. He perceives her as a passive object that is there for him to examine and to shape according to his will, based on the laws of psychology. Or, when he does grant his vis-à-vis agency, it is always the individual personalities who are ascribed such autonomy. In the process, he overlooks the following understanding of Miss Beauchamp: Let us assume, for example, that Miss Beauchamp awakes on a sunny day and, while waking, immediately notices that it is a sunny day. Although the weather changes toward midday, Miss Beauchamp still recalls in the afternoon what a sunny morning it was. Now, let us assume it is the personality "Sally" that Miss Beauchamp acts out in the afternoon, whereas she expressed the personality "BI" in the morning. Nonetheless, it is *Miss Beauchamp* who comes to believe in the morning that it is sunny, and maintains this conviction about the morning weather into the afternoon. Of course, in the afternoon, Miss Beauchamp will claim *as Sally* that she—Sally—was present in the morning as a subconsciousness alongside BI and that she came to the conclusion about the weather conditions separately from BI. But this is just the imaginary world that Miss Beauchamp lives out as Sally. It is not surprising that Miss Beauchamp, as Sally, makes such claims: she—*Miss Beauchamp*—remembers the morning well, and now claims, since she is acting out her Sally personality, that she—*Sally*—observed the weather in the morning as a subconsciousness alongside BI. However, what in fact happened is simply that she—*Miss Beauchamp*—observed the weather in the morning and still remembers it well now that it is afternoon. Nothing in Prince's nearly 600-page case study rules out this interpretation. Since this is the case, we should accept this interpretation, and not succumb to the fantasies that Miss Beauchamp propagates as Sally.

If we accept this interpretation, how are we to understand Miss Beauchamp and her personalities? The distinction between the question of the identity of fundamental entities, the question of the identity of personalities, and the question "Who am I?" is helpful here, as is the commitment criterion and the narrative self-constitution theory. The commitment criterion explains why, in the morning and afternoon, we are dealing with one fundamental entity. In the morning, one person—as BI—comes to a conclusion about the weather conditions; she maintains this belief into the afternoon when she acts as Sally. This is a case of commitment continuity, which, according to the commitment criterion, means that BI in the morning and Sally in the afternoon are phases of one and the same fundamental entity. Even so, BI and Sally might be two *personalities* of one and the same fundamental entity. It is not my aim to defend any theory of the identity of personalities, but we could apply the *narrative self-constitution theory* from the last chapter to this example in order to explain the possible existence of two personalities in one and the same fundamental entity. In other words, the commitment criterion explains why we are dealing with one and the same fundamental entity, and the narrative self-constitution theory then helps resolve the issue of the identity of personalities.

At different points in time, Miss Beauchamp displays radically different preferences, ideals, temperaments, and character traits. *As each of her personalities*, she also has quite particular attitudes toward the attitudes and characteristics of the other personalities. This is especially interesting in the case of the personalities that Dr. Prince refers to as the "New BI" and the "New BIV." As the new BI, Miss Beauchamp has memories of her mental states and actions as BIV (and, as the new BIV, of her states and actions as BI). As BI, she can recall her states as the new BI, and thus also her states and actions as BIV (in this way, she can, as BIV, remember her states and actions as BI). As the BI who has acquired these memories, Miss Beauchamp is "humiliated and ashamed" about her states and actions as BIV, which she sees as her own. She feels "remorse" and asks Dr. Prince to forgive her (407–410). Likewise, as the BIV who has gained memories of herself as BI, Miss Beauchamp regards BI's states and actions as her own but, otherwise, her reaction here is a completely different one: as the BIV who has these memories of herself as BI, Miss Beauchamp feels no "repentance or remorse," but responds with "disgust," "anger," and "contempt" for herself (411–412). Here we must view Miss Beauchamp as a person who is in conflict with herself, not only with respect to her first-order attitudes, but also with respect to her stance toward these attitudes.

Corresponding to these different stances and attitudes, we could describe Miss Beauchamp as a person who narrates various stories about her life and lives out these different stories in different ways of living.[31] This can help us understand the relations that Miss Beauchamp as BIV cultivates with her friends. As BIV, Miss Beauchamp finds the friends she made as Sally frivolous and repulsive, whereas the friends that she made as BI bore her and are too conscientious and idealistic for her tastes. When Miss Beauchamp finds herself in the company of these people as BIV, she is completely unable to come to grips with the situation. She is utterly incapable of assuming the role that she plays as BI or Sally (478–479). We could say that Miss Beauchamp as BIV has and cultivates a certain self-understanding and would also like to lead a life that corresponds to that self-understanding. She tells herself a story about who she is and strives to act according to this narrative.[32] Since Miss Beauchamp as BIV is incapable of coming to terms with situations like those that arise with BI's and Sally's friends, she tries to ensure that she no longer ever acts as BI or as Sally. When she realizes that she cannot win this battle with herself as Sally, she, as BIV, makes a pact with herself as Sally, which explicitly regulates the time that she spends as BIV and as Sally (476–487, 498–504). In summary, we can say that Miss Beauchamp is one and the same fundamental entity the entire time. But, as BIV, her attitudes, character traits, and self-understanding are completely different than when she acts as BI or Sally. The story that she lives as BIV and would like to tell about herself would take a completely different course than the story she tells as BI or Sally. This gives rise to violent feelings toward herself and conflicts about how she conducts her life.

Having distinguished the different questions in this area, we can also grant Dr. Prince a certain insight with respect to the question "Who am I?" As a *dissociation psychologist*, Dr. Prince cannot decipher a Real Miss Beauchamp. In light of the radical splits between personalities, it cannot be said that any one personality expresses her "true self" more than the others. As a thesis regarding the question "Who am I?" I would be prepared to accept this claim. I doubt that every human has only one "true self" to which it should attempt to remain loyal in order to lead an "authentic" life. Dr. Prince, however, takes it upon himself—as a *savior prince* and *master chemist*—to distinguish one of the personalities as the Real Beauchamp. What is objectionable about his attitude is not only that he bases his therapy on fixed and chauvinistic criteria of gender identity, but also that he sees it as *his* task to determine Miss Beauchamp's true identity. It should be the task of Miss Beauchamp—the fundamental entity that interacts with Dr. Prince—to decide how to deal with her inner conflicts, even if she might possibly need help from other persons in the process. Dr. Prince fails to respect Miss Beauchamp's autonomy. Furthermore, he *cannot* restore Miss Beauchamp's true identity, since Miss Beauchamp's attitudes inevitably play a key role in the making of her identity as a personality: Miss Beauchamp's identity *as a personality or self is constituted, among other things, by her own active attitudes.*[33] Whether Miss Beauchamp would or should distinguish *one* personality as her "true" self remains an open question.

Up to now I have argued that we can understand the Beauchamp case as follows: Miss Beauchamp is a fundamental entity that at times lives out her own story of BI and, at others, acts as Sally or BIV. This interpretation of the case is not wrong, but to comprehend the Beauchamp case, we must consider an additional decisive component: the inner perspective of the personalities. How, for instance, does Miss Beauchamp understand herself when she sees everything from Sally's point of view? Since Sally is the most fully developed personality, and most strongly regards herself as an independent person, the focus in the next section will be on her perspective. We cannot understand Miss Beauchamp until we have understood Sally.

3 SALLY ON HERSELF

Sally consistently views herself as an autonomous person who is to be distinguished from the other persons.[34] This is exemplified by the following dialogue between Dr. Prince and her:

> "But why do you hate her [BI]? You are only hating yourself, for she is yourself."
> "No, she isn't." <With resentment.>[35]
> "Yes, she is."
> "No, she isn't. I won't have it so! We are not the same person. We don't think alike, and we don't have the same thoughts," etc., etc. (168–169; see also 27–28,[36] 30–31, 39–40, 49, 55, 130)

Here Sally makes two points, which she repeatedly stresses throughout the work in order to distinguish herself from the other persons. First, "we don't think alike." With this statement, she emphasizes that she differs *in content* from the other personalities. She is and thinks *differently*. She says, for instance, that BI is "stupid," does not "know half the time what she is about" (28, cf. 53), and does not "enjoy wickedness" (56). Furthermore, BI loves books (129–130) and other things that Sally finds boring (310). All of this, of course, contrasts with Sally.

The second point that Sally emphasizes is: "We don't have the same thoughts." Here she is not referring to the difference between the contents of the thoughts. She already did so in the first sentence. She and BI might have the same thoughts in terms of content. They might both think that it is Monday. But they carry out these same-content thoughts separately. Sally is a person and she thinks for herself; BI is another person and thinks for herself. The following exchange between Dr. Prince and her offers an example of this:

> "What were you doing at the time?" I asked.
> "What was I doing? I wasn't doing anything. She was brushing her hair. She was thinking about school, when the wind began to blow outdoors. I, too, heard it and felt it. The window was open; the air blew on her face, and then she began thinking of church; and the music, the Hallelujah Chorus, came; and she went off to sleep, and she looked very silly, and she settled down so <illustrating contemptuously>."
> Chris [that is, Sally] also corroborated everything that Miss Beauchamp [that is, BI] had said in her narrative of the original episode, stating that whenever either Miss Beauchamp or herself heard that peculiar sound of the wind, the scene in the church came back to them, no matter where they might be. Chris was reminded of it by the sound, as well as Miss Beauchamp.

> "'She' heard the music, and I heard it, too," Chris explained. When 'she' heard it last night 'she' saw the whole thing over again, and 'she' wanted to sit down and cry, but 'she' wouldn't. 'She' just sat in the chair and looked like a fool. 'She' sat down, dropped back, and did so—<illustrates position>. 'Her' eyes were not shut."
> "What were you doing?"
> "I was meditating."
> "What about?"
> "How silly 'she' looked." (89–90)

Sally relates with utmost clarity that she and BI think, act, and perceive separately (see also 47–49, 316, 372–374, 381–385). For Sally, this—along with the difference in content between her and BI—means that she and BI are separate people. How are we to understand this distinction that Sally draws between herself and others in philosophical terms? Sally does not have any philosophical theory of personal identity. But she works with philosophical ideas. Let me return to thesis 1* from Chapter 2:

> *Thesis 1**: Vicky and similar characters in cases of multiple personality understand themselves in a way that, if thought through philosophically, implies the assumption that each is respectively one fundamental entity among two or more in one body.

This thesis is certainly true of Sally. She assumes that the different personalities in her body are separate subjects of thought, action, and perception. She and the others think, act, and perceive separately from each other. Besides the different personalities, there is no subject of thought, action, and perception. When a particular thought, action, or perception takes place, it is not the human being who thinks, acts, or perceives. Rather, it is either she—Sally—or one of the other personalities who thinks, acts, or perceives. Sally does not use the terminology "subject of thought, action, and perception." Nevertheless, saying that she thinks that she and the other personalities are separate subjects of thought, action, and perception is here merely meant as a rendering of what she surely believes: that she and the other personalities think, act, and perceive separately from one another. Now, if the different personalities are separate subjects of thought, action, and perception, this implies—as will be argued in Chapter 10—that these personalities are separate fundamental entities. So Sally understands herself in such a way that, if philosophically thought through, implies that she is one of several fundamental entities in one body.

Now, is there a philosophical theory suitable for articulating Sally's position? Let me consider two empirical approaches, each of which is an answer to the question "What am I?": bundle theory and the authorial correlate approach. I will argue that Sally could not accept bundle theory as an articulation of her standpoint and that the authorial correlate theory is more promising.

Bundle theory may be explained as an account resulting from adding certain assumption to elements of Prince's dissociation psychology. According to Prince's dissociation psychology, the different personalities of a human being are nothing but bundles of psychological states.[37] The additional assumption—yielding bundle theory—is that fundamental entities are nothing but such bundles. It must then be asked how different fundamental entities are individuated according to such a theory: how are the boundaries drawn between different fundamental entities—these being bundles of psychological states? Prince thinks that personalities can overlap—that they can have psychological states in common. This is also how most bundle theorists think of fundamental entities. If fundamental entities are nothing but bundles of psychological states, it is hard to see how one can rule out the possibility that fundamental entities—being mere bundles—can overlap. It can also be asked just how much overlapping between two bundles is compatible with their continued existence as two fundamental entities. Are two bundles that share 98 percent of their psychological states two fundamental entities? What about 76 percent, 51 percent, etc.? It is hard to see how a bundle theorist can view any decision on this matter as being closer to the truth. In this sense, bundle theory needs to view this as an arbitrary decision.

Assuming that bundle theory must allow overlaps between fundamental entities and view the decision as to how many fundamental entities exist in one body as arbitrary, can Sally accept bundle theory as an articulation of her standpoint? In my view, she cannot. In the preceding quotation, Sally explains how she perceives and thinks separately from BI. If there are overlaps between BI and herself, at least one of their thoughts or perceptions must be shared. But if a thought is shared, *who* thinks that thought? There are only two possibilities: either they think the thought *together*, or *each thinks it for herself.* Sally cannot at all accept that they think it together. For her, a decisive feature of the division between herself and BI is that they think separately from each other.

If, however, the sharing of a thought is understood as meaning that each thinks it herself, we must explain how this is compatible with saying that the thought is *shared*—with saying that in this thought there is an overlap between BI and Sally. The bundle theorist might offer the following explanation: The *scientific or philosophical truth of the matter* is that BI and Sally are each merely groupings of mental states, and these groupings can overlap. *Scientific or philosophical representations*—such as the one offered by Prince of BI and BIV (see Figure 8.2)—make clear that this means that thoughts are shared. The question of whether each person thinks the thought herself is a question that arises only in *everyday language.* From a philosophical or scientific point of view, it is irrelevant how this question is answered in everyday language. In everyday language, we might just as well say that each fundamental entity thinks the thought herself.

Sally cannot accept this account. For her, it is a crucial issue whether the thoughts "in" Miss Beauchamp are thought together or separately. Sally believes that she thinks her thoughts, while BI thinks BI's thoughts. Therefore, Sally *must* say that they think separately from each other. Consequently, it *cannot* be an *arbitrary* decision whether she and BI can overlap. Because she and BI are two persons, they *cannot* overlap.

According to the authorial correlate theory, each of us is fundamentally an agent who is a correlate to psychological relations. This seems quite fitting as a philosophical articulation of Sally's standpoint. First, for Sally, it is decisive that she and BI think separately. The authorial correlate theory can give philosophical expression to this aspect of Sally's standpoint by saying that Sally is one agent and BI is another. That is why they are two fundamental entities. Second, Sally distinguishes between herself and BI on the basis of the empirical differences between them. The authorial correlate theory as such does not give any account of the individuation of fundamental entities (question 4). However, given that, according to this theory, each one of us is a correlate to psychological relations, it seems likely that individuation will have something to do with the psychological relations that each fundamental entity has to itself but not to others. And as we shall see, this is precisely the case (see Chapter 12).

> Generosity. A willingness to share. This he may be willing to do with material things, but not with his inner thoughts and feelings. His inner thoughts and feelings are just for him. Others may get themselves the same thoughts and feelings if they like, but sharing he won't. That is not only egoistic, but plain stupid. It is plain economic to share thoughts. If the thought is already there, why can't we share it? Why does he also have to have another thought exclusively for himself? He calls my way of thinking "bundle theory." Why does everything have to be a theory for him? (Answer: so that he can disprove it and rid himself of it. But that's not the point here.) I don't have a theory. My independent existence consists in my thoughts, feelings, sentiments, etc. These are my thoughts, my feelings, not his. But as long as I can keep some for myself, I am willing to share others. He first claims the whole territory for himself, and then he wants to exterminate all life in my part of it. Is there no justice in his philosophy?

I have argued that Sally's self-understanding, if philosophically thought through, implies that she and BI are two fundamental entities in one body. I have also argued that Sally is factually mistaken: she is not one of several fundamental entities in one body. On the contrary, Miss Beauchamp is one fundamental entity and Sally, BI, and BIV are several personalities of the one fundamental entity. However, according to the coexistence thesis, Sally is metaphysically right: each of us is fundamentally an entity of which there could exist more than one in the same body. Is the coexistence thesis true?

And if it is true, what are the conditions for the existence of more than one fundamental entity in one body? In the next chapter, I shall provide an overview of philosophical theories of multiple personality. I shall argue that the empirical theories among them are unsuccessful in the following sense: even if the conditions formulated by these theories are fulfilled, we do not have a case of more than one fundamental entity in one body. Non-empirical approaches may be more successful in this regard, but they are metaphysically problematic. In Chapter 10, then, I shall argue for the coexistence thesis and for certain sufficient conditions for the existence of more than one fundamental entity in the same body.

9 Philosophical Theories of Multiple Personality

This chapter provides an overview of philosophical theories of multiple personality.[1] However, my discussion is guided by a specific interest. I want to know the conditions under which more than one fundamental entity can be said to exist in one body. Thus, the main question of this chapter is whether any of the theories in the literature have captured these conditions.[2] The answer is no.[3]

1 AGENDA AND PERSONALITIES

In *Divided Minds and Successive Selves*, Jennifer Radden formulates conditions for the presence of more than one self in a single body:

> 1. *Separate-agency condition* Separate selves will have separate agendas.
> 2. *Separate-personality condition* Separate selves will exhibit distinct, non-agential personality traits singly or jointly. These two conditions (separate agency and separate personality) will suffice for interself and intraself identification and reidentification.
> 3. *Continuity condition* Separate selves will persist through time.
> 4. *Disordered-awareness condition* Disordered awareness on the part of at least one self will result in disordered memory in the subject in excess of that found in normal people. (41)[4]

By "self" Radden means "an embodied repository of integrated psychological states" (11). Since Radden always talks about selves, she may not regard these four points as conditions for the presence of more than one fundamental entity in a single body.[5] I will nonetheless show that the fulfillment of all four conditions is compatible with the existence of only one fundamental entity.

Let us begin with the first two conditions that Radden regards as sufficient for the identification and reidentification of selves.[6] The first condition is fulfilled when separate sets of propositional attitudes—"beliefs, values, goals, desires, and responses" (39)—are present. "These will be expressed in distinguishable patterns of motivation and behavior—separate agendas" (39). The second condition is meant to capture those personality traits not expressed in the separate "agendas." As examples of such traits, she names the following: "Physical and emotional style, temperament, gender and cultural identity, moral disposition, idiosyncratic history, and self-concept" (39).

To discuss Radden's theory and other approaches, it is helpful to introduce some terminology. We want to talk about people like Miss Beauchamp who show different personalities at different points in time (we are thus assuming that we are dealing with only one body or human being). When Miss Beauchamp exhibits the personality *BI*, for instance, I will speak of the *fundamental entity* displaying this personality as the *person in the BI-state* (*P-BI*, for short). When Miss Beauchamp exhibits the personality BIV or Sally, I will speak of the person in the BIV-state (P-BIV) or the person in the Sally-state (P-Sally). P-BI is a fundamental entity at a specific point in time, and this manner of speaking leaves open whether this fundamental entity is identical to P-BIV. It is thus compatible with all accounts of the individuation of fundamental entities. According to biological approaches, for example, P-BI is identical to P-BIV because each of these persons is identical to the human being who has the personalities BI and BIV. Words such as "BI" and "BIV" are thus labels for personalities, whereas terms like "P-BI" denote a fundamental entity at specific times—at all the points in time at which this fundamental entity displays the personality BI.

Against the backdrop of this terminology we can now show that Radden's first two conditions are insufficient for one body to embody more than one fundamental entity. On the basis of these conditions we could certainly distinguish BI from BIV: BI and BIV clearly have different agendas (first condition) and personality traits (second condition). Does this mean that P-BI is not identical to P-BIV? Not at all. These two conditions do not rule out the possibility that P-BI has memories of the psychological states of P-BIV. This is how it was in the Beauchamp case: as described in the last chapter, the "New BI" has memories of the mental states of P-BIV, so P-BI also has such memories. And P-BI reacts to these recollections with shame: she is ashamed that *she herself* while being P-BIV felt and behaved in a specific way. I believe that each of us understands this reaction by P-BI and can imagine having precisely this attitude toward ourselves in another state. Thus, even if Radden's conditions are fulfilled by BI and BIV, P-BI and P-BIV are thereby not two fundamental entities. Each of us can imagine being P-BI when she thinks of P-BIV and says, "I am ashamed that in this state *I* display that sort of personality and those feelings." When we imagine this, we rely on the distinction between the identity of fundamental entities and the identity of personalities: the fulfillment of Radden's first two conditions might mean that we are dealing with more than one *personality*, but not more than one *fundamental entity.*

Radden herself writes that Dr. Jekyll and Mr. Hyde in Stevenson's novel are a paradigmatic case[7] for the fulfillment of the four conditions (42–43, 56).[8] I have no intention of calling this into question. Still, the novel confirms my thesis that the fulfillment of the first two conditions is not sufficient for there to be two fundamental entities. In a part of the novel entitled "Henry Jekyll's Full Statement of the Case," Henry Jekyll describes the situation as follows: "Though so profound a double-dealer, I was in no sense a hypocrite; both sides of me were in dead earnest; I was no more myself when I laid aside restraint and plunged in shame, than when I labored, in the eye of the day, at the furtherance of knowledge or the relief of sorrow and suffering."[9] This makes clear that Henry Jekyll regards both personalities as a part of himself. Just as P-BI can think of P-BIV as herself, each of us can easily imagine having Henry Jekyll's attitude toward ourselves if we were ever so radically split as Henry Jekyll.

Radden's first two conditions thus do not suffice for the presence of two fundamental entities in one body. As Radden says herself, we can view the third condition either as an independent condition or as a presupposition of the first two conditions (40). For this reason the fulfillment of the first *three* conditions is naturally also insufficient. Now, I assumed above that P-BI has *memories* of the feelings and actions of P-BIV. Might there exist two fundamental entities if P-BI is not aware of the psychological states of P-BIV (and vice versa)? This brings me to Radden's fourth condition.

2 STREAMS OF CONSCIOUSNESS

In the fourth condition, the concepts *awareness* and *memory* both appear. I thus turn not directly to the fourth condition but discuss another possible condition that concerns memory only. This other possible condition may be termed the "*memory condition*"—a condition not proposed by Radden—and formulated as follows ("X" and "Y" refer to different personalities like BI and BIV): *the person in the X-state (PX) does not recall the states and actions specific to the person in the Y-state (PY), and vice versa.* Naturally this condition cannot be understood as meaning that PX has absolutely no memories. She recalls, to a greater or lesser extent, the states and actions of PX. These memories are of two kinds: on the one hand, they are *specific* memories about states and actions that express the personality X. On the other, they are *general* "memories-that" and "memories-how": for instance, *that* one gets wet in the rain and *how* one goes about walking.[10] Without such general memories, PX would be completely incapable of acting and it is doubtful whether she should count as a person at all. Without general memories, specific memories would presumably not be possible either.

Now, since PX has such general memories, it is reasonable to assume that she *shares* certain memories with PY. PY certainly remembers, for example, that one gets wet in the rain. If this is the case, however, the fulfillment of the memory condition does not mean that PX is not identical to PY. There may be just one fundamental entity here who, *as* X, does not remember the states and actions expressive of the personality Y and, *as* Y, has a corresponding amnesia with respect to the personality X. PX could then say, for example: "I can't recall my actions *as* Y, but they are nonetheless *my* actions." We can also imagine that PX later on remembers the actions of PY, and then says accordingly: "I didn't know that *as Y I* behaved that way and can only feel contempt *for myself* for this kind of behavior."

This is a good objection to the memory condition because this condition does not rule out that PX and PY *share general* memories. It could now be suggested that PX and PY are not identical to one another if they *do not* share *any memories*. Here one would need to discuss what *sharing* of memories means. However, because the question as to what it means to share states of awareness is decisive for the interpretation of Radden's fourth condition, let me turn directly to this condition.

The fourth condition states that disordered awareness leads to disordered memory. What Radden means by "disordered awareness" here can be expressed as follows: at least one "separate self," who at a certain time is correctly ascribed to a certain human being, has at this time no "introspective awareness" of some of the "conscious contents" of the human being at this time (41). When Radden speaks of an *introspective* awareness of conscious contents, I assume she means that one is directly conscious of this content without relying on evidence such as behavior.[11] According to Radden, one may ascribe a self to an individual at a certain time, even if this self at this time has no control over the behavior of the individual and at this time is not conscious. This is possible because the concept of a self is *dispositional*: "To have a self is to be inclined to respond in certain ways" (45).[12] Consequently, we must understand the fourth condition as follows: if a self has disordered memory in the sense of the fourth condition, it is not that the self lacks a memory of something that it previously experienced or knew. The disordered memory is to be traced back to a disordered awareness, which means that *this self never* had introspective awareness of what it now lacks a memory. But this also means that disordered awareness is the key notion in the fourth condition. Disordered memory is merely a consequence of disordered awareness.

For reasons just given, limiting the disordered memory in the fourth condition to specific memories will not yield a plausible condition for the presence of two fundamental entities. Accordingly, I understand the fourth condition as meaning that PX cannot remember *any* of the conscious states of PY, since PX and PY *do not share any conscious states*. Herein lies the disorder awareness of the individual. At one point Radden writes: "Perhaps even Dr. Jekyll and Mr. Hyde, who shared little but abilities and general knowledge, are best seen as aspects of the same self" (191).[13] In my terminology this means that, if the person in the Jekyll-state *does not share any* conscious states with the person in the Hyde-state, then these persons are two fundamental entities. But what does it mean to say they do not share any awareness states? It could mean that the conscious states have *no* common *content*. This understanding of the fourth condition, however, would be far too restrictive. It would mean that we would not have two fundamental entities in one body unless, for instance, they share no belief content. If PX believes that the earth revolves around the sun, PY could not hold this conviction. Otherwise, they would not be two fundamental entities. Thus, the fourth condition must be understood as meaning that PX and PY, *numerically speaking*, do not share any conscious states. However, they might, for example, have beliefs with the same content. In their common body, a belief of this sort would then simply be present twice: PX would have a token of this belief and PY another.

Understood this way, the fourth condition is a plausible candidate for a sufficient condition for the presence of two fundamental entities in one body: if PX and PY, numerically speaking, do not share any single conscious state, they are two fundamental entities. But why does this seem to be a plausible candidate for a sufficient condition? We are searching for a criterion that distinguishes between two possibilities: assuming that PX and PY have many conscious states with the same content, we must distinguish between two possibilities. The first possibility is that we are dealing here with *one* fundamental entity who has two personalities. If PX and PY have a conscious state with the same content (e.g., a particular thought), it is this one fundamental entity who has this conscious state (thinks this thought). The second possibility is that PX and PY *each* are a fundamental entity. The conscious states with the same content would then always appear *twice*. For instance, a thought with the same content is thought by each fundamental entity separately. Yet what are the conditions under which a case falls under the second possibility? Here it is useless to say: the second possibility is realized in a given case *because* PX and PY do not share any *token* conscious state. This answer is worthless because it merely *claims* that the second possibility is realized. What we want to know are the conditions under which the first possibility and the second possibility are each realized. Thus, the fourth condition only appears as a plausible candidate for a sufficient condition because this condition merely *assumes* that more than one fundamental entity is present.

This failure of Radden's fourth condition is nonetheless instructive. Radden lacks an informative answer to the question as to when the mental states of PX and the mental states of PY are states of two fundamental entities. We may suppose that the answer to this question has something to do with the *relation* that PX has to her mental states, but not to the states of PY. One possible characterization of this relation would be that PX has a *first-person relation* to her own mental states, but not to those of PY. PX would have *one* continuous first-person perspective and PY *another*. Such a characterization of the relation is offered by Carol Rovane, whose approach is discussed in the fifth section of this chapter. Another possibility is that PX has a *narrative relation* to her own mental states, but not to those of PY. This proposal will be discussed in the next section.[14]

3 NARRATIVE CENTERS

We are seeking the conditions under which a human being can be said to consist of not one but at least two fundamental entities. Daniel Dennett's theory of the self as a fictional character appears at first glance especially well suited to this. According to Dennett, a human being can have more than one self. These selves are created without there being a central agent that actively or intentionally creates them.[15] Such a theory initially seems to offer precisely what we are looking for: several personal unities in one body that cannot, however, be traced back to any basic personal unity. Let us thus take a closer look at Dennett's theory.

Dennett compares selves with fictional characters in novels. If we open up Melville's *Moby Dick* and read on the first page "Call me Ishmael," this of course does not mean that Melville should be called Ishmael. Melville merely created a fictional character and this character is called Ishmael.[16] Here an author has created a fictional character. According to Dennett, characters of a novel can emerge without an author. He imagines a computer that has been programmed to write novels. It has not been programmed to write a specific novel, but is supposed to produce novels based on the information it receives. The computer is turned on and the first sentence pops up: "Call me Gilbert": "What follows is the apparent autobiography of this fictional Gilbert. Now Gilbert is a fictional, created self but its creator is no self . . . I am *stipulating* that this is not a conscious machine, not a 'thinker.' It is a dumb machine, but it does have the power to write a passable novel."[17] Dennett wants to convince us that a character in a novel can be created without an author. Since we are interested in the selves of a human being, the thought experiment becomes particularly interesting when Dennett turns the computer into a robot: the computer is on wheels, has a camera, and can move. Dennett now assumes that the computer reacts to the environment by continuing to tell the story. If you hit the robot with a baseball bat, part of the story will be that Gilbert was hit with a baseball bat by somebody similar to you. And if the robot is locked up in a closet, it will say "help me."[18] Although "the robot's *brain*, the robot's computer" is not a self telling a story, the account produced is a "narrative of a self."[19] For our purposes, things get even more interesting when more than one self exists—more than one fictional character. In the same text, Dennett refers to the famous case of Sybil, the case of multiple personality discussed briefly in Chapter 2:

> When Sybil went in to see her therapist for the first time, she was not several different people rolled into one body. Sybil was a novel-writing machine that fell in with a very ingenious questioner, a very eager

> reader. And together they collaborated to write many, many chapters of a new novel. And, of course, since Sybil was a sort of living novel, she went out and engaged in the world with these new selves, more or less created on demand, under the eager suggestion of a therapist.[20]

According to Dennett, Sybil—the patient who enters into psychiatric treatment—is like his novel-writing robot. When the patient says "I am Peggy Lou" or "I am Victoria," this should be understood in the same way as the robot's "call me Gilbert." The difference is only that the patient (her brain?) creates *many* selves. Still, just like the robot, the patient is not an author who writes a novel. Her stories, just like the stories of the robot, are created by her (her brain?) as a reaction to her surroundings. Thus, there is no "I" that stands behind the stories and creates them. The only "I's" that exist here are the fictional selves that are referred to by such phrases as "I am Sybil" and "I am Vicky."[21]

In my critical remarks on Dennett, I would like to question Dennett's philosophy of mind as little as possible,[22] but I nonetheless hope to show that he does not present sufficient conditions for the presence of more than one fundamental entity in one body. I am prepared to grant him that the patient Sybil, just like the robot, is "a novel-writing machine," whatever that is supposed to mean exactly. In the following argument, I am even ready to assume that the fictional selves are not created by the patient Sybil as an author, but are somehow simply produced in her.

If Dennett's approach is to be understood as an account of the conditions for a human being to embody more than one fundamental entity, it must be interpreted as follows: *a human being embodies more than one fundamental entity if she (her brain?) has generated more than one fictional self.*[23] But this is wrong. The conditions for the existence of more than one fictional self are not sufficient for the existence of more than one fundamental entity. Let us assume like Dennett that the patient Sybil does not consist of several persons before beginning therapy. She is "a novel-writing machine." We may assume that she has general knowledge and diverse abilities before starting therapy. After therapy has begun, the patient sometimes behaves like the novel character Peggy Lou that she has created, and sometimes like Vicky. The emergence of these selves does not mean, however, that the patient does not retain her abilities and knowledge in all these personality phases. For instance, the following could be the case: The patient could ride a bike before therapy and knew that the earth rotates around the sun. *She* retains this ability and this knowledge both *as Peggy Lou* and *as Vicky*. This shows that the emergence of the selves Peggy Lou and Vicky should not be understood as the emergence of two fundamental entities. Even if the patient has more than one self after beginning therapy, this may nevertheless be a case of just *one* fundamental entity that already existed before the beginning of therapy and now sometimes behaves according to the pattern of one of the selves and at other times according to the pattern of the other. Following the emergence of the "New BI," Miss Beauchamp *as BI* can understand the personality BIV as one side of herself of which she is ashamed, and in much the same way, there is nothing to prevent the patient Sybil *as one of her selves* from understanding another self as a part of herself. It thus turns out that the criticism that shows that Radden's first two conditions are inadequate for the presence of fundamental entities proves the same thing for Dennett's theory. If we thus distinguish between the identity of fundamental entities and the identity of personalities, we can understand Dennett's theory as an interesting account of the identity of personalities that says nothing about the identity of fundamental entities.

At this point it could be argued that the reason why Dennett's model of fictional selves is unsuccessful as a criterion for the presence of more than one fundamental entity is that in Dennett's theory several selves are generated *too easily*. If more than one self exists only under conditions that demand a more radical fragmentation and are therefore more difficult to fulfill, it could be that more than one fundamental entity is indeed present in a body when *these* conditions are fulfilled. The proposal is thus to retain Dennett's model in broad outline, but make the conditions for the existence of more than one self more difficult to fulfill. Owen Flanagan defends a theory of multiple personality that largely follows Dennett's approach but contains certain deviations and refinements. We must ask whether his theory can offer the solution just proposed.

Flanagan agrees with Dennett that a self is "what we tell stories of ourselves about."[24] Like Dennett, he believes that a self is the *product* and *not* the *origin* of a story, and that the emergence of the self *cannot* be traced back to the conscious or intentional actions of a given agent.[25] But once a self has emerged, in normal cases each of us can be viewed as the author of our own identity.[26] This is an important point for his account of multiple personality. He distinguishes between "multiplex" and "multiple" selves. The idea of the *multiplex* self is meant to explain what, in normal cases, identity consists in. Here, identity can exist despite diachronic transformations and synchronous conflicts since *narrative connectedness* exists between the various strains. This narrative connectedness is due to the "authorial work" of the agent, who tells the story of her life and thus manages to hold the different strains together. If this unifying authorship and thereby the narrative connectedness fall away, we are no longer dealing with *a multiplex* self, but with *multiple* selves. In this case we are *not* dealing with *one narrator*, but *several*. This is how we should understand multiple personality.[27]

The interesting question for us is whether the distinction between multiplex self and multiple selves coincides with the distinction between one fundamental entity in one body and several such entities. Since a multiplex self can have quite varied personality facets, perhaps the conditions for the existence of multiple selves in Flanagan's sense are not as easy to fulfill as the conditions for the existence of several fictional selves in Dennett's sense. Nevertheless, Flanagan's distinction is also not the right one for our purposes. This can be shown, e.g., by reference to the fact that the absence of authorship, which implies the presence of multiple selves, should not be equated with the absence of agency as such. Let us assume that neither PX nor PY is in a position to tell a story that establishes narrative connectedness between them. By drawing on arguments from previous chapters, it can be shown that this does not imply that more than one fundamental entity exists here. Let us assume that PX has acquired the belief at t_1 that the household is out of sugar and PY has this belief at t_2. Despite the lack of narrative connectedness, this may be a case in which one fundamental entity—one agent—acquires the belief that the household needs sugar *as X*, and retains this belief *as Y*.[28] Thus I conclude that the conditions for the presence of multiple selves in Flanagan's sense are not sufficient for us to be dealing with more than one fundamental entity.[29]

Other authors present an interpretation of multiple personality that is similar to the approaches of Dennett and Flanagan. Dennett sometimes describes the self as "the model the agent has of itself";[30] Flanagan says that self "is actually a self-representation."[31] Thomas Metzinger takes up this aspect of their views when he interprets dissociative identity disorder as a case of "multiple self-models."[32] This theory is of course just as unsuitable as Dennett's and Flanagan's accounts for formulating sufficient conditions for the presence of more than one fundamental entity: just as a fundamental entity can live and tell several stories about itself, so too can it have several self-models of itself.[33] We may thus draw the *general* conclusion that the presence of various narrative centers or self-models is not a sufficient condition for the presence of more than one fundamental entity.[34]

4 CONDITIONS OF PERSONHOOD

The main focus of Kathleen V. Wilkes's discussion of multiple personality is the Beauchamp case, which Wilkes analyzes thoroughly (112–119).[35] She asks whether Miss Beauchamp was three persons (corresponding to BI, BIV, and Sally) between 1893 and 1904, that is, from the time of the trauma which supposedly caused BI's emergence to the time the personalities were fused into the "Real Miss Beauchamp." Wilkes writes that more arguments speak for a positive response to this question than for the answer that there is only one person present.[36] That is, we "ought to say" that there are three persons, but this is not necessarily "what we do say." There is no unequivocal answer to the question just how the concept of a person is in fact used in this borderline case: "We have no clear consensus about what to say: the concept of a person fails to cope under this particular strain" (128). She nevertheless believes that much speaks for the presence of several persons here. I shall argue that the points she makes do *not* speak for it *at all*. Her main argument for the positive response is that the personalities

(BI, BIV, and Sally) fulfill Dennett's *conditions of personhood*.[37] She formulates these conditions as follows:

> (1) persons are rational. (2) they are the subjects of Intentional ascriptions. (3) a certain stance or attitude must be taken towards them, a point that introduces the idea that persons are, *inter alia*, moral objects. (4) they can reciprocate when such a stance is taken, which similarly introduces the idea that they are, *inter alia*, moral agents. (5) they are language users. Finally, (6) they have a special kind of consciousness, perhaps self-consciousness. (23)

Wilkes claims, without arguing the point, that BI, BIV, and Sally fulfill conditions (1)–(2) and (5)–(6) (cf. 120). But why should we say that it is the *personalities* BI, BIV, and Sally that fulfill these conditions "separately" and not *Miss Beauchamp* herself? Certainly we can say that P-BI, P-BIV, and P-Sally each fulfill these conditions. However, this gives us *no reason whatsoever* for assuming that there are *three persons* present here. It could just as well be the case that we are dealing with one person who fulfills these conditions in each of her three states (i.e., as P-BI, P-BIV, and P-Sally). The problem with Wilkes's argument is that these conditions may provide an answer to question 7 from Chapter 3 (What is a person in a descriptive sense?), but the fulfillment of the conditions does not as such settle the issue of the *individuation* of fundamental entities (question 4).[38]

Wilkes discusses conditions (3)–(4) in more detail (120–123). However, a simple application of these conditions is beset by a similar problem: here one might say that the confusion is between question 8 (How is the moral status *person* to be understood, and what gives an entity this status?) and question 4. Nevertheless, one might argue that condition (3) is a good starting point for addressing the issue of individuation: if it is intelligible and appropriate to view BI and Sally as *separate* moral objects, are they not two fundamental entities? With respect to the third and fourth conditions, Wilkes draws on Prince's stance toward his vis-à-vis. Regarding condition (3), Wilkes believes that Prince is conflicted. On the one hand, he views his patient as a single individual that is to be cured. On the other, each of the three personalities is "an individual object of concern. He was worried about the effects on *BI* of Sally's practical jokes; he sympathized, quite genuinely, with *B4*'s agony when she told him that he was killing her; and, although he deplored Sally's childishness and occasional spitefulness, he was also amused by this 'carefree child of nature'" (122). Wilkes agrees with Prince in both of his attitudes, that is, she believes that with the aid of condition (3) we can attain no clear answer about whether we are dealing with one or several persons.

As I argued at length in the last chapter, Prince's attitudes toward his vis-à-vis are fundamentally ambivalent. Wilkes is mistaken in assuming, however, that the attention that Prince pays to the personalities individually speaks in favor of the conclusion that this is a case of more than one person (more than one fundamental entity). Such individual attention is just as intelligible and appropriate under the assumption that this is a case of only one fundamental entity. Such care, compassion, or indignation may just as well always be directed at one and the same fundamental entity, but this fundamental entity either *as BI*, *as BIV*, or *as Sally*. We can thus be worried, for instance, about how this fundamental entity *as BI* feels when this fundamental entity *as Sally* performs one of her practical jokes. The problem is that Wilkes does not tell us under what conditions the attitudes toward BI, BIV, and Sally require that they be viewed as separate fundamental entities.

The same problem arises with respect to her discussion of condition (4). She does not tell us under which conditions the moral agency of BI, BIV, and Sally requires us to say that they are three fundamental entities. As I argued in the last chapter with respect to the actual Beauchamp case, there is no reason to regard the different personalities in this case as independent agents. On the contrary: the case must be understood in such a way that *one fundamental entity* is acting here, at times *as BI* and at others *as Sally*.

In addition to the conditions of personhood, Wilkes adduces five points that supposedly speak for understanding the Beauchamp story as a case of more than one person. The first point is that the personalities are so different (123–124). As my discussion of Radden's first two conditions shows, this does not support understanding something as a case of more than one fundamental entity. Second, Wilkes mentions that BI, BIV, or Sally each alone could have led the life of Miss Beauchamp (124). This observation, however, could easily be restated by saying that one fundamental entity (Miss Beauchamp) could have led her entire life, for instance, *as BI*. Third, Wilkes says that it can be doubted that BII is the Real Miss Beauchamp. This point is also irrelevant, since—as argued in the last chapter—the question of whether anyone deserves to be called "the Real Miss Beauchamp" and who that person would be is related to the question "Who am I?" (question 6) rather than the questions about the identity of fundamental entities (questions 1, 2, and 4).

The fourth point concerns the issue that one personality often insists that another personality is *not her*. It also deals with the issue that the personalities regard Prince's therapeutic efforts to make BII into the sole personality of Miss Beauchamp as *their death* (127). Point four—as Wilkes says—thus concerns "what it must have been like from the inside, from the first-person perspective" (126). As I argued in the last chapter, we must take seriously that Sally understands herself as one fundamental entity of more than one in the same body and not merely as a personality of Miss Beauchamp. I also argued, however, that Sally is mistaken in believing that she in fact is one of more than one fundamental entity in one body. We are still seeking the conditions for the presence of more than one fundamental entity in one body. Examining the relation of P-Sally to her own states and actions might be a promising start. She surely has a *first-person* relation to them. So we should ask whether there is more than one fundamental entity in one body if there is more than one *first-person perspective* in this body. This will be examined in the next section.

To comment on Wilkes's fifth and last point, it is helpful to introduce some more terminology. This terminology, which I adopt from Stephen E. Braude, serves to distinguish between different claims about multiple personalities.[39] It may be that the personalities X and Y are *alternately conscious*, that is, X and Y *exist* simultaneously but the states of the one personality are at this time *purely dispositional*. If, on the other hand, X and Y are ascribed *simultaneous occurrent states of awareness* (perception of the surroundings is perhaps ascribed to X, while lively memories of the past are ascribed *simultaneously* to Y), then X and Y are *co-active*. It is sometimes claimed that personalities X and Y *perceive* the *surroundings at the same time* (for example, when only Y has control of the body). Here we may say that X and Y are *co-sensory*. It is also often claimed that X *is conscious of the mental states of* Y, *at precisely the time* at which Y has these states. Here we may say that X is *intra-conscious* of the mental states of Y. When X is co-sensory with Y and intra-conscious of Y, X is *co-conscious* with Y. X exerts *intra-activity* on Y if X is able to influence the experience or behavior of Y. X and Y are *co-present* if they have control over the body simultaneously. It is important to emphasize that the use of this terminology does not imply that more than one fundamental entity is really present here. This terminology is merely needed to distinguish between different claims that get made about the personalities of a human being. At the same time, the content of such claims is in need of interpretation: for example, if it is claimed that the personalities X and Y are co-sensory, it must still be decided whether this means that two *fundamental entities* perceive the surroundings separately, or whether the claim is to be interpreted differently.

The last point Wilkes makes is that Sally is co-conscious with the other personalities (that is, that she is intra-conscious of and co-sensory with them) (125–126).[40] As argued in the last chapter, we must certainly interpret Sally as believing that she, as one fundamental entity, is co-conscious with the other fundamental entities in one body. But, as was just written, Sally is mistaken: she is not a fundamental entity, but merely a personality of the fundamental entity Miss Beauchamp. And, as argued in the last chapter, it is quite easy to explain how it can be that Sally believes that she is co-conscious with another fundamental entity, though she and the other personalities are one and the same fundamental entity. Of course, Miss Beauchamp is just one case. However, Wilkes also fails to tell us under which conditions we would be dealing with more than one fundamental entity if co-consciousness is presumed to be present in a person. In addition, as I shall argue in Chapter 13, one fundamental entity cannot be intra-conscious of the mental states of another fundamental entity. Overall, it must thus be concluded that Wilkes has failed to specify conditions under which two fundamental entities exist in one body.[41]

5 RATIONAL POINTS OF VIEW

Up to now we have chiefly discussed theories that offer a philosophical interpretation of multiple personality. By contrast, Carol Rovane defends a theory of personhood and personal identity.[42] However, since one consequence of her approach is that one body can embody several persons, her view is naturally of interest here. According to Rovane, the diachronic identity of a person consists in the continuity of her first-person point of view and the distinction between persons rests on the fact that each has her own *unified first-person point of view.* Rovane distinguishes her understanding of the first-person point of view from that of Locke, who she thinks understands it phenomenologically: I have direct phenomenological access to my states, but not to the states of others (14–15). Rovane, in contrast, understands the first-person point of view as the "rational point of view of an agent" (19): "A rational point of view is the point of view from which a person deliberates" (21). The aim of such deliberations should be to form a judgment about what we should rationally do and think, all things considered. So the aim is to form "all-things-considered judgments," that is, judgments about what one should do and think when one has taken *everything* into consideration and rationally deliberated about it (rational deliberation consists in resolving contradictions, ranking preferences, finding the means to one's ends, etc.). Put more precisely, "everything" to be considered is "everything in the deliberator's rational point of view." This "everything" is "intentional episodes," that is, "any phenomena that would figure in psychological explanations of a person's actions." Examples of such intentional episodes are beliefs, desires, and the actions themselves (21).

The aim of deliberation is rational unity among the intentional episodes that explain the actions of a person. But *which* person? Since persons are to be individuated over rational points of view, a given individuation cannot be presupposed. We cannot assume, for instance, that we are dealing here with all the intentional episodes that explain the actions of a *particular human being.* At this point, the notion of a "unifying project" (31, 163) plays a central role. The relevant intentional episodes are the ones linked together by such projects. A unifying project is a "substantive practical commitment" (31). Examples of such projects are "the personal projects and fundamental commitments around which individual persons organize their lives in the short and long term" (163). A "set" of intentional episodes required for the conceiving and carrying out of the projects forms around each such project. *These* intentional episodes are those that should be taken into consideration in the all-things-considered judgments (31, 173–176, 196): "Such a set of intentional episodes constitutes an individual person with its own distinct rational point of view" (31). A particular person is *nothing but* such a set of intentional episodes (134).

One consequence of Rovane's account is that *one human being* can embody *more than one person*. This is the case when within one human being more than one overall rational unity is aimed at, and an overall rational unity is "the state that a person achieves when it arrives at and acts upon all-things-considered judgments in a rationally optimal manner" (130). More than one overall rational unity is aimed at if no all-things-considered judgments are made between the intentional episodes belonging to the different sets of intentional episodes and if each of these sets is to be fashioned into an overall unity.

To illustrate this point, Rovane introduces an example of a human being who has three life projects: teaching, playing music, and doing philosophy.[43] If a human being pursues such projects, she normally weighs them against one another. For instance, if she asks herself how she should spend the day, the week, or the year, she asks herself how important the individual projects are to her and how she can best realize them in light of the priorities between the projects and their elements. In this way, she arrives at all-things-considered judgments made on the basis of intentional episodes from *all* of the projects. This is how it is normally. But Rovane wants us to imagine another possibility of carrying out such projects of a human being: here the projects are pursued in complete isolation from one another. When the philosophy project is being pursued, all-things-considered judgments are made that take only those intentional episodes into account that are relevant to the philosophy project. In these all-things-considered judgments, the projects are thus not weighed against one another. But overall rational unity is aimed at among the intentional episodes belonging to the respective project. If this is the case, *three persons* are present in one human being. This also holds if one of the three persons—say, the philosopher—is *intra-conscious* of the musician's desire to practice the piano for hours. Since this desire is not taken into account in the all-things-considered judgments of the philosopher, it does not belong to this person (the philosopher) (173–177).

Why didn't I think of that? Perhaps he will stop trying to kill me if I strike a bargain with him on the use of the body. I'll draw up a contract! I'll even offer him 60 percent of our time (all this thinking sucks up an awful lot of time)! Let me begin immediately: "Agreement on the Use of the Body of Logi Gunnarsson. Section 1: The parties to this contract (Logi and Skugga-Sveinn) agree, when they are out, not to engage in any activity that would undermine the other party's undertakings. Section 2: Neither of the two parties to this agreement may unilaterally—" But it's no use. He'll never sign. As far as he's concerned, there's nobody to make an agreement with. It just isn't fair. I am willing to make such an agreement and all he does is to draw up a document proving my non-existence—without ever mentioning me.

Understood as an account of the individuation of fundamental entities, Rovane's position is mistaken. First, her account is intuitively implausible. Even if the human being pursues each of the projects completely independently in this way, she still might regard all of the projects as her *own* projects. She could, for instance, say *as a philosopher*: "When I perform *as a musician* I can live out my emotions in a way that isn't possible for me *as a philosopher.* I can't and don't want to weigh my projects against one another but I love them both." The attitudes expressed in this statement must be understood as attitudes toward oneself: *as a philosopher* the person understands herself as someone who—*as a musician*—can live out passions that she cannot satisfy *as a philosopher.* Each of us has such attitudes toward ourselves, and such attitudes remain possible even if we have decided to let our projects run radically parallel to one another. The imagined utterance also shows that the human being making it regards herself as an *agent*: she has for the time being decided not to try to make these two sides of herself into a unified whole. Intuitively speaking, Rovane has described a case in which one fundamental entity pursues her projects in an unusual fashion, but not a situation in which three fundamental entities are present.

Second, even assuming that persons are to be individuated over rational points of view, Rovane offers the wrong account of the individuation of such points of view. As a way of preparing my argument for this claim, let me say a few words about one's own attitudes as the starting point for practical deliberations. Subjective theories of practical reason assume that one's subjective attitudes (such as one's own desires), which cannot be given objective justification, are the ultimate basis of practical deliberations. Objective theories assume that one's attitudes can be justified "objectively." Both theories must nonetheless assume that one's *own* attitudes play an important role that the attitudes of others cannot play. According to subjective theories, my own attitudes are simply the subjectively given basis of my deliberations. According to the objective theories, my deliberations must take those of my attitudes as a starting point that I have made my own by regarding them as well founded; the attitudes of others become indirectly relevant only after I myself have adopted these attitudes by taking them to be well founded. As I will now argue, this particular role of one's own attitudes brings out a central problem in Rovane's theory.

Rovane describes a situation in which three projects run independently of one another. She points out that in this situation desires belonging to the music project are irrelevant for the philosophy project (176). However, this situation is artificial: the person in the philosopher-state has decided to pursue the philosophy project in isolation from the others. The person in the musician-state has decided the same for the music project. In this artificial situation we can say that "music" attitudes are irrelevant for the pursuit of the philosophy project. But they are only irrelevant because it has already been decided to pursue the projects independently of one another. Now, if this decision—or the decision to do philosophy at all—is questioned by the person in the philosopher-state, *all of her attitudes* will become immediately relevant for her further deliberations.[44] But which attitudes are these? It would be absurd to assume that these are only the attitudes attributed to the philosophy project. Let us assume that the attitude to want mental stability has been attributed to the music project up to now. The person poses herself the question "Should I continue to pursue philosophy?" and is conscious of this attitude. *Of course* this attitude is relevant for answering this question, *regardless of which project it has been ascribed to previously*. This shows that this attitude was also *previously*—as the projects ran alongside one another—*her* attitude. This attitude was made irrelevant to the philosophy project only by the decision to have the projects run completely independently of one another and through its attribution to the music project. The attribution to a specific project does not mean, however, that the attitude has lost its fundamental relevance for the practical deliberations of the human being—a relevance that only one's *own* attitudes automatically have in contrast to the attitudes of others.[45]

A rational point of view is "the point of view from which a person deliberates" (21). I have just shown that such points of view cannot be individuated via a commitment to reach an overall rational unity within a specific project (for example, philosophy, music, or teaching). The attitudes upon which a person *fundamentally* bases her deliberations are part of the point of view "from which a person deliberates." Certain decisions could make some of these attitudes temporarily irrelevant for certain purposes. For example, certain attitudes could be irrelevant for the unquestioned further pursuit of the philosophy project. However, these attitudes, like the commitments to the project themselves, remain within the point of view from which the person deliberates. Rovane thus offers an implausible interpretation of the notion of a rational point of view that could serve to individuate persons.

A third problem with Rovane's theory has to do with judgments and beliefs that are project-neutral. Let us assume the following: the music project is pursued on Thursdays and the philosophy project on Fridays. On Thursday, the person in the musician-state is in a foreign city to give a concert. On the way to the concert hall, the person comes across a lovely café but has no time to go in. The next day, the person in the philosopher-state knows where the café is because of the previous day's discovery and goes there to read Schopenhauer. The belief concerning the location of the café is only one example of many *project-neutral* beliefs that the person in the musician-state obtained on Thursday. These are beliefs that have nothing specifically to do with any of the projects, but can be used in their pursuit.

How should we describe this situation? The best description is certainly the following: someone pursues a project on a Thursday, discovers a café during that time, makes a note of it, and on the following day goes there to devote herself to her other project. If Rovane is correct, however, this description cannot be right. According to her, there is no person that acts on Thursday *and* Friday. One person is active on Thursday and the other on Friday. But this is wrong. The correct view is that the person who noticed the café on Thursday used this knowledge on Friday in order to go to the café.

Rovane can surely provide a coherent description of this case. She assumes that persons can share a token of a type of belief.[46] In other words: persons can *overlap*. That is, the belief that the café is located on the market square could be shared as a token by the two persons (203–208). If persons are sets of intentional episodes, this is simply a logical description of the case. Still, this description amounts to a *reductio ad absurdum* of this position: someone obtained a belief on Thursday; someone who never obtained it then has it on Friday! Instead of accepting Rovane's description of the case, we should distinguish between the identity of fundamental entities and the identity of personalities. In terms of the identity of personalities, Rovane might be right: there are two "persons" who share a token conviction. But only one fundamental entity is present that obtains the belief on Thursday and retains it until Friday.[47]

6 NON-EMPIRICAL EGOS

Whereas Rovane is primarily concerned with the issues of personhood and personal identity, Braude's main object of investigation in *First Person Plural* is multiple personality disorder.[48] His aim is to provide a philosophical analysis and clarification of the phenomenon and the concepts related to it. I have already mentioned a few of the terms he introduces. His concepts of autobiographical and indexical states should also be noted. A state is *autobiographical* for an individual if and only if the individual *experiences* this state as his own. A state is *indexical* for an individual if and only if the individual *believes* this state is his own (71–77). These concepts are then used to define additional concepts. "S is an *apperceptive center*" is defined as follows:

> (a) *S* is a subject of autobiographical states, both occurrent and dispositional (e.g., sensations, emotions, beliefs, desires, ostensible rememberings, hopes, plans, etc.), and (b) most of those states are indexical for *S* (i.e., *S* believes that those states are its own). (78)

Accordingly, "X and Y are separate apperceptive centers" is defined in the following manner:

> The autobiographical and indexical states of each other are (respectively) largely non-autobiographical and non-indexical for the other. (88)

In describing the *inner perspective* of a personality like Sally, these concepts are indeed very useful. Sally claims to *experience* the states of the other personalities as *alien* states, and she is *convinced* that these are states *of another person*.[49] Accordingly, Braude rightly claims that by using these concepts we can distinguish multiple personality disorder from other dissociative phenomena (78–80, 89) and from role-playing. A person who engages in role-playing believes, in each of her roles, that it is *she* who is playing these roles. A personality like Sally, however, does not see it like that (86).

Nonetheless, I do not want to adopt Braude's concept of apperceptive centers. His definition of this concept says that *S*—the apperceptive center—is the *subject* of states. Braude also says that we can assume the *existence* of such centers in multiple personality (89–90). I believe the *inner perspective* of Sally can indeed be excellently described in terms of the concepts of autobiographical and indexical states. But I do not wish to assume in the description of such phenomena that *personalities* like Sally are the *subjects* of the states attributed to Miss Beauchamp. We should not rule out in the *description* of the phenomena that we are dealing with just *one subject* of different states that sometimes understands itself *as Sally* and other times *as BI*.

With his terminology, however, Braude may not want to assume the existence of several subjects in one body in any strong sense. In fact, he argues that multiple personality disorder presupposes a fundamental unity. His argument is that we can *best explain* the characteristics, emergence, and maintenance of multiple personality disorder in a person if we assume this sort of fundamental unity. I do not want to consider his argument in detail, and I will just briefly remark on some aspects of it. The personalities of a multiple person normally have many abilities in common. It would be implausible to assume that each ability appears twice. A better explanation is that these abilities are to be attributed to "a single unifying ego" (172). Moreover, for multiple and non-multiple persons alike, the experience of an inner conflict presupposes a "synthesizing subject" (174). Finally, the emergence and maintenance of multiple personality disorder in a person is best understood as the reaction of a "single underlying synthesizing self" (174) to trauma and conflict (170–180).

How are we supposed to understand this underlying ego? Braude calls it "a kind of Kantian transcendental synthesizing self" (174). He compares his argument with Kant's reaction to Hume. Hume argued that we cannot discover the self in experience. Kant agreed, but argued that we must postulate a transcendental ego that makes experience possible through synthesis (166–169). According to Braude, the assumption of such an underlying ego is compatible with his assumption of different apperceptive centers.

Braude's position cannot be applied to the topic of the present investigation without further ado. The present work proceeds from the question "What am I fundamentally?" It is not clear whether Braude would answer the question "What am I fundamentally?" with "a transcendental ego." Even if the assumption of such an ego is necessary, this does not mean that each of us is fundamentally a transcendental ego. Braude's discussion of the concept of a person does not help settle this issue since he assumes that there are different concepts of a person that fit different contexts. As a result, it may sometimes be appropriate to treat the personalities of a multiple as separate persons; in other contexts, it might be appropriate to regard the multiple herself as a person (206–208).[50] However, the relation of this account of the concept of a person to the transcendental ego and to the topic of the present study is not clear.[51]

There is a further sense in which Braude's approach cannot be readily applied to the investigation in this book. One of my central questions is whether each of us is fundamentally an entity of which there *could* be more than one in one body. Braude is interested in a given phenomenon—multiple personality disorder—and argues that the affliction of a human being by that phenomenon presupposes the existence of *one* transcendental ego for that human being. Has he thereby ruled out the possibility that there *could* be *more than one transcendental ego* in one body? Is the assumption of two transcendental egos in one body *coherent*? If the *phenomena were different*—if persons with multiple personality disorder were more radically divided than they actually are—would we then *have to* assume more than one transcendental ego? His text offers no answers to these questions.

Like Braude, Stephen R. L. Clark offers a non-empirical account of unity in multiple personality. According to Clark, unconnected or only loosely connected thought fragments constantly flow through our minds, and the emergence of these thoughts is largely out of our control. Nonetheless, they are all objects of our *own attention*. Different objects are present here but only *one* "light of consciousness," only *one* "attention." Each of us has in a certain sense many selves: objects of attention that come to light like foreign objects without their being under our control. But none of us *is* such an object. Each of us consists only of *one self*, of the light, before which these objects appear. Disregarding the objects, the self is the light that illuminates these objects. The identity of this one self can be neither psychologically nor physically analyzed; it cannot be rationally analyzed at all.[52] This is also how we should understand multiple personality. Many personalities are present as objects of one self.[53]

We must now ask whether there can really be only *one* such light in each body. Since according to Clark there are no identity criteria for such a light, in principle we cannot rule out that, in one body, *two lights* shine on their respective objects. If that is so, we could ask whether such a non-empirical account of more than one fundamental entity in one body is superior to the empirical approaches discussed in previous sections. On the one hand, the answer is yes. The empirical criteria considered in this chapter are all compatible with the existence of only one fundamental entity in one body. Non-empirical theories like those of Clark, if understood to account for the existence of more than one fundamental entity in one body,[54] do not have this problem. The attention I devote to my different sides is essentially mine. If such attention is present twice in one body, we must be dealing with two fundamental entities.

On the other hand, the answer is no. Since there cannot be any empirical criteria whatsoever for the individuation of entities such as one light of consciousness in contrast to others in one body, non-empirical accounts of *individuation* must be rejected, just as non-empirical theories of *diachronic identity* were rejected in previous chapters. This comparison of empirical and non-empirical approaches sets the task for the next chapters: the conditions for the existence of more than one fundamental entity in one body must be empirical, but must also avoid the problems of the empirical theories discussed in this chapter.

10 The Coexistence Thesis

In this chapter, I offer a defense of the coexistence thesis. Section 1 prepares the ground by contrasting this thesis with animalism. Sections 2–3 provide two arguments for the coexistence thesis. This argument is then completed by offering, in section 4, a sufficient condition for the presence of two fundamental entities in one body.

1 THE COEXISTENCE THESIS VS. ANIMALISM

Each of us is fundamentally an entity, of which there could exist two or more in one body. This is the coexistence thesis. I am interested in fundamental entities who begin their existence as human beings and I would therefore like to defend the coexistence thesis for *human* bodies. I leave aside the issue whether fundamental entities can exist in other kinds of bodies. This means that *animalism*—the view that each one of us is fundamentally a *human being*—is the important opponent of the coexistence thesis.

Animalism has been much more frequently applied to the issue of diachronic identity than to the question of individuation. So let me start by considering two versions of animalism that deliver diverging answers to the question of when the existence of a human being ends. Brain damage may lead to the irreversible loss of higher mental functions. A being exists in a purely vegetative state, breathing and digesting, but entirely without consciousness. This being does not feel or think and will never do so in the future. Some reflexes may be exhibited—for example, coughing as a reaction to a blockage of the throat—but any intentional or coordinated movements are impossible. The ethically controversial case of Karen Quinlan was such a case.[1] Here the question is metaphysical: does the human being who I was until the loss of these brain functions continue to exist in this vegetative state or has she—have I—ceased to exist?

According to one application of animalism, the human being who I am continues to exist as long as the vegetative system is still working.[2] Another version of animalism, in contrast, holds that the human being who I am no longer exists when the mental functions are irreversibly lost. To be a human being means, among other things, to have the basic capacities for a human life. A being in such a vegetative state does not have these capacities and will never regain them. Thus, according to this account, I—the being who existed until the loss of these capacities—am not the being in the vegetative state. I have ceased to exist.[3]

The concept of an organism plays a central role in both of these versions of animalism: my existence is exactly as long as the existence of the *human organism* that I am. But what are the necessary and sufficient conditions of the continued existence of a human organism? One issue concerns the loss or replacement of biological organs by artificial parts fulfilling the same function as the biological[4] organs.[5] If the organs were to be slowly replaced by artificial parts that successfully fulfill the same functions, would the same human organism still exist? Another issue relates to the significance of the different organs. Can a human organism survive the loss or replacement of certain types of organs, but not of others? These issues can then be combined in questions such as: can I survive with an artificial heart, but not with an artificial brain? Thus, both versions of animalism need to be supplemented by some criterion for deciding when we no longer have a case of one and the same human organism maintaining its vegetative or mental functions.

One possible criterion is that it is necessary and sufficient for the continued existence of the organism that the *central organ controlling the organism* continues to exist. One and the same human being continues to exist if enough of the central controlling organ—the brain, perhaps—continues to exist so that the functions of the organism are maintained. A combination of this criterion with one of the two versions of animalism just discussed would mean that the human being continues to exist as long as the organ responsible for controlling its vegetative functions—the brain stem, perhaps—continues to maintain these functions.[6] A combination with the other version of animalism would mean that the human being continues to exist as long as the organ responsible for its mental functions—the cerebral cortex, perhaps—continues to maintain these functions.

Against this backdrop, we can now turn to animalist approaches to individuation. The issue of individuation is the question as to how human organisms are counted. For example, how many human organisms exist in the case of conjoined twins?[7] If two human organisms exist, then conjoined twins are two fundamental entities. According to one version of animalism, the number of fundamental entities is the same as the number of human organisms understood as a system of vegetative functions. This position would need to be supplemented by a criterion X for the individuation of a human organism as a system of vegetative functions. Let me call this view "the vegetative approach." According to another kind of animalism, the number of fundamental entities is the same as the number of human organisms understood as a system of mental functions. This account would need to be further specified by a criterion Y for the individuation of a human organism as a system of mental functions. I call this view "the Aristotelian approach."

In my argument against animalism, I shall work with versions of criteria X and Y that assume that human organisms are individuated over the central controlling organ. Thus, as will become clear when we consider cases of conjoined twins, this kind of animalism implies that if one human body were successively controlled by *two separate controlling organs*, this would be a case of *two human beings*. The difference between the vegetative and the Aristotelian approach to individuation would then be the following: According to the former, the number of human organisms is the same as the number of human biological centers controlling the vegetative functions of a human body. According to the Aristotelian account, it is the number of human biological centers controlling mental functions that matters.

Although my argument will work with these two examples of criteria X and Y, it is equally applicable to all versions of animalism about individuation. My argument will be that one human being can embody more than one subject of action, thought, and perception and that it can therefore embody more than one fundamental entity. It is possible to defend the view that if one human body embodies two subjects of action, thought, and perception, then this human body embodies *two organisms*, no matter how organically unified it is in other respects—e.g., whether it has exactly one biologically integrated brain to maintain its mental and vegetative functions. Such a view is compatible with the coexistence thesis and I would not regard it as a version of animalism. My argument is directed at all positions according to which the number of fundamental entities is the same as the number of human organisms understood as biological unities (or other material unities, assuming that human organisms can survive extensive replacement of organs by artificial material).

2 FIRST ARGUMENT FOR THE COEXISTENCE THESIS

A very simple argument can be offered for the coexistence thesis. Let me start with a real case of conjoined twins and then consider a series of imagined cases, the last one involving a single human being with only one organ controlling mental functions. The idea is that one should say that the real conjoined twins are two fundamental entities and that the grounds for saying so mean that we should say the same about all the other cases. At least the last case is a case in which we have two fundamental entities embodied by a single human body or human being.

The conjoined twins Abigail and Brittany Hensel, mentioned in Chapter 3, have a total of two arms and two legs. Abigail moves one arm and one leg and Brittany controls the other arm and the other leg. Below their separate heads and necks, they have what seems to be a common body to others. They have two hearts and two spinal cords, but one circulatory system and reproductive organ. Their movements are well coordinated; for example, they play sports like basketball and volleyball and can drive a car.

Having started with this real case, let us add four imaginary cases:

(I) Abigail and Brittany Hensel; two arms, two legs, two heads; Abigail controls one arm and one leg, Brittany the others
(II) Same as (I), except: each controls the whole body at separate times
(III) Same as (II), except: not two heads, but only two brains
(IV) Same as (III), except: not two brains, but one biological center of control for purely vegetative functions (= one brain stem?) and two biological centers of control for mental functions (= two cerebral cortices?)
(V) Same as (IV), except: a single whole brain

I think that it is clear that case (I) is a case of two fundamental entities who are connected bodily with each other. I could have started with other cases in which this is even clearer: cases in which the two conjoined twins have basically entirely separate human bodies and are just conjoined at, say, the hip. However, Abigail and Brittany's case is itself a clear case of two fundamental entities. The important point is that Abigail and Brittany are two entirely separate sources of passive psychological states, active attitudes, actions, and capacities. Let us first consider passive states. When Abigail sees or feels something, Brittany does not thereby see or feel it (and vice versa). Their perceptions may have a common object (they may be looking at the same tree) and their feelings a common cause (the itch may come from a fly on their chest), but their perceptions and feelings are entirely separate. Even if Brittany sees or feels something, Abigail does *not thereby* see or feel it; *she*—Abigail—would *also* need to see or feel it. The same holds for *active attitudes*, for example, beliefs and emotional attitudes. If Brittany acquires the belief that John Adams was the second American president, Abigail does *not thereby* acquire this belief; she would *also* need to acquire it. Assuming that Abigail was also paying attention in history class, it is not unlikely that she will also acquire this belief, but she need not. The same point is equally true of Brittany's and Abigail's *capacities.* If Brittany learns to serve a volley, Abigail does not thereby know how; she must also acquire this ability.[8] Again, the same is true of their actions. Their actions are based on separate attitudes and capacities and are different intentional actions: they each need to perform the intentional action of throwing the basketball. Given that Abigail and Brittany are such entirely separate sources of passive states, active attitudes, capacities, and actions, it is clear that they are two fundamental entities.[9]

Case (II) differs from (I) in the following way: each of the twins is in control of both arms and legs, but they are in control at separate times. It is not important how this switch takes place. To maintain a parallel structure with my later cases, it is simplest to assume that the one is unconscious when the other is in control.[10] B. and A. are independent here in all the ways described for (I).[11] If anything, their independence is even clearer in this case: If A. is conscious on a Tuesday and learns to serve a volley, B. will not know how to do it when she is conscious the next day. She must learn to do so separately.

Case (III) differs from (II) in that the body now has only one head, but it has two brains inside this one head. If (II) is a case of two fundamental entities, this one must surely be such a case as well. The twins are just as independent of each other as before. It is just that they have only one head to express it. However, the fact that B. and A. use the same head to express their feelings and attitudes does not make these feelings and attitudes any less independent.

Case (IV) shows the vegetative approach to be false. This case differs from (III) in that now there are not two whole brains present. There are still two brain centers responsible for the control of mental functions (two cerebral cortices?), but there is only one brain center responsible for the vegetative functions (one brain stem). Thus, the vegetative account must say that there is only one fundamental entity in this case. That is clearly false. Although there exists one center of control for vegetative functions, the independence of A. and B. with respect to passive states, active attitudes, capacities, and actions remains just the same. Each of A. and B. is just as much an independent source of all of these as before. So they are two fundamental entities.

Case (V) differs from (IV) because exactly one whole brain exists here. There is only one biological control center for mental functions.[12] According to the Aristotelian approach, this is thus one human being and one fundamental entity. It is true that it is only one human being, but it is still a case of two fundamental entities. What has changed in comparison to (IV) is that there is only *one biological control center* for mental functions. In other words, there is only *one organ* to be found which controls mental functions. But the independence of A. and B. has not changed. They are just as independent as they are in case (II). If they are different fundamental entities in (II) on account of this independence, they must also be two fundamental entities here.

3 SECOND ARGUMENT FOR THE COEXISTENCE THESIS

Defenders of the vegetative approach can object that it is simply wrong that in (IV) *A.* and *B.* are the agents performing the relevant actions. According to the vegetative approach, there exists only one human being in (IV). The objection to my argument is that it is *this human being* who acts in (IV); sometimes the human being acts *as A.* and sometimes *as B.* The Aristotelian can make similar claims about (V). I will start by laying out a schematic argument against the vegetative position—an argument that can then be turned into an argument against the Aristotelian position and a second argument for the coexistence thesis:

(A) Since there exists only one vegetative control center in case (IV), there exists—according to the vegetative approach—only one human being in case (IV).
(B) The actions in case (IV) have two separate sources; they cannot be traced back to the single vegetative control center.
(C) The actions in (IV) are not—by the standards of the vegetative approach—performed by the human being; from (A), (B).
(D) The actions in (IV) are performed by two separate agents; from (B), (C).
(E) If I were to exist in case (IV), I would be acting.
(F) If I were to exist in (IV), I would be one of two agents in one body; from (D), (E).
(G) According to the vegetative approach, I am fundamentally a human being.
(H) The vegetative approach must falsely claim that I would not act in case (IV); from (C), (E), (G).

Premises (A) and (B) need no defense here: (A) is simply a consequence of the vegetative understanding of individuation. (B) has been adequately defended in the previous discussion of (IV). The first important question is why (C) is supposed to follow from (A) and (B). Let us first consider what the defender of the vegetative approach should say about intentional action in normal cases (cases in which there is clearly only one source of intentional action and one whole brain). Surely the advocate of the vegetative account cannot defend the claim that the *vegetative control center* performs an *intentional action* whenever the human being does. One might say that the vegetative system digests or that it controls digestion, but it surely performs no intentional actions. It is the human being—not the vegetative control center—who catches balls and throws stones. Intentional action is not possible unless the human being already has certain abilities and then it is the human agent and not the vegetative system that performs these actions.[13]

Now, what is the defender of the vegetative view to say about (IV)? Who acts in this case? If the vegetative control system does not act in normal cases, it does not act here either. In normal cases, there is no problem about saying that the human being acts. In such cases, there is only one source of agency. But in case (IV) there are two sources of action. Neither of these sources serves to individuate the human being; according to the vegetative approach, the human being is individuated over the vegetative system. So the vegetative approach cannot say that the human being acts in (IV), sometimes as A. and sometimes as B. This answer to argument 1 for the coexistence thesis is simply not open to the advocate of the vegetative position. Whatever or whoever acts in (IV), it is not the human being. (Proposition (D) makes explicit that there are two agents in (IV). This could be accepted by the Aristotelian for case (IV) and she could still insist that there are two human beings acting here, given that Aristotelian individuation of the human being runs over the biological center of control for mental functions and there are two such centers in (IV).)

The defender of the vegetative account could make a different objection to argument 1. Instead of saying that in (IV) the human being acts, she could say that the question who acts in (IV) is simply irrelevant to the question as to how many fundamental entities exist in (IV). There is only one fundamental entity in (IV)—namely, the human being—and this entity does not act. The argument involving (C), (E), (G), and (H) serves to answer this objection. (C) has already been discussed. (G) simply states the vegetative answer to the question of what I fundamentally am. Premise (E) says: "If I were to exist in case (IV), I would be acting." This is the crucial premise. It would surely beg the question against the vegetative approach to assume that whenever I exist, I must be a capable of action. After all, according to the vegetative approach, I can exist in a purely vegetative state. However, it seems to be a reasonable requirement for any answer to the question "What am I fundamentally?" that I am fundamentally a sort of entity by whom—*if* intentional human actions take place—intentional human actions are performed: whenever intentional human action takes place, it is performed by a fundamental entity.[14] Now, it cannot be denied that *actions take place* in (IV). But, according to the vegetative approach, I would not—none of us would—perform these actions if I—any one of us—were to exist in (IV). Instead I would be the human being and the human being does not act in (IV). Thus, the vegetative approach leads to the *paradoxical* result that intentional actions take place in (IV), but these actions could not be performed by me if I were to exist in (IV). This involves a violation of a *reasonable requirement for answers to the question "What am I fundamentally?"*[15]

Proposition (F) is only true if we individuate the body in accordance with the vegetative approach. Since (F) plays no role in the argument against the vegetative approach, let me now turn to the criticism of the Aristotelian account:

(A)* Since there exists only one biological center of control for mental functions in case (V), there exists—according to the Aristotelian approach—only one human being in case (V).

(B)* The actions in case (V) have two separate sources; they cannot be traced back to the single biological control center.

(C)* The actions in (V) are not—by Aristotelian standards—performed by the human being; from (A)*, (B)*.

(D)* The actions in (V) are performed by two separate agents; from (B)*, (C)*.

(E)* If I were to exist in case (V), I would be acting.

(F)* If I were to exist in (V), I would be one of two agents in one body; from (D)*, (E)*.

(G)* According to the Aristotelian approach, I am fundamentally a human being.

(H)* The Aristotelian approach must falsely claim that I would not act in case (V); from (C)*, (E)*, (G)*.

Cases (IV) and (V) are importantly different. On this basis, one might argue that (B)* is false, though (B) is true. Intentional actions can surely not be traced back to the vegetative system. However, they can be traced to the biological control center for mental functions. Thus, there are two important differences between (B) and (B)*. First, the sources of action can in (B) be traced back to systems that are different from the vegetative system in a *biological sense* and are themselves *biologically distinct* from each other. In (B)* the two sources of actions are two distinct mental systems. There is no biological difference between them and the brain and they are not biologically distinct from each other. Second, in (B) intentional action cannot be traced back to the vegetative system *at all*. In (B)* intentional action can be traced back to the biological control center for mental functions; the two mental systems are within the boundaries of this biological center.

Despite these differences, in the intended meaning of propositions (B)*, (C)*, and (D)*, they are true. The Aristotelian approach offers a biological account of individuation: the control center for mental functions is understood *biologically*; it is a certain *organ*. As long as there is one of these organs, there is one human being. Now, I said earlier that the vegetative system does not perform intentional actions. Although it may be less obvious, the same is true of the parts of the brain involved in intentional action. The brain does not perform any intentional actions.

In normal cases, a human being who has developed certain abilities becomes a human agent, and it is the human agent who performs the actions. Case (V) is not a normal case. It is assumed about (V) that A. and B. are here just as separate as in the other cases. If that is so, what has happened in (V) is that one human being has not become one human agent, but two. With respect to all of their passive states, active attitudes, capacities, and actions, A. and B. in (V) are just as separate as Brittany and Abigail in (I). If we *individuate* human beings *over* central controlling *organs*, there is just one human being in (V). But that which makes up agency we do not get once, but twice. If A. is able to read and B. is able to read, that is what we have: *A.* is able to read *and B.* is able to read. A. and B. must acquire these capacities entirely separately. Thus, there is not *one* agent here who acquires the capacity to read; there are two. If we individuate the human being over the central controlling organ, we must therefore say that the human being does not perform any intentional actions at all. The human agent who performs the actions must be individuated differently. So (B)*, (C)*, and (D)* are true.

I commented on (D) by saying that it "makes explicit" that there are two agents in (IV). Similar comments could be made about (D)*. The summary of the argument says that (D)* follows from (B)* and (C)*. As the argumentation in the last paragraph makes clear, one cannot really decide whether (B)* and (C)* are true without at the same time considering whether (D)* is true. So one might say that (D)* makes explicit what one must already accept in accepting (B)* and (C)*. (D)* is the first premise in argument 2 for the coexistence thesis:

(D)* The actions in (V) are performed by two separate agents.
(E)* If I were to exist in case (V), I would be acting.
(F)* If I were to exist in (V), I would be one of two agents in one body; from (D)*, (E)*.

As I just said, the arguments given for (B)* and (C)* are also arguments for (D)*. And the reasons for (E) also speak for (E)*. Now, the coexistence thesis follows from (F)*. Whereas one could say that in (IV) there exist two human beings on account of the two existing organs controlling mental functions, this is not an option for (V). No animalist can claim that in (V) there exist two human beings or bodies. So we can conclude from (F)* that I am—that each of us is—an entity of which there can be more than one in a single body.

Arguments 1 and 2 are different, but related, arguments. Argument 1 says that if one has a certain view about conjoined twins, then one must also accept the coexistence thesis. Argument 2 makes no direct use of the comparison with conjoined twins. Also, principle (E)* plays no direct role in argument 1. In argument 1, one is not directly asked about either (IV) or (V). One is asked to consider the case of conjoined twins and to produce an explanation as to why one thinks that there are two fundamental entities in this case. Consistency with the relevant explanation then requires one to say that there are two fundamental entities in (IV) and (V). Nevertheless, the arguments are related: although I could have argued directly for (D)*, I did in fact support (D)* by appealing to the case of conjoined twins ("A. and B. in (V) are just as independent as A. and B. in (II)"). In addition, one might say that principles (E) and (E)* amount to an implicit premise in argument 1: without implicitly accepting these principles, how could one claim that the crucial ontological difference between Abigail and Brittany is their separate agency rather than their separate brains?

4 THE CAP CRITERION

I have argued against the Aristotelian position by saying that there exist two agents in case (V). I said that A. and B. are two agents in (V) because A. and B. are just as independent in (V) as in the previous cases. Now, that claim might be questioned. It might be doubted that in a human being with one whole brain there can ever be independence of agency of the sort possible when there is some bodily difference between agents (as there is in cases (I)–(IV)).

I will respond to this objection by formulating a sufficient condition for the coexistence of two fundamental entities in one body. Let me start by going back to my discussion of the differences between the two agents in cases (II) and by introducing some terminology. Remember that I assumed that A. and B. are never conscious at the same time (to use the terminology of the last chapter: they are never co-active). And as I said, A. and B. are subject to *passive states* (for examples, perceptual states and urges) entirely independently of each other. And they acquire *active attitudes* (for example, beliefs and emotional attitudes) [16] and *capacities* (for example, the ability to read) entirely independently of each other. It is important to add that their *memories* of these passive states, active attitudes, and capacities (*CAPs*) are also independent of each other. A. will normally be able to exercise capacities that she acquired earlier and she will often remember her experiences. However, B.'s CAPs are separate from A.'s. Thus, although they may have acquired or had the *same kind* of CAPs, each one can only remember her own CAPs. It is clear that *if* A. and B. in (V) are just as independent with respect to their CAPs and the memories of them as in (II), they are two agents and thus two fundamental entities. Now we just need to formulate a sufficient condition for this independence.

Recall the terminology from the last chapter: "The person in the X-state" ("PX") refers to a fundamental entity at those times when the fundamental entity displays the personality X ("the person in the Y-state" ["PY"] is understood analogously). Let us now make the following assumptions about PX and PY in the rest of this chapter and in the next chapters: PX and PY share the same human body. PX and PY are not co-active: PX is active at odd times (t_1, t_3, etc.) and PY is active at even times (t_2, t_4, etc.). Let us also assume that PX is a fundamental entity that exists over time and that the same holds for PY (this assumption does not rule out that they are the same fundamental entity; each fundamental entity may perhaps be identical to the human being). Now we only need to assume that PX and PY are just as independent of each other as A. and B. in (II): if PX (at an odd time) acquires a CAP—a capacity, active attitude, or passive state—then PY does not thereby have any of these CAPs or a memory of them. On the contrary, in order to have such CAPs or a memory of them, PY (at an even time) *would herself* need to *acquire* the CAP. The same holds for PX (at odd times) with respect to CAPs that PY acquires (at even times). This can be formulated in terms of *incapacities* that PX and PY have with respect to each other's CAPs:

> *The CAP criterion*: (1) PY is incapable of having any of the types of CAPs that PX acquires (at odd times) or memories of them, unless PY

acquires these types of CAPs herself (at even times). (2) PX is incapable of having any of the types of CAPs that PY acquires (at even times) or memories of them, unless PX acquires these types of CAPs herself (at odd times). (3) PY is a fundamental entity existing over time. PX is a fundamental entity existing over time. If (1)–(3) are fulfilled, PX and PY are two fundamental entities.

The notion of the *acquisition of a CAP at a certain time* is to be understood as meaning that the person gains the relevant CAP in some other way than *by the normal causal connection within the brain of this human being* between the relevant CAP at this time and a CAP gained at an earlier time by the same human being. A typical case of the *acquisition* of a belief would involve somebody acquiring a belief at a certain time based on her perceptual experience at that time. A typical case of the maintenance of a belief would involve somebody continuing to have a belief she acquired in this way at an earlier time. PX and PY are separate in the sense that each has to acquire their CAPs for themselves. There are no causal connections between the CAPs each acquires within their common brain.

If the CAP criterion is fulfilled, things can hardly be said to be normal since PX and PY are radically independent of each other with respect to experience, thought, and action. Considered for themselves, however, PX and PY are perfectly normal subjects of experience, thought, and action. They do not differ from normal human beings in the way in which they have experiences and thoughts and perform actions. What it means for PX and PY to acquire a CAP at a certain time does not differ from what it means for a normal human being to acquire a CAP at a certain time. Thus, for the purposes of employing the concept of the acquisition of a CAP in the CAP criterion, it does not have to be decided whether it would count as an acquisition of a CAP if somebody were to come to have a CAP in some way which—as described in some thought experiments—deviates from the normal manner of acquiring a CAP. The concept of the acquisition of a CAP employed in the criterion is simply the notion of acquisition familiar to us from normal cases.

It might be objected that the CAP criterion is not sufficient for the coexistence of two fundamental entities in one body. Even if this condition is fulfilled, one might object that this is just a case of one fundamental entity with a strangely systematic amnesia: at even times, this fundamental entity is amnesic with respect to odd times, and vice versa.

This objection plays on an ambiguity in the concept of amnesia. One can use "amnesia" simply to mean that PY does not have any of the CAPs that PX has acquired or memories of them, unless PY acquires them herself (and vice versa). However, one is not permitted to move from this use of the word to the concept of amnesia as something that holds between the states of one and the same fundamental entity. It begs the question to assume that case (V) or the relationship between PX and PY is a case of amnesia in this latter sense. In fact, it seems to me that (V) is not a case of amnesia in this sense at all. First, amnesia in this sense is never really complete: only if a portion of CAPs has been retained can one say that somebody is amnesic about some other portion of her CAPs. Second, A. and B. in (V) (and PX and PY) are just like case (II) in the following respect: A. has simply never acquired the CAPs that B. has acquired or she must acquire them for herself if she is to have them. And one cannot be amnesic about something one has never acquired.

Here another objection could be made concerning memory. There is an important difference between (II) and (V). A. and B. in (V)—and PX and PY—have the same whole brain. Thus, in contrast to (II), PX and PY can in principle retain and remember each other's states. Thus, PX and PY are one fundamental entity.

In response to this objection, let us consider two kinds of interference with the normal course of events in (II). First, we may keep A. and B. physically distinct, but somehow transport CAPs and "memories" between them. For example, whenever A. acquires a certain belief, this belief is somehow copied and transported to B. Or when A. has an experience, an apparent memory of having had this experience is created. Here A. and B. remain distinct fundamental entities. It is just that whenever A. acquires a belief, B. acquires a belief with the same propositional content, and whenever A. has an experience, B. has the false impression that she has had this experience, too. Second, we may at t_n perform a physical fusion in such a way that after it A. and B. form one physical system that is able to retain and remember the CAPs that either A. or B. acquired. This integration of CAPs and memories would not mean that A. and B. were one fundamental entity all along. Rather, they were each one fundamental entity until t_n and the existence of this fundamental entity ends at t_n. After that, there exists another fundamental entity that retains and remembers the CAPs of A. and B.

Now, two different scenarios in the case of PX and PY must be understood in the same way as these two interferences in (II). First, we can create apparent "memories" in PY of PX's CAPs (and vice versa) in the same way that they are created in the first interference in (II). But that would not make PX and PY the same fundamental entities. It would simply be the case, for example, that PY would be provided with a belief with the same propositional content as a belief that PX has acquired. It begs the question against the CAP criterion to assume that, because PX and PY have a common brain, real memory of experiences or recovery of beliefs or capacities between PX and PY must be possible. Second, PY may at some point actually become able to retain or remember PX's CAPs. In that case, there now only exists one fundamental entity, though *prior* to this PX and PY were two fundamental entities. As long as the mutual incapacities with respect to their CAPs hold, PX and PY are two fundamental entities. Thus, the fact that PY (or PX) may gain this capacity does not show that PY and PX were one fundamental entity before PY gained this capacity.[17]

Under what conditions do these mutual incapacities hold? Although I will not provide any general answer to this question, there are clear cases in which PX and PY are incapable of remembering or retaining the other's CAPs and clear cases in which they are. In order to count as being able to remember or retain them, PX does not need to be able to do so all on her own. For example, if hypnosis were needed to help PX recall certain beliefs or experiences, she would still count as capable of recalling these beliefs and experiences. If, however, nothing—e.g., hypnosis, psychotherapy, pharmaceuticals, or brain surgery—can help PX recall PY's CAPs, then PX is surely incapable of recalling them. So it surely makes sense to assume that PX and PY may have capacities or incapacities this way.

I conclude that the coexistence thesis is true: each one of us is fundamentally an entity of which there can exist more than one in the same body. But what is then the relationship between the fundamental entities and the body they share? This question will be discussed in the next chapter.

11 Sharing My Body

If two fundamental entities share a body, what is their relationship to the shared body? This chapter discusses this question by explaining how two fundamental entities can be materially constituted by a single living being (section 1), how they can travel precisely the same spatiotemporal route through the world (section 2), how their bodily awareness can be understood (section 3), and how the shared body can express their respective mental states (section 4).

1 TWO IN ONE: MATERIAL CONSTITUTION

In section 6.2, it was argued that each of us is *not identical* to a living being or a body, but is rather *materially constituted* by a living being and a body. This makes it possible for two fundamental entities to share a body: they are materially constituted by the body they share.[1] It must now be discussed in more detail how one living being and one body can materially constitute two fundamental entities.

What it means for two fundamental entities to be materially constituted by one living being becomes clear if we consider one such example. So let's assume that, initially, only one fundamental entity is materially constituted by a particular living being. Even earlier—before the fundamental entity came into being—this living being already existed. When the living being became complex enough, the fundamental entity came into being. However, the existence of the fundamental entity does not mean that we now have two organisms: one organism maintaining the vegetative functions and another organism responsible for the mental functions. Rather, when the fundamental entity came into existence, we were left with one organic unity that includes the vegetative and the mental functions. We may assume that the mental states of this fundamental entity rest on certain brain processes and other material happenings.

At a later point, an additional fundamental entity comes into being in the same living being. When this second fundamental entity is thinking something that the first fundamental entity isn't thinking, then the thoughts of the second fundamental entity must also rest on certain material processes. Because the mental processes of the two fundamental entities are separate, there must also be a difference in the material processes they are based on. Nevertheless, the second fundamental entity is materially constituted by the same living being as the first one. Before the first fundamental entity came into being, the living being already existed and it continued to exist when the second fundamental entity came into being. This living being may also continue to exist when the two fundamental entities have ceased to exist. But each of these fundamental entities forms an organic unity with the living being. Within each of these organic unities, the material processes on which the mental episodes of this unity rest take place and these processes are not part of the other organic unity.[2] In such a case, there exist *two material beings*, but each of these beings is materially constituted by *one and the same living being.*

One may raise the following objection to this account: If the living being L materially constitutes the fundamental entity FE1, then L and FE1, at each point in time during their existence, consist of the same material parts. The same holds for L and FE2. According to the account just offered, there is supposed to be a material difference between FE1 and FE2. That is impossible, assuming that FE1 and FE2 are materially constituted by one and the same living being L and that, during the existence of FE1 and FE2, there is at no time any material difference between these two fundamental entities and L.

To overcome this objection, my account must be supplemented by the following clause: if fundamental entities FE1 and FE2 are materially constituted by one and the same living being, then in each case—in the material constitution of each of these fundamental entities—not every part of the living being participates in the material constitution. This principle can be explained by considering case (IV) concerning the conjoined twins A. and B. discussed in section 10.2: this is a case in which there exists only one biological center controlling the purely vegetative functions (the brain stem, we may assume), but two biological centers controlling the mental functions (two cerebral cortices, we may assume). In this case, a fundamental entity comes into being when the mental functions begin. Prior to this point in time, there exists only *one* living being. This living being can survive the death of the two fundamental entities that come into existence later than this living being. But not every part of the living being participates in the material constitution of FE1. The one cerebral cortex plays no part in it. Thus, this cerebral cortex is not part of FE1. Nevertheless, there is only one living being that exists before the two fundamental entities come into being, and it can survive both of them. This is also how the case of PX and PY must be understood—the case in which there are two fundamental entities but only one biological organ controlling the mental functions. Here there exists only one living being which materially constitutes two fundamental entities, but not every material process taking place in this living being participates in the material constitution.

There are naturally differences between the case of the conjoined twins and the case of PX and PY. In the first case, it is clear that a *part* of the living being does not participate in the material constitution of one of the fundamental entities—that part being one of the cerebral cortices. In the case of PX and PY, it is not possible to specify any such part independently of the mental episodes of the two fundamental entities. Accordingly, I have talked about the material processes on which these mental episodes rest. These material processes might be considered parts in a broad sense. It is, however, not important whether we speak here of parts or material processes. The important point is that the fundamental entities PX and PY are materially constituted by one and the same living being and that certain material processes that participate in the material constitution of PX do not take part in the material constitution of PY (and vice versa).[3]

2 TWO IN ONE: SPATIAL SELF-LOCATION

In his 1968 paper "On Being in the Same Place at the Same Time," David Wiggins defends the following principle: "No two things *of the same kind* (that is, no two things which satisfy the same sortal or substance concept) can occupy exactly the same volume at exactly the same time."[4] If the fundamental entities PX and PY can be materially constituted by one and the same living being, then Wiggins's principle is false. Even if there are material differences between PX and PY—because the respective mental episodes rest on different material processes—they are materially constituted by a living being occupying a certain volume at the same time. Thus, two fundamental entities occupy the same space at the same time. In the original paper, Wiggins offers a few reasons for this principle. However, in a 1997 postscript to a reprint of the paper he questions these reasons. In this postscript he argues as follows for the principle:

> Insofar as we continue to take material substances of this or that particular kind seriously, and insofar as this seriousness of ours engages with an interest in the casual [causal?] explanation of the interactions of bodies in the physical world, the substance concepts that we cherish will be concepts of things that *compete* for space in the world, things that do not slide into one another and out of one another again and that exclude one another from a given place. These are concepts of things that oppose one another and *interact*, dependably.[5]

PX and PY—the fundamental entities individuated by the CAP criterion—are subjects of experience and action and are materially constituted by a living being. As such, they are capable of causal interaction with other fundamental entities and with other objects. So the reference to causal explanation or interaction offers no reason for accepting Wiggins's principle. His comment about "things that do not slide into one another and out of one another again" does surely also not present a problem for my position. And why should fundamental entities not be capable of sharing a place? Wiggins simply offers no argument for that claim. So we must look elsewhere for an argument for this intuition.

One might argue that fundamental entities must necessarily be—or necessarily understand themselves as—subjects of experience who, over time, travel a certain spatial route through the world and who, from the vantage point of that route, experience other objects as standing in certain spatiotemporal relations to themselves (the subjects).[6] Even if that is so, this does not mean that such a spatiotemporal route serves to *individuate* fundamental entities. A fundamental entity can understand herself as a subject who experiences objects from the vantage point of a certain spatiotemporal route, while at the same time understanding herself as a fundamental entity who travels exactly the same spatiotemporal route through the perceived world as other fundamental entities with whom she shares a body. The fundamental entities PX and PY who—because they share a body—travel exactly the same spatiotemporal route through the world can be individuated on the basis of other factors than this spatiotemporal route. If PX fulfills the commitment criterion, then PX is a fundamental entity existing over time. The same holds for PY. If PX and PY also fulfill the other conditions of the CAP criterion, this suffices to individuate them, despite the fact that they experience objects from the viewpoint of exactly the same spatiotemporal route.

It might still be argued that this way of individuating fundamental entities is problematic. After all, the CAP criterion allows that PX may be entirely unconscious at even times. And each of these even times may be very long. And if the CAP criterion is fulfilled, PX will have no memories of the experiences PY makes at even times. So if PX observes object O_1 at t_1 from a certain point in space, has no experiences at t_2, has at odd times no memories of the experiences had at t_2, and t_2 is very long, then PX at t_3 has experiences of objects that she may—on account of the missing experiences at t_2—not be able to connect spatiotemporally with the object O_1. And without being able to make such spatiotemporal connections—so runs the argument—PX cannot understand her experiences as experiences of an objective world. And, as one might argue, being able to understand one's experiences in this way is a necessary condition for being a fundamental entity.[7]

It is true that, under these conditions, PX may have severe difficulties in finding her way in the world when she gains control of the body at t_3. These are, however, purely *practical* difficulties. PX need not have any difficulties in understanding what it means that she at t_3 experiences the same object, O_1, as at t_1. PX need only assume that at t_2 she stood in a certain spatiotemporal relation to O_1, though at t_2 she was—to use the terminology of Chapter 9—not active and thus not able to have any experiences. It makes perfect sense to assume that PX at t_2 stood in a spatiotemporal relation to O_1 even if at t_2 only PY was active. As the discussion of coma in section 5.1 shows, the commitment criterion can explain why PX exists continuously as one and the same fundamental entity from t_1 to t_3 even if PX is not active at t_2. So PX can at t_3 assume that she existed at t_2 and stood in a certain spatiotemporal relation to O_1, though at t_2 she is not aware of this fact. Thus, PX will have no difficulties in grasping what it means that at t_3 she has experiences of the same object, O_1, as at t_1. Overall, we may conclude that we have found no reason not to assume that two fundamental entities may travel exactly the same spatiotemporal route through the world.

3 TWO IN ONE: BODILY AWARENESS

In Chapter 9, I doubted that two fundamental entities can share mental states. The coexistence thesis means that two fundamental entities can share one and the same body. It might now be argued that this position necessarily implies a false account of awareness of one's own body. If fundamental entities cannot share mental states, but they can share the body, then—so runs the argument—the body can *only* appear as the *object* of consciousness. In other words, for the consciousness of each of the fundamental entities, the shared body can only serve as a shared object of each consciousness. However, this involves an entirely misguided understanding of the awareness of one's own body. If we distinguish between objective body and phenomenal body, then we may say that the objective body (as opposed to the phenomenal body) can only appear as an *object* of consciousness. In contrast, when I am conscious of my own phenomenal body, the phenomenal body *cannot* function *only* as an *object* of consciousness. The coexistence thesis—the view that two fundamental entities can share a body—implies that *everything non-mental can only occur as an object of consciousness.* This implies, in turn, the false view that the phenomenal body can only function as an object of consciousness. Therefore, the coexistence thesis must be rejected.

This is the bare structure of an argument that must now be fleshed out. In particular, it must be explained what it means to say that the own phenomenal body "cannot function only as an object of consciousness." To elaborate the argument, I will sketch a view that can be developed by taking Maurice Merleau-Ponty's theory as a starting point. I am looking for a position that understands the phenomenal body to be on the *perceiving* rather than *perceived* side in such a way that it will seem impossible to assume that one living being can embody two fundamental entities. The view I will develop based on Merleau-Ponty's theory is such a position if any view is. Thus, if I then succeed in showing that this view is compatible with the existence of two fundamental entities in one living being, then one may assume that this also holds for other such positions. Merleau-Ponty writes:

> If I can, with my left hand, feel my right hand as it touches an object, the right hand as an object is not the right hand as it touches: the first is a system of bones, muscles and flesh brought down at a point of space, the second shoots through space like a rocket to reveal the external object in its place. In so far as it sees or touches the world, my body can therefore be neither seen nor touched. What prevents its ever being an object, ever being "completely constituted" is that it is that by which there are objects.[8]

As the talk of constitution indicates, it would not be possible to do justice to Merleau-Ponty's own theory without taking into account certain assumptions it shares with transcendental philosophy. This aspect can be ignored here because I am only concerned with a specific point that one can make based on Merleau-Ponty's ideas. One might say that the perceiving subject principally eludes perception. If the perceiving subject tries to make itself an *object* of perception, then it again eludes perception as the *subject* of *this* perception. In this passage, Merleau-Ponty takes up this view of the perceiving subject in his account of the touching hand or the touching (phenomenal) body. (Although he does not use the terminology in this passage, the touched body is the objective body, the touching body the phenomenal body.)[9] For our purposes, the following is Merleau-Ponty's crucial thought: The phenomenal body is not an object of perception. It is not something lying between the perceived object, on the one hand, and the perceiving subject or the perceptions or thoughts of this subject, on the other. "My body has its world, or understands its world, without having to make use of my 'symbolic' or 'objectifying function.'"[10] Here my own body fulfills the role usually assigned to the perceiving subject or the perceptions. The perceiving body is not something more primitive than perception or a link between the perceived object and the perceiving subject. Rather, my body is the place where perception takes place. In contrast to a subject that is assumed to exist *in* a body, my own (phenomenal) body cannot be understood as something that stands over against the things. Rather, my phenomenal body is itself in touch with them. "In the action of the hand which is raised toward an object is contained a reference to the object, not as an object represented, but as that highly specific thing toward which we project ourselves, near which we are, in anticipation, and which we haunt."[11] The reference to the object, the consciousness of the object, is not achieved by something inner—something essentially separate from the object and the body—but rather by the (phenomenal) body itself that can in the end touch the object.[12]

On the basis of this view, an argument can now be put forth against the coexistence thesis: This thesis can only be sustained if a fundamental entity is understood as something inner. Only if fundamental entities are something inner can two separate such entities exist over time in the same body. According to the view just sketched, perception of things (or more generally, consciousness of things) cannot be understood as something inner that is separate from the phenomenal body. Although one's own phenomenal body cannot be identified with one's own objective body as a possible object of consciousness, one's own phenomenal body is something bodily—something that can literally touch its object. Thus, there can be only *one* body that is one's own phenomenal body. So it follows that, because the perceiving subject is not something inner that is separate from the phenomenal body, there cannot be more than one perceiving subject. Therefore, the coexistence thesis must be rejected.

This argument can be further supported by drawing on Merleau-Ponty's deliberations on another example:

> It was also said that the body is an affective object, whereas external things are from my point of view merely represented. This amounted to stating for a third time the problem of the status of my own body. For if I say that my foot hurts, I do not simply mean that it is a cause of pain in the same way as the nail which is cutting into it, differing only in being nearer to me; I do not mean that it is the last of the objects in the external world, after which a more intimate kind of pain should begin, an unlocalized awareness of pain in itself, related to the foot only by some causal connection and within the closed system of experience. I mean that the pain reveals itself as localized, that it is constitutive of a "pain-infested space". "My foot hurts" means not: "I think that my foot is the cause of this pain", but "the pain comes from my foot" or again "my foot has a pain".[13]

The (phenomenal) body *cannot only* be understood as something in which the pain is *localized*, but *the (phenomenal) body is itself something that has experiences*: the phenomenal body occupies the position which most theories assign to the perceiving subject. However, the pain is *also* localized in the (phenomenal) body—in something that is bodily. When touching something, one is conscious of the position of the hand as the hand is touching it. Analogously, the phenomenal body experiences the pain in the foot.[14]

One might argue that this position is incompatible with the coexistence thesis. There can exist two fundamental entities in one body only if each of the fundamental entities experiences pain on its own. If, however, the (phenomenal) body is itself both localized in space and that which experiences the pain, then there cannot exist two fundamental entities in the same living being separately experiencing pain. The phenomenal body is that which experiences the pain and each living being has only one phenomenal body.

I do not want to take a stand on the position which has been developed here based on elements in Merleau-Ponty's work. I only want to discuss one question: if this position is right, does this mean that there can exist only one fundamental entity in one body? A positive answer to this question rests on the assumption that each living being can have only one phenomenal body in the sense of this position. This assumption, however, is false. If the Merleau-Pontean position is right, PX's phenomenal body is something that perceives things. The perceiving subject is not an inner subject. Rather, the perceptions are had by the phenomenal body itself—perception is literally bodily. This holds of course for PY. Now, the following is perfectly possible: PY has no (bodily) memories of the (bodily) perceptions and experiences that PX has, unless PY has had such perceptions and experiences herself (and vice versa). And PY has none of the (bodily) capacities that PX has, unless PY has acquired these capacities herself (and vice versa). Nevertheless, these (bodily) memories, perceptions, and capacities are understood in the Merleau-Pontean sense. In other words, it is possible that PX and PY fulfill the CAP criterion *and* that perceptions and other characteristics are understood along the lines of the Merleau-Pontean position. If the CAP criterion is fulfilled in this way, then PX's bodily way of being functions entirely separately from PY's bodily way of being. PX's bodily engagement with the world has nothing to do with PY's bodily engagement. In Merleau-Ponty's terminology, we might say that PX has one phenomenal body and PY has another one. But it is not important whether we employ this terminology. The crucial points are the following: If the CAP criterion is fulfilled, then PX and PY are two fundamental entities. They are materially constituted by one living being. This does not give us any reason to understand PX's and PY's perception as a purely inner phenomenon. We may understand their perception in the Merleau-Pontean sense as a bodily phenomenon through and through. If PX's bodily way of being in this Merleau-Pontean sense functions entirely separately from PY's bodily way of being and the other conditions of the CAP criterion are fulfilled, then PX and PY are two fundamental entities in a single living being.

It might be objected that this overlooks a point central to the Merleau-Pontean position: according to the commitment criterion, a fundamental entity does not begin to exist until a material being makes a commitment. But the material being's phenomenal body exists earlier. Therefore, it cannot be the case that there exist two fundamental entities in one living being, each with its own phenomenal body. Because the phenomenal body itself perceives, there can only exist one fundamental entity in each living being. Each division within a living being must take place against the backdrop of the unity of the phenomenal body.

In response to this objection we must make a distinction between two points. First, the objection questions the plausibility of the assumption that the existence of a fundamental entity does not begin until a commitment has been made by a material being. This objection was discussed in section 6.3. Second, the objection concerns specifically the possibility of the existence of two fundamental entities in one living being. I have claimed that two fundamental entities with a shared (objective) body can have two entirely separate bodily ways of being. Now, it cannot be denied that the physical processes in the shared (objective) body equally influence both of the fundamental entities. It can also not be questioned that, before the two fundamental entities come into existence, the material being will have acquired certain capacities that the two fundamental entities now have. For example, a child may learn to crawl and walk before it becomes capable of making commitments. After the fundamental entities have come into existence, they keep these capacities. The objection is that one cannot distinguish clearly between the two fundamental entities' bodily ways of being, on the one hand, and the bodily way of being they share, on the other. If that is so, it seems that a Merleau-Pontean position cannot allow for the existence of two fundamental entities in one body. This—so runs the objection—can only be allowed if we understand the two fundamental beings as purely mental beings separate from the body. In that case we would have rejected the Merleau-Pontean position in favor of a dualistic picture of the relationship between a fundamental entity and its body.

To answer this objection, let us return to Merleau-Ponty's example "my foot has a pain." Let us assume that PX has had a bad foot injury. PX is in pain. Then, at an even time, PY becomes active and PY is now also in pain. This is entirely compatible with the assumption that PX's bodily way of being functions entirely separately from PY's bodily way of being. The injury is a physical happening. The fact that PX and PY are both in pain means only that PX and PY both react with pain to this physical occurrence. This does not mean that PX and PY experience pain in the same way. PX may experience it as a stabbing pain in a particular part of the foot. PY may experience it as a burning sensation in the foot that she cannot further localize. It would be in the spirit of the Merleau-Pontean position to describe these as two very different bodily experiences of pain. One might say: PX's phenomenal body experiences things very differently from PY's phenomenal body. This opens up the possibility that PY's bodily experience of pain does not come from PX's bodily experience of pain. Rather, PY's bodily experience of pain is PY's bodily reaction to the physical occurrence to which PX reacted in her own way with her bodily experience of pain. So it seems that the Merleau-Pontean position does not exclude a distinction between the physical occurrence and the bodily ways of being of the two fundamental entities in one living being. On the contrary, it seems to *call for* such a distinction: beyond the physical occurrence itself, a bodily way of dealing with the occurrence is constitutive of the experience of pain. There can be two entirely separate bodily ways of dealing with physical occurrences in a single living being.

The example of walking must be interpreted in the same way. Before the fundamental entities PX and PY come into existence, the living being that materially constituted PX and PY learns to walk. We must distinguish between the capacity to walk, which was acquired before PX and PY came into existence, and the "styles of walking" that PX and PY acquire. PX and PY may walk very differently—they may have cultivated two very different "styles of walking." These two different styles of walking are a part of PX's and PY's different bodily ways of being. The fact that PX and PY could both already walk when they came into being does not mean that there exists only one fundamental entity here. Only if PY had the style of walking that PX has acquired, though PY has not acquired this style of walking herself (or vice versa), would this be a case of one fundamental entity.

4 TWO IN ONE: BODILY EXPRESSION OF MENTAL STATES

I want to conclude this chapter by discussing the bodily expression of intentional states. This topic is Lynne Rudder Baker's starting point in an argument to the effect that one body cannot embody more than one fundamental entity, or "person," to use her terminology:

> If there were any time at which you could share your body with another person, then both of you would have a first-person relation to your body at that time. Part of what it means to say that you have a first-person relation to a body is that that body expresses your intentional states: We can see the coach's frustration in the way he walks down the sideline; we can see the sprinter's effort in the grimace on his face and the strain of his muscles. The athlete's body itself reveals that the athlete is making enormous physical effort. If S_1 and S_2 are two human persons, then it must be physically possible that S_1 is making an enormous physical effort at a certain time and S_2 is totally relaxed at that time. But if S_1 and S_2 shared a body at time, *t*, then it would not be physically possible for S_1 to be making an enormous physical effort at *t* and for S_2 to be totally relaxed at that time. For it is not physically possible for a single body to express both enormous physical effort and total relaxation at the same time. Therefore, there is no time at which S_1 and S_2 share a single body. So, a person's body at a time distinguishes her from all other persons at that time.[15]

Baker's argument presupposes that two fundamental entities can only share a body if this body can express their intentional states *at the same time*. This presupposition must of course be rejected. As the CAP criterion makes clear, we can have two fundamental entities in the same body even if they are never co-active. If a fundamental entity is not active, then the body does of course not express its intentional states. However, a fundamental entity must not be active to exist; it does not lose its beliefs or capacities even if it is not active. Therefore, a fundamental entity can share the body with another fundamental entity even if they are never co-active. This rejection of Baker's presupposition would suffice as an answer to her argument. However, with it, one only shows that two fundamental entities can share a body if they are alternately active. In the next chapter, I shall elaborate further on the possibility of co-activity. Here I merely want to argue that one body can simultaneously express the mental states of different fundamental entities.

Let us first consider, by way of comparison, the case of *one* fundamental entity who has different emotions. A fundamental entity may, for instance, love and despise somebody. She may simultaneously express her love and contempt with a smile. One might say that she is smiling both lovingly and contemptuously. In the case of *two* fundamental entities in one body, one of the fundamental entities might love somebody, whereas the other fundamental entity might despise this person. Here two possibilities must be distinguished. The first possibility is that the two fundamental entities are co-active without being co-present, i.e., without having simultaneously control over the body. The second possibility is that they are co-present. The first possibility is easily conceivable. One can imagine, for example, that the smiles quickly alternate between being loving and contemptuous. The one time, one of the fundamental entities would be smiling, the other time the other. But what would happen if the two fundamental entities were co-present? This possibility must be distinguished from the case of only one fundamental entity. If there exists only one fundamental entity, its smile is a way of expressing love and contempt at the same time. If two fundamental entities are co-present, then there is also only one bodily movement. However, this bodily movement is the result of the separate attempts by the two fundamental entities to express their own feelings. The one fundamental entity wants to express its love. The other wants to express its contempt. The resulting bodily movement can be described as a smile that is simultaneously loving and contemptuous. But it is not the smile of one fundamental entity, but rather a bodily movement that is the result of the attempts of two fundamental entities who want to smile at the same time. Thus, the case of one fundamental entity must be distinguished from the case of two co-present fundamental entities, but the case of two co-present fundamental entities expressing their feelings at the same time is nevertheless possible.

This is also how one can understand the previous example of the pain in the foot. An injury to the foot does not determine how the injury is experienced. One does not have to understand the experience as something "purely inner" to be able to distinguish the experience of pain from the injury. Even if one understands the experience of pain as a bodily experience in the Merleau-Pontean sense, then a living being can have two different bodily experiences of the injury. These could be experiences of two fundamental entities. If they are co-active without being co-present, then they might perhaps express the different experiences of pain quickly one after the other. If they are co-present, then the simultaneity of the different bodily experiences may mean that the bodily expression of the two different expressions of pain remains ambiguous.

The bodily condition of a human being does of course limit what kind of feelings or emotions she can have. It may perhaps be physically impossible to be completely relaxed while engaging in extreme forms of mountain climbing. Baker may thus be right that it is impossible that one of two fundamental entities in the same body is completely relaxed while the other one is just about to finish a marathon race. But this is a point about the limits that the body of one fundamental entity imposes on her possible mental states. This holds independently of whether the body embodies one or two fundamental entities. Two fundamental entities in one body may have different feelings and express these feelings at the same time, but the body may set limits on what they are able to feel at each time.

12 A Criterion of Individuation

I have argued that the CAP criterion presents *sufficient* conditions for the existence of two fundamental entities in one body. But does it also present *necessary* conditions? In this chapter, I will argue that it does.

> I've had a rather devastating realization. He's using YOU to kill me. Why else would he plan to publish this book? He wants to convince all of you that I don't exist. The theses, the arguments, the definitions—they are just a means to the real end: your mind. If his theories alone won't kill me, your BELIEF in them will. If no one recognizes my existence, I don't exist. So I beg you not to believe him. I need your recognition. PLEASE.

To do so, I must start by considering the relationship a fundamental entity has to her own passive states (section 1). This lays an important foundation for the rest of the chapter. In section 2, I consider two rival candidates for the individuation of fundamental entities and elaborate on the CAP criterion. The remaining sections then lay out the argument for this criterion.

1 THE PRIORITY OF ACTIVE ATTITUDES

According to the authorial correlate theory, I am fundamentally an agent who is a correlate to the psychological relations for which this agent is minimally responsible. Now, I am not only in psychological states for which I am minimally responsible. For example, I am minimally responsible for the commitments I make, but I am not responsible for the experience on which I may base these commitments. Let us call the psychological states for which I am minimally responsible "active attitudes" and my other psychological states "passive states."[1] The authorial correlate theory implies an answer to the question concerning the basis for counting active mental states as *my* mental states—as the mental states of a particular fundamental entity. My active attitudes—the states I am minimally responsible for—are my correlates. So they are mine because I am minimally responsible for them in the sense explained in Chapter 4. The authorial correlate theory does as such not imply any answer to the question as to the basis for counting *passive* mental states as *my* mental states.

> On what basis does a mental state at a certain time count as the mental state of a certain fundamental entity as opposed to another fundamental entity? (*Ownership Question*)

Three remarks should be made about this question. First, it is a question about the ownership of a mental state at a *specific time*. Second, it asks for an *explanation* of the ownership of a mental state. What is the *basis* for counting a mental state as belonging to a particular fundamental entity? Third, it concerns the attribution of mental states to one *fundamental entity* as opposed to another fundamental entity. This means that this question has nothing to do with the questions "Who am I?" or "Which mental states are truly mine?" In other words, if a fundamental entity experiences some of her mental states as not truly hers—if she is alienated from certain of her own mental states—this presupposes that these mental states are nevertheless hers in a sense.[2] And it is this presupposed ownership of mental states that is at stake in this question. Moreover, this question does not concern the basis of the attribution of mental states to one personality as opposed to another personality of a single fundamental entity.

We can distinguish two radically different ways of answering the ownership question. According to the *empiricist* answer, a mental state is mine because I have *phenomenological access* to it.[3] Different authors will elaborate differently on the notion of phenomenological access, but the basic idea is always the same. It is assumed that we have a basic understanding of what it means to be immediately aware of a mental state. If I am immediately aware of a mental state in this basic sense, then the mental state is mine. This notion of phenomenological awareness or immediate awareness has, as such, nothing to do with rational relations between mental states. Thus, the sense in which a passive mental state is mine can be explained entirely independently of the notion of an active mental attitude or the possible rational relations between passive and active mental states.

Although the authorial correlate theory, as such, does not imply an answer to the ownership question, I think that it invites a rationalist response. To explain the rationalist response, let me make three assumptions about two categories of passive mental states—desires and perceptions. (1) The content of perceptions and desires can be expressed *propositionally*:[4] one perceives that something is the case; one desires that something would be the case. (2) Perceptions and desires do not imply any *judgment*. For example, I can perceive that such and such is the case without judging that such and such is the case (without committing myself to its being true that such and such is the case). Perceptual illusions that one recognizes as such are an example. I may be unable *not* to experience things as being so and so even if I judge that they are not so and so; I know that I am subject to a perceptual illusion. (3) Perceptions and desires have a common element in different variations. In both cases, things appear to one in a certain way. In the case of perceptions, it appears to one that such and such is the case. In the case of desires, it appears to one that it would be good if such and such were the case. To have a desire means simply that things appear to one in this way.[5]

The *rationalist* answer has two parts. First, in contrast to the empiricist account, it does not explain ownership of mental states in terms of phenomenological access. I distinguished between active and passive states by saying that the active attitudes are those for which a fundamental entity is minimally responsible. Although this does not exclude an empiricist answer to the ownership question—a question involving no distinction between active and passive states—it already suggests a rationalist account of the ownership of *active* attitudes. According to rationalism, the very nature of active attitudes—as states for which a fundamental entity is minimally responsible—explains why they belong to a particular fundamental entity: they belong to the fundamental entity who is minimally responsible for them.

Second, the rationalist answer assigns *priority* to the *explanation* of the ownership of *active* mental attitudes. Active attitudes, e.g., beliefs and emotional attitudes, can be based on passive states. As an example of passive states, let us first consider perceptions. In the case of perceptions, it appears to me that such and such is the case. If I make a judgment on the basis of a perception, I am committing myself to things being the way they already appeared to me to be. Here we have the key to the rationalist answer to the ownership question with respect to passive states. The rationalist answer begins with an explanation of the ownership of active attitudes. Now, when I take up an active attitude based on a passive attitude in the preceding way, *I am assenting* to things being the way that they *already appear to me*. The appearance may well have a phenomenological component. However, this is not what it means to say that things appear to me in a certain way. To say that things appear to me in a certain way is to say that things present themselves to me as being a certain way and that I, in making a judgment on the basis of this appearance, would be assenting to things being that way. In doing so, *I* must necessarily be *assenting* to things being the way they *appear to me*—not the way they appear to somebody else. So we have a rationalist answer to the ownership question with respect to passive states:

> *The Rationalist Principle:* (1) A passive state belongs to fundamental entity FE1 as opposed to other fundamental entities on account of the relationship between the active states of FE1 and the relevant passive state. (2) For a fundamental entity to be in a certain passive state means that, to this fundamental entity, it appears that *p*. (3) A certain passive state—the appearance that *p*—belongs to fundamental entity FE1 as opposed to another fundamental entity on account of the fact that, in making a judgment to the effect that *p* based on the appearance that *p*,

> *FE1* would necessarily be making a *judgment* based on the way things *appear to FE1* as opposed to other fundamental entities.

The authorial correlate theory invites supplementation by the rationalist principle. As I already said, this theory implies a rationalist account of active attitudes. If the ownership of active attitudes is explained in terms of minimal responsibility rather than phenomenological access, then a unified approach would also give a rationalist account of the ownership of passive states. By explaining the ownership of *active* attitudes in terms of minimal responsibility, the activity of the agent who has these active attitudes plays a crucial role in the explanation. In the rationalist explanation of the ownership of passive states, the activity of an agent also plays a role: the ownership of *passive* states is explained in terms of the fact that an agent can base her judgments on such states. Thus, I conclude that the authorial correlate theory should also accept a rationalist account of passive states—in other words, that it should accept the rationalist principle.

The rationalist principle explains not only the ownership of perceptions but also of desires. To say that I desire something is to say that it appears to me as good if so and so were the case. On the basis of this appearance, I could make the judgment that *p*: that it would indeed be good if things were that way. According to the rationalist principle, the desire counts as mine on account of the fact that, in making judgment on the basis of this appearance, I would necessarily be making a judgment based on the way things appear to me as opposed to the way things appear to other fundamental entities.

In addition to perceptions and desires, there is a third category of passive states: feelings or sensations. Although it may be less obvious, the rationalist principle also accounts for the ownership of states in this category. For example, when a fundamental entity is in pain, something appears to her as painful. On this basis, the fundamental entity to whom this appears as painful could then judge that something is exactly as it appears to her—namely, painful. The pain thus counts as a mental state of this fundamental entity as opposed to another fundamental entity on account of the fact that, in my making this judgment, this fundamental entity would be assenting to things being the way they already appear to her.

The rationalist principle now enables us to address an issue related to the question of the individuation of fundamental entities. This issue is the following possibility: can a fundamental entity share a *token* passive state with other fundamental entities? Or putting it more plastically (describing passive states as experiences): can two (or more) fundamental entities share one and the same token stream of experiences? If we accept the authorial correlate theory and the rationalist principle, then the answer must be no. The authorial correlate theory understands fundamental entities as agents who form their active attitudes—for example, make their commitments—separately from each other. Fundamental entities are not bundles of mental states.

Rather, if an agent makes a commitment, another agent does not have this kind of commitment unless that latter agent makes the commitment herself. Thus, two fundamental entities cannot share a token *active* attitude.

If we now apply the rationalist principle, it follows that fundamental entities cannot share token *passive* states either. Let's assume, for example, that each of the two fundamental entities has committed itself to its being true that a certain plant is blue on the basis of the appearance that the plant is blue. Can the two fundamental entities have separate token commitments that are based on a shared token appearance? According to the rationalist principle, the appearance that the plant is blue belongs to the fundamental entity FE1 on the basis of the fact that, in making this judgment based on this appearance, FE1 bases this judgment on something that appears to FE1 as opposed to other fundamental entities. This implies that the appearance that the plant is blue belongs *exclusively to FE1*. Of course, FE2 can have another token appearance of the same type. It can also appear to FE2 that the plant is blue, but in making her own judgment that the plant is blue based on this appearance, FE2 would be basing the judgment on her own token appearance.

Is the rationalist principle really correct? Is it the correct articulation of a rationalist approach? Why can we not say that two fundamental entities make their own commitments for themselves, but base these commitments on shared tokens of passive states? The rationalist principle explains what it means to say that a passive state belongs to a particular fundamental entity. It means that, in making a judgment based on an appearance, the fundamental entity is assenting to things being the way they already appear to that fundamental entity. In accepting the appearance, the fundamental entity is, as it were, giving in to something that already tempts her: things present themselves to her as being a certain way and, in making the judgment, the subject accepts that things are as they present themselves as being. It is essential to this explanation that the subject accepting the appearance is assenting to things being the way they already present themselves to *her*. If we were to assume that two fundamental entities could share a token passive state, this explanation would get lost. What would it mean to say that two fundamental entities share a token passive state? We could not say that, in making the relevant judgment, each fundamental entity would be responding to the way things already appear *to her*. This has a clear meaning provided by the rationalist principle, but then it would mean that each fundamental entity is responding to her own token appearance. Thus, the defender of the position that two fundamental entities can share the same passive token state while making commitments on their own must come up with a different explanation as to what it means to say that the shared passive state belongs to both fundamental entities. One possibility would be that things do not appear to each separately, but that the appearance is genuinely common: things appear not to me *and* you, but genuinely to us. But how is that to be explicated in a rationalist manner? Another possibility would be that there are three subjects here: the two fundamental entities making the commitment and then a subject of a common token appearance. I won't elaborate on these possibilities. In either case, I submit, we will no longer be able to say that, in making a judgment, a fundamental entity is assenting to things being the way they already appear to her.

I conclude that the defender of the authorial correlate theory must also accept the rationalist principle. And acceptance of the rationalist principle means that the following possibility is incoherent: two fundamental entities existing at a specific time, separately making commitments, but sharing token passive states. It should be noted that this of course does not mean that we cannot have a single fundamental entity radically conflicted in her commitments. These conflicts might indeed be so radical that we would want to say that one fundamental entity has two personalities. However, this would not be a case of two fundamental entities separately making commitments, but a case of one fundamental entity making conflicting commitments.

Let me close this section by noting how the rationalist principle enables us to put my criticism of Rovane's theory in Chapter 9 on a systematic footing. According to Rovane's account, "the philosopher" can have phenomenological access to the desires of "the musician" who shares a body with the philosopher. I argued that, if the philosopher were to radically reconsider her life, the desires belonging to the musician would be of relevance and that this shows that these desires are the desires of one fundamental entity with two radically different projects (philosophy and music). Now, the rationalist principle explains why this is so. The reason why the desires belonging to "the musician" are also the desires of "the philosopher" and thus the desires of one fundamental entity is *not* that "the philosopher" has phenomenological access to them. Rather, the reason is that the desires are appearances that can serve "the philosopher" as the basis of her commitments. And these appearances can serve both "the musician" and "the philosopher" as the basis of their commitment. Therefore, "the musician" and "the philosopher" are at best two personalities of a single fundamental entity rather than two fundamental entities.

2 TWO CRITERIA OF INDIVIDUATION

In Chapter 10, I defended the CAP criterion as a *sufficient* condition for the individuation of fundamental entities. Recall that the CAP criterion presupposes that PX and PY are not co-active. PX is active at odd times (t_1, t_3, etc.) and PY is active at even times (t_2, t_4, etc.).

> *The CAP Criterion:* (1) PY is incapable of having any of the types of CAPs that PX acquires (at odd times) or memories of them, unless PY acquires these types of CAPs himself (at even times). (2) PX is incapable of having any of the types of CAPs that PY acquires (at even times) or memories of them, unless PX acquires these types of CAPs himself (at

odd times). (3) PY is a fundamental entity existing over time. PX is a fundamental entity existing over time. If (1)–(3) are fulfilled, PX and PY are two fundamental entities.

The question we now need to address is whether the CAP criterion is also a *necessary* condition for the individuation of fundamental entities. Let us consider the following example, in which PX and PY are not co-active and condition (3) of the CAP criterion is fulfilled. We may even assume that condition (3) is fulfilled on account of the commitment criterion. There exists commitment continuity between PX at t_1 and PX at t_7. The same holds for PY at t_2 and t_8. According to the commitment criterion, PX is thus one fundamental entity existing over time and the same holds for PY. However, there exists no commitment continuity between PX and PY at all. Despite this lack of commitment continuity between PX and PY, PY at t_8 has memories of the passive states of PX at t_3. To facilitate the discussion, let's assume that these are experiential memories. We have an instance of experiential memory when somebody remembers from the inside how she experienced something at an earlier time.[6] This is not an instance of remembering from a third-person point of view that somebody had an experience at an earlier time. Rather, it is remembering from the inside how it was to have the experience. So we are assuming that PY has an experiential memory of an experience that PX had. This means that PY remembers an experience that was had when PY was not active. Our example is characterized by four assumptions: (A) PX and PY are not co-active; PX is active at odd times, PY at even times. (B) PX and PY, by the commitment criterion, each exist as a fundamental entity over time. (C) There exists no commitment continuity between PX and PY. (D) PY has experiential memory of an experience that PX had at an earlier time. The question is: are PX and PY one or two fundamental entities?

If the CAP criterion is a necessary condition for the presence of two fundamental entities, PX and PY are not two fundamental entities in this example. Recall that "CAP" is an abbreviation for "capacities, active attitudes, and passive states." PY remembers a passive attitude of PX's. So if the CAP criterion is such a necessary condition, PX and PY are one fundamental entity. I think that the CAP criterion does indeed present such a necessary condition. However, before I present the argument for this claim, I want to consider the case for saying that PX and PY are two fundamental entities in this example.

The commitment criterion is an account of diachronic identity. According to this criterion, PX at t_1 and PX at t_n are one and the same fundamental entity on account of the commitment continuity existing between them. However, if there were no commitment continuity between PX at t_1 and PX at t_n, then PX at t_1 and PX at t_n would not be one and the same fundamental entity. Commitment continuity is a *necessary* condition for the *diachronic identity* of fundamental entities. Now, there is no commitment continuity between PX and PY in our example. It would seem that, if the commitment criterion is a correct account of diachronic identity, then—with respect to the issue of *individuation*—commitment continuity should also be *necessary* for the presence of one rather than two fundamental entities. If there is no commitment continuity between PX and PY, they should thus count as two fundamental entities. We thus arrive at an alternative to the CAP criterion, again assuming that PX and PY are not co-active and that PX is active at odd times (t_1, t_3, etc.) and PY at even times (t_2, t_4, etc.).

> *The Generalized Commitment Criterion*: (1) The commitment criterion is the correct account of diachronic identity. (2) PY is a fundamental entity existing over time. PX is a fundamental entity existing over time. (3) PX and PY are one and the same fundamental entity if and only if there is commitment continuity between them.

What speaks in favor of the generalized commitment criterion is that it offers a unified account of diachronic identity and individuation. In both cases, the matter is decided by the presence or absence of commitment continuity. Nevertheless, I think the generalized commitment criterion offers a false account of individuation. In my view, the commitment criterion offers the correct account of diachronic identity and the CAP criterion the right theory of individuation.

Why should one accept two different accounts, depending on whether we are dealing with diachronic identity or individuation? The basic answer to this question is that these two accounts are two parts of a fundamentally unified approach. This approach starts with the authorial correlate theory. The application of this theory to the problem of diachronic identity yields the commitment criterion. A fundamental entity is an agent who maintains her identity over time by maintaining commitment continuity. If there is a break in commitment continuity, we can no longer say that we have one and the same agent. Now, agents are also subject to passive states and we must ask which passive states belong to one agent as opposed to another. Here the rationalist principle comes in. It is a principle about the ownership of passive states at a particular point in time. It says that the passive states on which a certain agent bases her commitments belong to that particular agent. Now, an agent may also have a relationship to a past passive state in experiential memory. In our example, PY at t_8 has experiential memory of the experiences PX had at t_3—a time when PY was not active. The question is whether there exists only one fundamental entity here and whether this fundamental entity *as PY* remembers the experiences it had at t_3 *as PX*. I think the answer to that question is yes. This positive answer does not follow from the rationalist principle—a principle that holds for a certain point in time. However, the basic assumption behind the rationalist principle is that the boundaries of fundamental entities extend all the way out to their passive states. Passive states belong to one agent as opposed to another on account of their relations to active attitudes. Thus, contrary to the generalized commitment criterion, it may be that PY's experiential memory of a past experience amounts to a relation that establishes the past experience as a mental state of PY.

It remains to be shown that this is indeed the case. This will be argued in the next section. I will use the rest of the present section to elaborate the CAP criterion and my overall position. After all, it is rather unusual to employ different criteria for diachronic identity and individuation. In particular, I need to explain how it can be a coherent position that commitment continuity is not necessary to establish that PX and PY are one and the same fundamental entity, even though this continuity is needed for diachronic identity.

I said that PY has experiential memory of an experience PX had at an earlier time—a time at which PY was not active. However, given that one can only have a *memory* of one's own mental states, does this not presuppose that PY existed at t_3 and had the experience at that time? Saying that it is memory does presuppose this, but there are good reasons for counting it as memory. I think we are justified in saying that PY has experiential memory of an experience PX had if certain conditions are fulfilled. The next section will explain why this is so. Here I merely want to state these conditions and explain my position. In this discussion, please keep in mind that, as defined in Chapter 9, "PX" and "PY" denote the person in the X-state and the person in the Y-state, respectively, and that the person in the X-state and the person in the Y-state share the same body.

> *The Memory Principle:* (1) PY at t_8 is in a mental state that presents itself as a memory of an experience had at t_3. (2) PX at t_3 had this experience. (3) PY at t_8 and PY at t_3 are one and the same fundamental entity. (4) The way in which PY's mental state at t_8 is causally related to PX's experience at t_3 fulfills the conditions for counting PY's mental state at t_8 as a memory of an experience rather than as, say, an image of an experience acquired by PY on the basis of somebody's report of the circumstances of this experience. (5) The conditions mentioned in (4) do not include the assumption that PY and PX are one and the same fundamental entity. (6) If conditions (1)–(5) are fulfilled, then PY at t_8 has experiential memory of PX's experience at t_3.

In my view, if conditions (1)–(5) are fulfilled, then PY at t_8 has experiential memory of the experience of PX at t_3. In that case PY and PX are one and the same fundamental entity even if there is no commitment continuity between PY and PX. I shall argue this in the next section. But is it even coherent to maintain such a position in conjunction with the commitment criterion as an account of *diachronic* identity? My answer is yes, and let me begin my explanation by discussing the reasons why a notion of experiential memory plays no role in my account of diachronic identity.

Let us consider a case of a single human being who at t_8 is in a mental state that presents itself as a memory of an experience that the same human being had at t_3. Moreover, let us assume that there exists no commitment continuity between these two times in the life of this human being. According to the commitment criterion, this means that the entity at t_8 is a different fundamental entity than the subject at t_3, even though a single human being exists here. If that is so, however, the human being at t_8 cannot be *remembering* what happened at t_3. Memory presupposes identity and the entities existing at the two times are not one and the same fundamental entity.

If the conditions of the memory principle are fulfilled, the situation is very different. The crucial difference between this situation and the previous case is that here PY at t_8 and PY at t_3 are one and the same fundamental entity. This means that when PY at t_8 is in a mental state that presents itself as a memory of an experience at t_3, it is *possible* that this is *genuine memory*. It is *possible* that PY is a fundamental entity who had this experience at t_3. Here the issue of diachronic identity has already been settled: PX at t_3 and PX at t_8 are one and the same fundamental entity; the same holds for PY. It remains to be settled whether PY and PX, each a fundamental entity existing over time, are one and the same fundamental entity. In my view, if the conditions of the memory principle are fulfilled, then PY at t_8 has a genuine memory of the experience that PX had at t_3. Thus, because the conditions of the CAP criterion for there being just one fundamental entity are thereby fulfilled, PY and PX are one and the same fundamental entity. This does not show that the CAP criterion is a necessary condition for the existence of two fundamental entities, but it shows that it is perfectly *coherent* to appeal only to commitment continuity with respect to diachronic identity *and* also let experimental memory count with respect to the issue of individuation.

To further explicate my approach, it is useful to contrast it with an account offered by Walter Sinnott-Armstrong and Stephen Behnke. They are interested in the topic of responsibility in cases of multiple personality disorder. They formulate a *sufficient* condition for the existence of one person in one body and think that this formulation shows that in cases of multiple personality disorder there always exists only one person. According to Sinnott-Armstrong and Behnke, persons A and B are one and the same person if they have the same body (including the brain)[7] and the memory chains of these persons converge on some token experience.[8] There exists a chain of memories between person P_1 at t_1 and person P_n at t_n if person P_n at t_n remembers an experience P_{n-1} had at t_{n-1}, P_{n-1} at t_{n-1} remembers an experience P_{n-2} had at t_{n-2}, etc. Two chains of memories converge on a token experience if in both chains there exists a memory of the same numerical experience.[9] The authors mention two possible cases of such a convergence in cases of multiple personality disorder. In the first case, the remembered experience occurred before the onset of multiple personality disorder, i.e., at a time when only one person existed in the currently shared body. This seems to be their favored case: since there exists only one person at the time of the experience, it is clear that the memories converge on numerically the same experience. In the second case, A and B both have memories of an experience that took place after the human being starts suffering from multiple personality disorder.

Before I discuss the difference between my position and theirs—which has to do with the fact that Sinnott-Armstrong and Behnke do not distinguish between diachronic identity and individuation—let me make a few additional remarks: (1) Because Sinnott-Armstrong and Behnke do not explicitly rule out the possibility that A and B are co-sensory, they cannot assume that, if the relevant experience was had after the onset of multiple personality disorder, there exists only one *token* of phenomenologically the same experience. If A and B were two co-sensory fundamental entities at the relevant time, then each of these fundamental entities could have had this experience separately. Therefore, the authors have to concentrate on the first case mentioned earlier. (2) If that is so, then their criterion delivers no verdict on cases in which there exists no memory of an experience that took place before the onset of multiple personality disorder. In contrast, the CAP criterion can also deal with such cases. (3) In contrast to the CAP criterion, their account provides no answer for the case in which neither PX nor PY has the relevant experiential memory. (4) Another important difference is that, in addition to the shared body, the authors only mention experiential memory as sufficient for the presence of only one person. In contrast, according to the CAP criterion, it would also be sufficient if PY had an active attitude or a capacity that PX had acquired, without it being the case that PY had acquired that attitude or capacity herself. (5) Finally, the CAP criterion delivers not only a sufficient but also a necessary condition for the existence of only one fundamental entity in the body.

In their discussion, Sinnott-Armstrong and Behnke do not explicitly distinguish between individuation and diachronic identity. They present their sufficient condition as if it were also sufficient for diachronic identity: there exists a chain of experiential memories between P_1 at t_1 and P_n at t_n; at least if the chain exists within one and the same body, this is sufficient for P_1 at t_1 and P_n at t_n being one and the same person. I reject this thesis for fundamental entities. In my view, the existence of a chain of experiential memories between a fundamental entity at t_n and a fundamental entity at t_1 is not a sufficient condition for their diachronic identity. In his criticism of Sinnott-Armstrong and Behnke, Steve Matthews describes a fission case in which, from a converging point of two chains of memory, these two chains of memory reach to a point in the future at which the two fission products with these chains of memories are not identical to each other.[10] Since experiential memory plays no role in my account of diachronic identity, this sort of criticism simply does not apply to my position. The commitment criterion is decisive for diachronic identity and, as argued in Chapter 5, there can be no commitment continuity in fission.

I argued in Chapter 10 that the CAP criterion successfully fulfills a task at which the empirical theories discussed in Chapter 9 fail. These theories present criteria for different persons existing in one body. However, the fulfillment of these criteria shows at most that there are two personalities present in a single fundamental entity. In contrast, the fulfillment of the CAP criterion means that there are two fundamental entities present. A presupposition of the CAP criterion on which I have not yet commented plays a crucial role here: PX and PY are not co-active. The purpose of this condition is to enable us to distinguish between two cases: the case of two personalities of a single fundamental entity and the case of two fundamental entities in one body. If we were to allow the possibility that two fundamental entities in one body are co-sensory, then we would not be able to distinguish the two cases. According to the CAP criterion, PX and PY are one and the same fundamental entity if PY has experiential memory of an experience of PX's (or PY has a capacity or an active attitude of PX's without having acquired that capacity or attitude herself at an even time). If we were to allow that two fundamental entities are co-sensory, then we could not rule out the possibility that in such a case PX and PY are two fundamental entities who have the same type of experience *separately* but *at the same time* (or who acquire the same type of capacity or belief separately but at the same time). Therefore, we must exclude that two fundamental entities are co-active.

Another way of phrasing this point would be to say that the co-activity of two fundamental entities must be excluded in order to be able to distinguish between the following two cases: the presence of a token active attitude (or a token passive attitude or a token capacity), on the one hand, and the presence of two tokens of the same type of active attitude (or two tokens of the same kind of passive attitude or capacity), on the other. The second case would be one in which two fundamental entities each have their own token. The criticism of Radden's fourth condition was that it fails to set out the conditions for distinguishing between these two cases. Sydney Shoemaker's account of individuation suffers from the same flaw. According to Shoemaker, we have two fundamental entities if and only if two functional units can be distinguished in such a way that the mental states of the two units together cannot possibly rationally cause a certain effect.[11] Now we may explain an action performed by PX by reference to a desire that PX and PY share. But is it a token desire shared by PX and PY or do PX and PY each have their own token of a desire of the same type? In order to apply his theory, Shoemaker would need to be able to distinguish between these two cases, but he does not offer us the means to do so. The CAP criterion is designed to distinguish between such cases. It does so by excluding co-activity and by then asking for information about the relationship between PX and PY at different times.

It is important to realize that this does not mean that we must say that two fundamental entities in the same body cannot be co-active. To apply the CAP criterion, we need to assume that we are confronted with a case at a particular time that is not a case of two fundamental entities being co-active at that time. Now, the CAP criterion has two possible results: (1) either PX and PY are a single fundamental entity or (2) they are two fundamental entities. Let us consider these in turn. (1) If either PX or PY later has a CAP that the other acquired at the earlier time (or a memory of it) without having acquired it herself at the later time, then PX and PY are a single fundamental entity. This is a result easily arrived at. We only need to find a *single case* in which a CAP is "transported" in this way from PX to PY (or vice versa). (2) The other result is much harder to arrive at. In this case we need to show for PX and for PY that each is *incapable* of having the CAPs acquired by the other one, unless they have acquired the respective CAP themselves. As before, to show this, we need to focus on cases at particular times that are not cases of two fundamental entities being co-active at the relevant times. It is not clear how many cases we need to test in order to show that PX and PY are incapable of this. However, when we have shown that they are incapable of this, then we may conclude that they are two fundamental entities. And having concluded that, we may then assume that there can be cases in which these two fundamental entities are co-active.

3 IN DEFENSE OF THE CAP CRITERION: EXPERIENTIAL MEMORY

To a defender of the authorial correlate theory, two criteria of individuation invite themselves: the generalized commitment criterion and the CAP criterion. I have offered some general reasons why the CAP criterion is a necessary condition for the presence of two fundamental entities, but I must now defend this criterion in detail. The basic difference between the two criteria is that the CAP criterion assumes that, in addition to separate active attitudes, two fundamental entities cannot be linked by memory of passive states or the retainment of capacities. This section concerns the memory of passive states (I focus on experiential memory) and the next one on capacities. In this section, I will present an argument for two theses. First, if conditions (1)–(5) of the memory principle are fulfilled, then PY at t_8 does indeed have experiential memory of PX's experience at t_3. Second, if PY at t_8 has experiential memory of PX's experience at t_3, then PY and PX are one and the same fundamental entity.

The argument for the first thesis takes up most of this section. Here it must be shown that, under these conditions, PY has genuine *memory* of PX's experience rather than something that does not count as memory though it resembles memory in many ways (imagined memory). Let me start by considering how the distinction between genuine memory and imagined memory is drawn in the normal case in which a human being embodies only one fundamental entity. The person is in a mental state that presents itself as a memory of an experience had at an earlier time. To count as genuine as opposed to imagined experiential memory, three possibilities must be ruled out: (a) *Nobody* ever had the experience that the fundamental entity "remembers." (b) *Somebody* had the experience, but *not the fundamental entity* who "remembers" it. (c) The fundamental entity had the experience that she "remembers," but the fundamental entity simply imagines that she *remembers* it.

As an example of possibility (c), let us consider the following situation: The fundamental entity has forgotten her experience, but a friend describes in detail the event that the fundamental entity experienced. The fundamental entity might then imagine that she remembers her experience of the event. However, since the mental state that presents itself to her as a memory is caused by the detailed description given by the friend and is *not caused in the right kind of way by the original experience*, this mental state would not be a case of memory. Naturally there are countless other ways a person can imagine that she remembers something when the way she has acquired the "memory" precludes its counting as genuine memory. The point of condition (4) in the memory principle is to exclude such possibilities.[12]

In practice, it may be difficult to be sure that none of (a)–(c) holds. Nevertheless, if these three possibilities can be excluded in the normal case, then we have genuine memory. In our case—the case specified in the memory principle— both (a) and (c) can be excluded. Since PX at t_3 had the experience, possibility (a) can be excluded. Our case is just like the normal case in that we have one human being whose brain has not been manipulated in any way. So, *if* we can exclude possibility (c) in the normal case, *then* we can also exclude it in our case. Therefore, the important question is whether we can also exclude (b) for our case.

If conditions (2) and (3) of the memory principle are fulfilled, it seems that we can also exclude (b)—the possibility that *somebody* had the experience but *not the fundamental entity* who "remembers" it. Condition (2) says that PX at t_3 had the relevant experience. This means that the experience was had by a fundamental entity embodied by the human being who embodies PY. Condition (3) says that PY at t_8 and PY at t_3 are one and the same fundamental entity. This means that the fundamental entity who, at t_8, has the impression that she remembers the experience existed at the time of the experience (at t_3) and was at that time embodied by the same human being. It seems to me that these are *sufficient* conditions for excluding possibility (b). Given that (a) and (c) have been excluded, it is not in dispute that an experience that was actually had at t_3 has the right sort of causal connection with a mental state that a fundamental entity has at t_8 for that mental state to count as a memory of the experiences. The only step that needs to be taken with the exclusion of (b) is that this fundamental entity recalls *her own experience* at t_3 and that this is thus a genuine memory of that experience. This step must be taken. There is no difference between the relationship between the fundamental entity at t_8 and the experience at t_3 in our case, on the one hand, and the relationship between a fundamental entity remembering an experience and the experience itself in the normal case, on the other. In both cases, the fundamental entity exists at both times. In both cases, there exists one human being embodying that fundamental entity. In neither case has the brain of the human being been manipulated in any way. Thus, I see no good reason to deny that in our case the fundamental entity is remembering her own experience if we say this about the normal case. The fact that PX has the experience at t_3 is not a good reason for denying this. That PX has this experience means only that, at the time of the experience, the human being was acting out the personality X. In the normal case, the fact that we were acting out a different personality gives us no reason to assume that we cannot remember the experiences we had at the time. Thus, I conclude that we can exclude possibility (b) if conditions (2) and (3) are fulfilled. If the conditions of the memory condition are fulfilled, the fundamental entity PY has at t_8 memories of her own experience at t_3.

This does not yet show that PX and PY are one and the same fundamental entity. To reach this conclusion, two possibilities must be excluded. First, it must be excluded that PX and PY had the same kind of experience at t_3 but had their own token experience separately. This possibility is excluded by assumption: we are discussing the CAP criterion and it assumes that PX and PY are not co-active. PY was not active at t_3, so PX and PY cannot be two fundamental entities who had experiences separately at t_3. Second, it must be excluded that PX and PY are two fundamental entities who, though they do *not* have the same kind of experience *separately* at t_3, can share the same token experience. According to this possibility, even if at t_8 PY is remembering her own experience at t_3, she might be remembering a token experience she shared with another fundamental entity—namely, PX. This possibility is excluded by the rationalist principle, which excludes that two fundamental entities can share a token experience. I conclude that the fact that PY has experiential memories of the experiences that PX had at t_3 means that PX and PY are one and the same fundamental entity.

4 IN DEFENSE OF THE CAP CRITERION: CAPACITIES

Obviously, I have not yet defended the requirement of the CAP criterion that two fundamental entities must acquire their capacities entirely separately. Actually, I have not even defended the requirement that this holds for all active attitudes. If we accept the arguments for the commitment criterion, this must clearly hold for commitments: if PY at an even time has the commitments that PX has made at an earlier odd time and PY has not acquired these commitments herself at an even time, then PY and PX are one and the same fundamental entity. What about active attitudes other than commitments, e.g., emotional attitudes? Just as in the discussion of experiential memory, we must focus on the issue of individuation and separate this from the question of diachronic identity. PX has acquired a certain emotional attitude at an odd time. PY has this emotional attitude at a later even time, even though PY has not acquired this attitude at an even time. On account of commitment continuity, PY exists at both of these times as one and the same fundamental entity, even though PY is not active at odd times. In this case, one can only explain the fact that PY has this emotional attitude by assuming that PX and PY are one and the same fundamental entity and that this fundamental entity acquired this attitude when PX acquired it at an odd time.

An active attitude is something that one must take up. PY has not taken up the relevant attitude at an even time. Thus, PY must have acquired it at an odd time and PX and PY must be a single fundamental entity. This argument is even more obviously correct for capacities. Nobody has a capacity that she has not acquired. If PY has a capacity at an even time that she has not acquired at an even time, then she must have acquired it at an odd time. However, at odd times, PY is not active. Thus, PX and PY must be a single fundamental entity and this fundamental entity acquired this capacity *as PX*.

So it must be concluded that the separate acquisition of capacities is a necessary condition for the existence of two fundamental entities.[13] However, it must be noted that only certain capacities are intended in the CAP criterion. Not all capacities are acquired by fundamental entities. On the one hand, there are personal and sub-personal capacities. Personal capacities are acquired and exercised by fundamental entities. Sub-personal capacities, in contrast, are not exercised by the fundamental entity. For example, the capacity to digest food is a sub-personal capacity which the digestive organs rather than the fundamental entities have. On the other hand, there are capacities that, according to the commitment criterion, a human being has before a fundamental entity comes into existence. In the last chapter I discussed the capacity to walk. The human being can walk before the fundamental entity comes into existence. Nevertheless, it is not a sub-personal capacity. After the fundamental entity comes into existence, this capacity is exercised by the fundamental entity. However, as we saw in the last chapter, if there are two fundamental entities in one body, they may give this capacity different forms. For example, two fundamental entities may have different styles of walking. These different styles would be acquired by fundamental entities and the CAP criterion would apply to these capacities.

> He's winning, isn't he? While I've been mocking him, he's been spinning his web. With each move I just get more entangled. And I can barely breathe. When I'm dead, he'll wander around our house asking himself what is missing. He's always ignored me. So he'll never know why he is so lonely.

I have now reached the end of the main discussion of individuation in Part III. I have defended three main theses: (1) the coexistence thesis, (2) the thesis that the CAP criterion is a *sufficient* condition for the presence of two fundamental entities in one body, and (3) the thesis that the CAP criterion is a *necessary* condition for this. It should be noted that one does not have to accept the whole package in order to accept some of these theses. One may, for example, accept the coexistence thesis without thinking that the CAP criterion is a sufficient condition for the presence of two fundamental entities. And one may accept that the CAP criterion is a sufficient condition, but think that the generalized commitment criterion is the correct account of individuation. It should also be stressed that the generalized commitment criterion presents a possible extension of the authorial correlate theory and the commitment criterion to the issue of individuation. I think that it is not the correct extension, but perhaps some readers are willing to go down the road with me without going the whole way.

13 Multiple Personality in Therapeutic and Biographic Discourses

In the final two chapters, I return to the interpretation of multiple personality. Doing so serves two purposes. First, the philosophical argument for the coexistence thesis and for the CAP criterion needs to be supported in a certain way by a discussion of multiple personality. Second, having now completed the presentation of my account of personal identity, this account can now be employed to cast light on multiple personality. Let me start this chapter by elaborating on these two points, starting with the first.

In Chapter 10, I offered purely philosophical arguments for the coexistence thesis—arguments not dependent upon any assumptions about multiple personality. As such, the success of these arguments does not depend on whether the relevant theses and concepts are of importance outside of philosophy. However, these arguments are naturally controversial. One objection to my arguments could be that in these arguments the concept of an *I* or a fundamental entity has been employed outside of its conditions of application. One aim of the final two chapters is to show that this is not the case. How does one accomplish this? What I need to show is that, in various contexts outside philosophy, people work with assumptions that—if thought through—imply that more than one fundamental entity exists in one body. The aim of my philosophical argument was to demonstrate the coexistence thesis—the thesis that each one of us is a fundamental entity of which there could be more than one in one body. The aim of the discussion in these final two chapters is to show that this thesis does not take us outside of the conditions of application of the relevant concepts. On the contrary, the thesis merely makes philosophically precise certain ideas entertained in various perfectly intelligible contexts outside of philosophy. Here the final two chapters take up the thread from Chapter 8. The case of Miss Beauchamp was one case in which such ideas were entertained. This chapter and the next show this for other cases and contexts.

By showing that such ideas are entertained in various discourses about multiple personality, I will at the same time be achieving the second aim of these two chapters: interpreting multiple personality. However, part of this interpretation will consist in showing that multiple personality is more complicated than that. I am talking about texts about multiple personality and people who understand themselves or others as having multiple personality. These texts and people do indeed often entertain the idea that there are several fundamental entities in play in such cases. However, they rarely do so unambiguously. They will equally work with the idea of a single fundamental entity radically divided into distinct personalities. Part of my account of multiple personality is that in such real cases we never in fact have more than one fundamental entity. Even literary cases must be interpreted as cases of a single fundamental entity so radically alienated from itself that it experiences parts of itself as another—on account of the depth of the alienation often understanding the other as another fundamental entity, but often also realizing that the other is part of itself.

In this study, the authorial correlate theory—together with both the commitment criterion and the CAP criterion as elaborations of this theory—has been defended as an account of the concept *I* as it occurs in the question "What am I fundamentally?" This chapter will explore how this concept appears in recent psychotherapeutic and biographical discourses on multiple personality. It is of course impossible to provide an overview of these discourses here. Nor is that my aim. Rather, I wish to examine the use of the concept *I* in these discourses by way of example. The main text of the chapter will discuss the 1998 work *Amongst Ourselves: A Self-Help Guide to Living with Dissociative Identity Disorder.* I will focus on one work in the main text since it is important for me to reach a phenomenological density of description. Thus, the notes in this chapter (and the next) have a significance that extends beyond their normal role, since it is naturally important that the theses defended here have a validity beyond this one work.

I have selected *Amongst Ourselves* because it links psychotherapeutic discourse with autobiographical writing. The authors are Tracy Alderman, who holds a doctorate in clinical psychology, and the licensed clinical social worker Karen Marshall. Alderman and Marshall understand Karen Marshall as a person who has dissociative identity disorder. Alderman and Marshall are partners but Marshall was in treatment with another therapist (vii–viii). On the one hand, the work consists of an "informational text" (1) whose coauthors are Alderman and Marshall. On the other, the text is interrupted by contributions written by Marshall's various personalities (or "alters," as they are called in contemporary discussions of these issues): some by the alter usually in control, Karen, and the majority by the other alters. Because of this circumstance, among other things, this work naturally differs radically from Morton Prince's *The Dissociation of a Personality.* As shown in Chapter 8, Dr. Prince understands his vis-à-vis as a passive object that is to be studied and then returned to its natural state, according to the laws of psychology. The three functions of Karen Marshall—as the coauthor of the theoretical interpretations, as the voice of the alter Karen, and as the voice of the other alters—indicate that the theoretical attitude toward persons with multiple personality is entirely different from Dr. Prince's: the joint text by Alderman and Marshall is probably intended to lend the whole work scientific weight, but at the same time their theoretical account is clearly meant to be close to the standpoint of the alters.

My interpretation of this text will draw on the philosophical account offered so far. However, in section 2, I will also add some further philosophical reflections on the consciousness a fundamental entity can have of its own conscious and unconscious states and of the mental states of other fundamental entities in the same body. This will help us interpret ideas often entertained in studies of multiple personalities, such as the idea of an inner communication between the various personalities of a person with multiple personality.

1 THE OTHERS IN MY BODY—THE OTHERS IN MYSELF

Let me begin the interpretation of *Amongst Ourselves* with the following passage, which exemplifies the formal structure of the book and offers a suitable entry into its content:

> Because you have many people all living in one body, things can get a bit crowded and confusing at times . . . Basically, your body is a container for many others and each of these beings has their own desires, interests, and ways of being. Whenever you have to share such limited supplies (the body) with so many people (the alters), you're bound to have confusion and other organizational difficulties . . . You and your body are limited supply, yet the interests and commitments of your alters could keep you busy twenty-four hours a day . . .
>
> We have a bunch of us who live inside. We like it a lot. We have a set of twins we call the screamers (guess why) . . . These ones came because of the pain. They never let the noise out and only scream inside. They are afraid that if anyone ever heard them we would be killed. (81–82)1

The passage in Roman type is the "informational text" by Alderman and Marshall, and the part in italics is by the alters (Roman and italic will be used to show this difference in subsequent quotations as well). The theoretical text takes on the inner viewpoint of the alters. ("Talking about yourself as a plural is actually more accurate than referring to yourself as 'I,' because it includes all of you, not just the one personality who is speaking at that moment" [25].)[2] What is of central importance here is the talk of the body as a "container" for many "beings" or "people."[3] This evokes the image of an interior space in which these beings—the alters—can scream or verbally communicate without a person outside this space being able to hear them. However, the alters residing in this space can hear the voices. ("People with DID [dissociative identity disorder] will have conversations with alters . . . These voices or sounds stemming from inside the head are actually the chatter of the alters. The alters may be communicating with each other or with the one who is out at the time . . . *At first when I was asked about hearing voices, I didn't understand what I was being asked. I always had conversations going on with all different voices in my head, so it was not unusual*" [24].)[4]

This mobile container—the body—is nonetheless always steered by at least one of the alters. A comparison with a school field trip suggests that one personality chiefly takes over this steering function (cf. 81-82). This is precisely how Alderman and Marshall see it. The "host personality" (12) is the alter personality that usually represents the "system" (13)—the entirety of the alter personalities—to the outside world.[5] On the inside, the other alters communicate with each other or with the host personality about what and when something should be done and by whom:[6]

> Imagine that you are running a small company and that each decision you make about the company has to be approved by a board of directors . . . Well, this is what living with DID is like. People who have multiple personalities are forced to live life as a committee. Each personality has a say in what takes place, and in some circumstances, consensus must be reached before an action takes place . . .
>
> The big one [Karen] always gets to be in charge. At first, we all wanted to be in charge. It was fun to be out and have time to play. But we had to learn if the big one wasn't in charge, we wouldn't get the fun things, like candy and ice cream . . . We also know that when the little ones stay and try to take over, we will have to spend hours looking for papers they hid or other stuff they didn't care about. When we were having bad days with flashbacks and stuff, we would all meet and agree to let the big one do what needed to be done. (77–79)

This hierarchy between the host and the other personalities, however, is of a purely practical nature. The comparison with a company makes this clear. Someone leads the firm, but each employee—boss or not—is just as much a being, a person, who works for this firm. So we cannot say that Karen is the real person and that the other personalities are only parts of her. Even more radically: the alter personalities are not at all parts of a being, a person, or an I who occasionally has inner monologues. These are not monologues but efforts to *communicate among various beings*, which ideally arrive at a common outcome. Accordingly, Alderman and Marshall comment on the first two conditions of the diagnostic criteria for dissociative identity disorder as follows:[7]

> Most people have different ways of being in different situations . . . However, when they're acting differently from what they would consider normal, they're acting based on a different role, not a different identity. If you have multiple personalities, each time a different identity appears, it carries with it a history and a distinct way of relating to the world. This is one of the key differences between roles and identities. Roles refer to the parts people play in different situations, while multiple identities refer to the presentation of different selves . . . In order for this second criterion to be met, this aspect of a person must be an entity and must control their actions and behaviors at least some of the time . . . Again, the distinction needs to be made between people with one personality, who have many sides or ways of presenting themselves, and one person who has more than one personality, each of whom guide or direct the behavior of that individual. (15–16)

This quotation must be read in light of other passages. A person with one personality is distinguished here from a system that consists of more than one "entity."[8] A person with one personality can have several sides or play several roles. At the same time, however, its actions are always carried out by one and the same entity. This is different in a multiple: here the actions can be traced back to different entities. This corresponds to other claims quoted previously: "*We would all meet and agree to let the big one do what needed to be done*"; different individuals meet to agree upon who must carry out certain actions. This also means that the actions of a multiple cannot be understood as someone occasionally acting *as one personality* and at other times *as another personality*. There is no subject that thinks or carries out actions. Several subjects exist in one body that communicate with one another and carry out actions separately ("Talking about yourself as a plural is actually more accurate than referring to yourself as 'I.' ")

Together Alderman, Marshall, and the alters sketch a picture of an inner and outer world. Several entities exist in this purely mental inner world, actively communicating and negotiating and initiating actions. In the outer world, the body acts, steered by one or another inner person. How are we to ultimately understand this? One possibility is the following: taken literally, such statements must be understood as Cartesian dualism, with the exception that Alderman and Marshall imagine *several* Cartesian subjects. Now, this is a self-help book. The dualism is thus just a *useful fiction* that the authors wish to convey to their readers so that readers can gain a better grip on their lives. Of course, the authors do not explicitly say that it is a fiction because the usefulness of the fiction is based on its being believed. This is surely one possible interpretation of the text.

But we can take the claims in *Amongst Ourselves* seriously in a philosophical sense without assuming a Cartesian dualism. We can understand the text in such a way that it works with the concept of an I, which in this study has been explicated in terms of the authorial correlate theory. And *Amongst Ourselves* shares with this study the acceptance of the coexistence thesis, which states that there can be more than one I (or in my terminology, more than one fundamental entity) in one body. Many statements in *Amongst Ourselves* can be expressed in terms of the authorial correlate theory. According to the authorial correlate theory, each one of us is fundamentally an agent who is a correlate to certain psychological relations. *Amongst Ourselves* does not need to be interpreted as assuming a Cartesian inner space in which several Cartesian subjects communicate with one another. Rather, to uphold the position taken in the text, one needs only to assume the existence of several agents understood as correlates to psychological relations who are each materially constituted by one and the same body. The conditions of individuation of such agents are specified by the CAP criterion. Thus metaphysically seen, *Amongst Ourselves* is flawless. The book is written in a *terminology* that evokes Cartesian associations in a philosopher, but might nevertheless be appropriate for the purposes of a psychological self-help book. Regarding the *fundamental assumptions themselves* that are defended in the book, there is nothing to be criticized from a metaphysical point of view.[9]

I think that this reflects our reactions in reading psychological reports and biographies about multiple personality. Such works frequently work with a certain concept of an I that is familiar to all of us. This is also what makes such reports so fascinating. We believe that we are hearing or reading about something incredible, which actually *could be true*: that more than one person exists in one human being. We then look more carefully into the matter because we want to know whether the case at hand is also a *real* case of two persons in one body. We want to know how radical the separation between the personalities really is. When we then learn that the separation is not all that radical, however, we draw the conclusion that it does not involve more than one person—that such cases do not in fact really exist. In other words, we assume that what is being reported is not some metaphysical absurdity. But we are skeptical that the conditions for the presence of more than one person are in fact fulfilled.

This would amount to interpreting *Amongst Ourselves* along the lines of the following theses from Chapter 2:

> *Thesis 1**: Vicky and similar characters in cases of multiple personality understand themselves in a way that, if thought through philosophically, implies the assumption that each is respectively one fundamental entity among two or more in one body.
>
> *Thesis 2*: Each of us is a fundamental entity, of which there could exist two or more in one body (the coexistence thesis).
>
> *Thesis 3*: The conditions for the presence of two or more fundamental entities in one body are never fulfilled in reality.

Alderman and Marshall take up Vicky's position as an account of alters, even in the main text of *Amongst Ourselves.* This means that they accept a position whose truth conditions are partially specified by the coexistence thesis. However, as thesis 3 says, the authors are wrong in assuming that in cases of dissociative identity disorder there is more than one fundamental entity.

However, this interpretation of *Amongst Ourselves* would be too simple. It would be naïve to think that this book only operates with an I concept correctly explicated by the authorial correlate theory (and its elaboration by the commitment criterion and the CAP criterion) or that this theory can do justice to all the statements in the text. Certainly the text operates with this I concept. The text frequently suggests that the sort of entity each one of us is exists multiply in dissociative identity disorder: in other words, that more than one fundamental entity is present in such a case. This is how we can interpret the talk of several entities or beings consulting one another, communicating, and allowing or denying one another the control over the body as their container. But we are dealing with a psychological self-help book here, and it would be mistaken to expect such a book to make distinctions that are important for a philosophical investigation of personal identity. Therefore, I think that the authors are not just operating with an I concept, which I have explicated in terms of the concept of a fundamental entity. At work here is *also* a concept of personality or identity, which needs to be distinguished from both the concept of a fundamental entity and the concept of a role.

A fundamental entity can play different roles, but in explicitly or implicitly engaging with the question "Who am I?" this entity can assume that she herself plays these various roles. A fundamental entity can also be so radically split that she has different personalities. *As the one personality,* she has other structures of interest and perception than she has *as the other personality.* (In deciding whether these are really different personalities, one would be answering the question of the individuation of personalities.) It may be that a fundamental entity has good reasons to distance one side of herself so radically from another. A theorist—a philosopher or a psychiatrist—might then say we are dealing with *one* fundamental entity; but the fundamental entity herself *as the one personality* might regard the other personality as another fundamental entity.[10] This is one way to understand the previously quoted passage in which the authors distinguish between role and personality. The following passage is also interesting in this context:

> It may appear that the individual is having rapid mood swings, but really the moods of each alter are remaining somewhat consistent—it's simply the alters that are changing. This is not to say that each alter will always have the same mood. Just like everyone else in the world, the mood of an alter will change based upon the circumstances . . .

> *The feeling is very strange, and as you get to know yourself better you will begin to understand what is happening. You can recognize when each alter is coming out and they are changing quickly, and you feel so different with each alter who is out.* (21)

The theoretical passage is best understood as talking about more than one fundamental entity. "It may appear" that the mood of one fundamental entity changes, but "really" there are different fundamental entities whose moods remain constant and who alternately take control. Here the text is really talking about different fundamental entities: each of them is "just like everyone else in the world," and accordingly, the mood of each of them could suddenly change independently of the others' mood. In the italicized text by the alters, however, something else is expressed: "*You feel so different with each alter who is out.*" How can this be understood other than as saying that we are dealing with *one* fundamental entity who feels differently depending on whether she acts *as the one* or *as the other personality*?

2 KNOWING MYSELF AND THE OTHERS

How are we to understand the notion of communication between different alters employed in *Amongst Ourselves* and other writings on multiple personalities? In what way can an alter have knowledge of the mental states of another alter? Can one alter X be conscious of the mental states of another alter Y at precisely the time at which Y has these states? In other words, can X be intra-conscious of the mental states of Y? Does it matter here whether we understand alters as distinct fundamental entities or as distinct personalities of one and the same fundamental entity? I will defend the following thesis:

> *No intra-consciousness thesis:* One fundamental entity cannot be intra-conscious of the mental states of another fundamental entity, even if the two fundamental entities share the same body.[11]

I cannot provide a detailed argument for this thesis here so I will limit myself to two points. (1) According to the authorial correlate theory, psychological states are correlates to the subject who has these states. In the case of a commitment, somebody has committed herself to something. In the case of an experience, something appears to somebody in such and such a way. If somebody commits herself to something or something appears to her in a certain way, then this person is normally directly conscious of committing herself in this way or experiencing things in this way. But can somebody (A) be directly conscious of the commitment or the experience of somebody else, that is, if A is not the one committing herself in this way or experiencing things in this way? I think that the answer is no; I don't know how one could make sense of this. A direct inner consciousness of something is consciousness of having committed *oneself* in such and such a way or of things appearing to *oneself* in such and such a way. Thus, if the authorial correlate theory is correct, one fundamental entity cannot be intra-conscious of the mental states of another fundamental entity.[12]

(2) I can be directly conscious of my own beliefs and emotions in such a way that I cannot be conscious of the beliefs and emotions of others. In the case of belief, I can ask myself whether it is really true that *p*. If I then judge that it is really the case, I am directly conscious of believing that *p*. This direct consciousness of my beliefs is not based on an interpretation of my actions or my inner mental processes. Rather, I am directly conscious of my beliefs by making a judgment about what is the case. A similar point holds for direct consciousness of my emotions. I can become conscious of my emotions toward somebody by directing my attention toward that person rather than my inner mental life or my actions. For example, by directing my attention toward a particular person, I may realize that my relationship to her is one of respect, though I may possibly judge that she does not deserve to be respected. I cannot be conscious of the beliefs and emotions of others in this way. In order to be directly conscious of my beliefs or emotions in this way, *I* need to make a judgment about what is the case or direct my attention to a person. This is an additional reason for thinking that I cannot be directly conscious of the mental states of another fundamental entity.[13]

Although I cannot be directly conscious of the mental states of another fundamental entity in the same body, I can naturally attribute mental states to her in the way I can attribute mental states to other human beings based on their actions. In this way, my relationship to the mental states of other fundamental entities is just like my relationship to my own unconscious mental states. I can say about myself: "I must unconsciously believe that my boss has betrayed me. If I think about it, I come to the conclusion that she has not betrayed me. But the only reasonable explanation for my behavior toward her is that I believe she has betrayed me. So I must believe this unconsciously." This way of talking about unconscious states is quite familiar and allows for the possibility that I am conscious of my unconscious states in the sense that I attribute such states to myself based on my behavior.[14] So I attribute unconscious states to myself just as I attribute mental states to other human beings. Despite this similarity, one may raise the question as to whether there is not a difference between my relationship to my own unconscious states, on the one hand, and the mental states of other fundamental entities, on the other—even if these fundamental entities share my body. There is this sort of difference, as will become apparent in the following account of unconscious states.

> *Unconscious states thesis:* A fundamental entity's relationship to her own unconscious states differs significantly from her relationship to the mental states of other fundamental entities, even if the fundamental entities share a body.

As just mentioned, I may attribute an unconscious state to myself to account for my behavior. Despite the fact that I am aware of it in this way, it is nevertheless an unconscious state. I may also be unaware of my conscious states and that would not make these states unconscious in the sense under discussion here. For example, I may divide my attention in such a way that I am unaware of consciously putting on my shoes while focusing my attention on a conversation with somebody.[15] The concept of an unconscious state explicated here cannot be understood in purely epistemic terms as a state of which I am unaware. Rather, the fact that a state is unconscious says something about my relationship to it other than the fact that I am unaware of it.

Elsewhere I have discussed this concept of an unconscious state in more detail.[16] I can only summarize it rather dogmatically here. To do justice to the difference between a person's relationships to her conscious and unconscious states, I will positively and critically take up a proposal by David Finkelstein. A person can express her mental states in various ways. For example, she can express her gratitude toward another by giving her presents or thanking her. Finkelstein notes the special status of avowals or self-ascriptions like "I am grateful to you." Self-ascriptions, namely, can fulfill two functions equally. By saying "I am grateful to you," one normally not only says that one is in a state of gratitude, but one also expresses this gratitude just as one would with a present. As we have seen, a person who has an unconscious state may be able to attribute this state to herself. According to Finkelstein, it is distinctive of the self-ascription of an unconscious state that it fulfills only one of the two functions. With the utterance "I have an unconscious hatred of my father," a person indeed *describes* a state that she attributes to herself based on her own acts, but she does not *express* the hatred. Only the *acts* that justify this self-ascription express the hatred. Here Finkelstein locates the distinction between conscious and unconscious states: "*Someone's mental state is conscious if she has an ability to express it simply by self-ascribing it. If she lacks such an ability with respect to one of her mental states, it is unconscious.*"[17]

I would like to adopt Finkelstein's criterion here, but I reject another aspect of his analysis: namely, an assumption he shares with most interpreters of the unconscious, from Freud to Davidson. Finkelstein thinks that the process of turning an unconscious state into a corresponding conscious state has to do with gaining the ability to express by self-ascription a state which the person was previously unable to express in this way.[18] But that would mean that the unconscious state involves the *same attitude* as the conscious one, that both cases, for example, involve the *same state of hatred*, which can be transformed from an unconscious state to a conscious one. This is precisely what I want to call in question.

If a person *unconsciously* believes that her boss has betrayed her, her relationship to this belief is different than to a conscious belief with the same propositional content. The person cannot attribute to herself the unconscious belief by asking herself whether her boss has actually betrayed her. On the contrary: if she answers this question, she will come to the conclusion that it is not true that her boss has betrayed her. This means that acceptance of the proposition "my boss has betrayed me" is not one of her mental states. This is an attitude she does not have. But if that is so, then the unconscious belief that one's boss has betrayed one is a different attitude from the conscious belief with the same propositional content. The attribution of this unconscious belief is justified because the person acts *as if* she accepts this proposition. But she does not accept it. Thus, conscious and unconscious beliefs are different attitudes.

An unconscious belief must be understood as a state that can be regarded as a *belief* only on the basis of its *rational connection* with a conscious belief.[19] If a person self-ascribes an unconscious belief, she thereby *presupposes* that she faces a *rational choice*: either she turns the unconscious belief into the conscious belief that her boss has betrayed her, or she continues to reject the proposition that this betrayal has occurred. But if she continues to reject it, then, rationally, she should change her behavior: the fact that she unconsciously believes that her boss has betrayed her means, after all, that she behaves as if the betrayal has occurred. The self-ascription of this unconscious belief thus *conflicts* with the rejection of the proposition that her boss has betrayed her. Summarizing, we can say that the self-ascription of an unconscious belief implies a *rational expectation*. It is the expectation that, as soon as one knows about one's own unconscious belief, one should either turn it into a conscious belief or change one's behavior. The unconscious state can be regarded as a *belief* precisely because of this rational connection with conscious belief.[20]

Now, it can be made clear how a fundamental entity's relationship to her own unconscious states differs from her relationship to the mental states of other fundamental entities (even if the fundamental entities share a body). My unconscious states are states that I am unable to express by means of self-ascription. An unconscious state counts in the first place as the kind of state it is—for example, as a belief—on account of its rational connection to a conscious belief. For instance, it must be possible for the unconscious belief to stand in rational conflict with the conscious belief. This, in turn, presupposes that the unconscious belief is a state of the same fundamental entity as the conscious belief. I express a different attitude to the world—to a state of affairs or an object—in my unconscious states than in the corresponding conscious states. For example, my unconscious hatred of my boss amounts to a different attitude than my conscious hatred of her. I do not stand in this complicated relationship to the mental states of other fundamental entities. Thus, my relationship to my own unconscious states is significantly different from my relationship to the mental states of other fundamental entities.

> So he's not quite as unaware of me as he pretends to be. He's clearly noticed some of my actions—actions I naturally perform with our common body. But of course he must see them as his actions. So he reinterprets them as actions expressing HIS UNCONSCIOUS states. He really takes whatever theory he can to define me out of existence. Sigmund Freud (1856–1939), Austrian psychiatrist, inventor of the unconscious, which he later called the "es" (it) and contrasted with the "ich" (I). You can google him too. So, according to Logi, I am an "it" and he is an "I." He can control his "it" as long as he is good at making himself conscious of it. Please! I am "I," not an "it." I read that Freud was refuted a long time ago. Outdated stuff. Doesn't he think anybody notices?

Against this backdrop, we can now return to the interpretation of *Amongst Ourselves* and its idea of an *inner communication* among the alter personalities. Alderman and Marshall distinguish *integration* and *communication* among alters as possible therapeutic goals. In integration, the personalities "integrate or merge into one" (35). "The goal of integration is to allow the person to continually have consciousness of and access to all areas of themselves" (35). Still, they do not present integration as a necessary goal of therapy. Communication between the personalities is a necessary step in this direction and a way to come to grips with everyday life (35).[21] Communication cannot be understood as intra-consciousness. Rather, Alderman and Marshall define co-consciousness between various personalities in terms of the concept of communication, describing it as "an awareness of and ability to communicate with the other alters" (77). The no-intra-consciousness thesis defended earlier fits this aspect of *Amongst Ourselves:* if different fundamental entities in one body have no intra-consciousness of one another, they will have to communicate with one another instead. According to the authorial correlate theory, each fundamental entity is a correlate to its mental states. Things appear differently to each of these fundamental entities. The purpose of communication is to convey one's perspective on things to the other fundamental entities. This is precisely the situation of the different alter personalities as it is described in *Amongst Ourselves*, at least when no integration has taken place.

It would be unreasonable to expect the authorial correlate theory to fit every aspect of *Amongst Ourselves.* If we really have a case of different fundamental entities, I think that *inner* communication—that the different fundamental entities speak to each other in inner space—is just as impossible as intra-consciousness between different fundamental entities. However, the talk of inner communication in *Amongst Ourselves* may also be understood as invoking communication among different personalities of the same fundamental entity rather than communication between different fundamental entities. Such inner communication among different personalities can be explicated with the help of my account of unconscious states.

How can we make sense of the assumption that different personalities of a single fundamental entity *communicate* with one another on the inside—that is, not by external signs such as written notes? I am unable to express my unconscious states by means of self-ascription. If I have more than one personality, it may be that I can express an emotion by self-ascription only as *the one personality.* Since I can express this emotion as one of my personalities, it is, strictly speaking, not an unconscious state. However, *as one of the other personalities* who cannot express this feeling, I stand in a relation to this emotion that is similar to my relation to unconscious emotions: I cannot express the emotion by self-ascription.

In this sort of situation, we can sensibly speak of an inner communication between the personalities of one fundamental entity, and this sort of communication also has a practical function. If we take the alter personalities *Rosalee* and *Nada* from *Amongst Ourselves* as examples, we can explain this as follows: let's assume that *as Nada*, the fundamental entity cannot express a certain emotion by self-ascription but *as Rosalee* she is able to do so. To try to get the fundamental entity *as Nada* to bring this emotion into focus, the fundamental entity *as Rosalee* may try to convey this emotion to the fundamental entity *as Nada* by way of *communication.* Of course, she may do this by way of written communication. However, this mode of communication is not what interests us here. We can also understand voices in one's head this way. *As Nada*, the fundamental entity has no direct access to the emotion. The fundamental entity must employ inner communication to tell itself that it has this emotion. On the one hand, this is similar to an *internal monologue* and therefore not communication in a narrow sense. It resembles a case in which a fundamental entity without multiple personality tells itself that it has an unconscious emotion. The fundamental entity can take note of the emotion, but not express it by self-ascription. On the other hand, it is similar to an *inner dialogue. As Rosalee*, the fundamental entity can express the emotion by self-ascription, but not *as Nada.* If the fundamental entity *as Rosalee* communicates the emotion on the inside, it must seem to the fundamental entity *as Nada* that it is a statement from someone else, since she *as Nada* cannot express this emotion by self-ascription.

Summing up, we can say that *Amongst Ourselves* works with the assumption that a body can embody more than one fundamental entity. This assumption is metaphysically correct, but there is probably no such actual case. Since the work is not a philosophical study, however, it would be wrong to say that Alderman and Marshall are mistaken. Moreover, they also work with the idea of more than one personality of *one* fundamental entity. If we assume that they are talking about different personalities of one fundamental entity, then—by appeal to the explication of unconscious states—we can make sense of the idea of an inner communication between the personalities.

14 Multiple Personality in Literary Discourses

Does the concept of a fundamental entity, of which there can be more than one in one body, occur in works of fiction? At first glance the answer clearly appears to be yes. Here we need mention only a few of the most famous works dealing with a shared body: *The Strange Case of Dr. Jekyll and Mr. Hyde*, *I'm Not Stiller*, and *Psycho*. At second glance, just the opposite appears to be the case. Dr. Jekyll actually sees Mr. Hyde as a part of himself. Stiller is merely fooling himself when he poses as White. He ultimately realizes this himself. If we understand *Psycho* simply as a filmic presentation of a psychiatric disorder—one in which Norman Bates is perhaps just a multiple personality[1]—then this work of fiction tells us nothing that we cannot already find directly in psychological and psychiatric research.[2] But fictional works like *Psycho* cannot be understood as one-to-one transpositions of psychic disorders. We may even presume that in stories of the double, the second self is *never* meant to be understood literally as a second fundamental entity in one body: the point of departure is always a single person, and its doppelganger primarily serves a symbolic function, which operates differently depending on the work. What is symbolized, for instance, are the inner psychic division within the relevant person, the division of the human being as such, or the battle between good and evil in the human being, etc. At any rate, this is how doppelganger stories are normally interpreted. In her study *The Fear of the Other: Approaches to English Stories of the Double (1764–1910)*, Astrid Schmid defines the doppelganger relation this way: "According to my definition, the double-ganger relationships in the literature selected reveal the following features throughout: the doubles *share* a rationally inexplicable inner-psychic entity, *a common mind*. It is in this *recognition of the self as being split* into two halves that the motif's inner dynamics are to be found. For in his appearance, the double-ganger externalizes the First Self's haunting process of becoming aware of those *repressed aspects of the self*."[3] In other words, the doppelganger is a literary means to symbolically express the conflicted inner-psychic processes of persons. Even authors not concerned with presenting a precise definition of *doppelganger* likewise assume that the doppelganger symbolizes the inner conflict within an individual's identity: "The origin in the *experience of a problematic identity* is just about the *only trait* of the modern doppelganger that *can be generalized*. All these doubled and halved humans . . . have had to experience that *their I* does not as a matter of course fit *with itself*."[4]

At second glance, it thus looks as if the concept of a fundamental entity, of which there could be more than one in one body, does not play a role in works of fiction. As I will demonstrate, however, on the third glance, this is not always the case. I will focus on a contemporary text: *Fight Club* by Chuck Palahniuk, published in 1996.[5] With the aid of contemporary terminology, the text refers explicitly to multiple personality as a psychiatric disorder ("dissociative personality disorder" [168]). When the one person in the novel describes himself as a split personality, another person immediately connects this with *Psycho* ("Just like Tony Perkins' mother in *Psycho*" [173]). Moreover, the film version of *Sybil* is mentioned as a possible illustration of the phenomenon (196). *Fight Club* thus deals with multiple personality as a phenomenon of our contemporary culture and is therefore a suitable object of investigation. I will show that the concept of a fundamental entity, of which there can be more than one in one body, in fact plays an important role in this text.

1 MY DOPPELGANGER AS MY OTHER SELF

Like many good literary works, *Fight Club* is open to many interpretations. In section 2, I argue that the novel plays with the idea of two fundamental entities in one body. However, it is obvious that *Fight Club* can also be interpreted as a work involving the identity problems of one and the same fundamental entity. This purpose of this section is to outline a few of the ways in which the book can be interpreted in this latter sense and thus to make clear that the interpretation in section 2 is compatible with acknowledging the text's other meanings. Thus, in this section I will sketch how we can understand *Fight Club* using models typical for interpretations of doppelganger novels: *existential*, *socio-psychological*, *moral-allegorical*, *psychoanalytic*, and *psychiatric* models.[6]

The protagonist in *Fight Club* tells the story in the first person, and we never learn his "real name" (172). He suffers from chronic insomnia and only finds temporary relief when he begins attending different support groups for people suffering from mostly fatal illnesses, none of which our protagonist has. As a result of his insomnia, the whole of reality has slipped away from him; everything is "a copy of a copy of a copy," and "you can't touch anything and nothing can touch you" (21 and 96). He does not find a solution until he joins the support group "Remaining Men Together" (for men with testicular cancer) and can cry between the sagging tits of "Big Bob." Here our protagonist can lose "all hope," "hit bottom," "die," and, after dying, be "resurrected." After every meeting he is "more alive." This is how he overcomes his insomnia for a period of two years until Marla Singer, a woman who also obviously has no fatal illness, shows up in all of his support groups. Confronted with her presence, he experiences himself as a liar and faker. He can no longer die and can thus no longer be resurrected and sleep (22–23).

We can already recognize the novel's *existential* characteristics here. Our protagonist leads a life in which he himself disappears as an individual. He can no longer feel himself and is not in touch with anything. In the car company he works for, he is responsible for using profit-oriented formulas for recalling defective products, which reduce people to purely mathematical values (30–31, 95–96). Like other people, he has become a slave to his "nesting instinct" (43). He wants to organize his life perfectly by furnishing the perfect IKEA apartment. But the result is: "The things you used to own, now they own you" (44). He has become a victim of a culture that extinguishes individuality (134). Everything—even he himself—is merely "a copy of a copy of a copy." Through the possibility of dying in support groups for fatally ill people, to then be resurrected, he thinks he has temporarily reclaimed freedom and life (22). But Marla Singer's presence exposes this as a lie: he does not really "hit bottom." He just pretends to. A little crying in support groups cannot liberate him from the things that own him; it cannot enable him to get in touch with himself.

The invention of a doppelganger as a liberator (46, 146, 173–174) becomes necessary for our protagonist. Our protagonist is of course initially unaware that Tyler Durden—the liberator—shares a body with him and undertakes actions when our protagonist believes he is sleeping or spends a sleepless night in bed (163–167). Until shortly before the end of the novel our protagonist believes that Tyler is another human being whom he has met by chance. Our protagonist can leave the support groups behind him when he invents "fight club" together with Tyler Durden (52).

In "fight club," from which the novel takes its name, the existential traits of the text become perhaps the clearest. "Fight club" goes back to the situation where the protagonist asks Tyler for a place to stay and Tyler agrees, on one condition: "I want you to hit me as hard as you can" (46 and 52). At first the protagonist does not want to. His doppelganger thus has to explain it to him. It is about "wanting to know more about himself. About self-destruction" (52). This first fight between the protagonist and his doppelganger is the beginning of what they develop into "fight club" in which men beat each other up in the basements of bars. It is always just two men who hit each other, without shirts and shoes, until one says "stop." "Fight club" is about self-destruction. But in a sense the destruction of the self is only a way to find oneself. The self that is destroyed in "fight club" is the self defined by society and in words (49, 51, 143). It is about achieving point zero through self-destruction—only then can the individual gain freedom (70).

If our protagonist aims to gain personal autonomy by first destroying himself in "fight club," he is bound to fail. When his apartment is destroyed by a gas explosion, *he*—as he himself says—has been destroyed: "That was my whole life . . . It was me that blew up" (111). In other words, his old self has been destroyed. But he did not have the courage to do it himself. He had to invent Tyler to do it. It was Tyler who blew up the apartment (172–176). This way our protagonist cannot attain the self-determination that he seeks. By inventing a doppelganger to carry out certain actions for him, he invents a power that increasingly controls his life. This brings me to the *socio-psychological* interpretation of the novel.

According to this interpretation of stories of the double, they are about the conflict between the individual and society. The individual feels that his identity or existence is rejected or leveled by societal norms. But the individual has also internalized the social expectations to such an extent that this conflict repeats itself as an internal division in the individual. The individual can resist society only by generating a new self that opposes society or is strong enough to gain power in society, whereas the old self still bows to it. Thus, the conflict between individual and society must repeat itself inner-psychically.[7]

Fight Club runs along just those lines.[8] Tyler incorporates the protagonist's feeling toward society's erasure of his identity: "Our culture has made us all the same . . . We all want the same. Individually, we are nothing" (134). Tyler comes and teaches our protagonist self-destruction in "fight club." But at some point this is not enough for our protagonist. One day in "fight club," he takes on a good-looking beginner, and completely destroys his "angel face": "I wanted to destroy everything beautiful I'd never have . . . I wanted the whole world to hit bottom" (123). As a result, Tyler decides he has to raise "fight club" to another level and invents—alone—"Project Mayhem" (123–124). "Project Mayhem" has a different goal and structure than "fight club." The goal is "the complete and right-away destruction of civilization," so that "we can make something better out of the world" (125). Tyler holds the reins of this project in his hands. "Fight club" now really serves only the aim of recruiting men for this project (135). The recruits shave their heads like neo-Nazis (157) and quote Tyler's life philosophy blindly and dogmatically (140–150). "No one guy understands the whole plan, but each guy is trained to do one simple task perfectly" (130). Each member is part of an organism that is Tyler Durden (155). Thus in his cultural revolt, our protagonist has become a victim of an organization that is more dictatorial than the society against which the fight was supposed to be.

Our protagonist no longer understands what is happening, and he hardly sees Tyler. He sets out in search of him. At this point in time, he does not know that he and Tyler share one body. After finally realizing that they have the same body, our protagonist wants to stop Project Mayhem but it is too late. The recruits follow only the rules of the project and no one—not even Tyler himself—can change these rules (178–179, 189). It is also not in our protagonist's power to prevent Tyler from taking control of the body and carrying out actions according to his own plan. He has no other option but to kill Tyler (194–197). With a pistol in his mouth, our protagonist shoots himself through his chin and ends up in the psychiatric ward (204–208).

We can also interpret *Fight Club* in a *moral-allegorical sense*. When our protagonist destroys the "angel face" in "fight club," it is the evil in him that wants to destroy "everything beautiful I'd never have" (123). Evil and beauty cannot be reconciled. When Tyler founds Project Mayhem in response to this, he is also equated with the power of evil: "Tyler said the goal of Project Mayhem had nothing to do with other people. Tyler didn't care if other people got hurt or not. The goal was to teach each man in the project that he had the power to control history" (122; cf. 77–78). Each of them is to become familiar with a power in himself that stops at nothing. In the scene in which our protagonist realizes that his fight with Tyler was a fight with himself, he refers to the author of his actions alternately as himself and as "the monster" (117). Just as Dorian Gray finally turns the knife against the evil in himself—against the painting that has grown ugly—our protagonist realizes shortly before he pulls the trigger on the pistol in his own mouth that "under and behind and inside everything I took for granted, something horrible has been growing" (202).[9]

In several respects, we can also interpret *Fight Club psychoanalytically*. *First*, it is suggested that sexuality is the determining element underneath all the stories that we tell about ourselves or live out. Tyler works, among other things, in old-fashioned movie theaters in which the film spool is changed in the middle of the film. Obviously, one can compare the changing of the film spools—a change that the audience does not notice—to the change between the two personalities (25–28). Now, a film normally tells a story. But is life not about something else than the story? When Tyler at one point causes a chemical burn in the protagonist's hand, Tyler says he should enjoy this one perfect moment: "Tyler says to pay attention because this is the greatest moment of my life. 'Because everything up to now is a story,' Tyler says, 'and everything after now is a story'" (75). As a film projectionist, Tyler splices pornographic pictures into the films. None of the viewers notices, but they feel nauseated or cry without knowing why (29–31). In other words, sexuality determines our actions, but we are unaware of it and tell ourselves stories about our lives. Sexuality goes deeper than the stories that our protagonist constructs around his two personalities.

Second, a suppression of sexual desires and a displacement of their object take place. Tyler screws Marla Singer. Naturally our protagonist believes that it is not him—but Tyler—who fucks Marla: he hears Tyler and Marla for nights in another room and dreams that he is screwing her (56–59, 64–65). Later our protagonist says: "I know why Tyler had occurred. Tyler loved Marla. From the first night I met her, Tyler or some part of me had needed a way to be with Marla" (198).

Even more important is perhaps the homoerotic relation between our protagonist and Tyler. Here *Fight Club* contains an element that characterizes so many doppelganger stories.[10] When the protagonist fights with Tyler, he is in an act of auto-aggression—he hits himself (116, 167)—fighting his own homoerotic inclinations and, at the same time, fulfilling these desires, by pretending to fight with Tyler. The actual fights in "fight club" are of course homoerotically connoted, and "fight club" is treated like a forbidden homosexual club. "The first rule about fight club is you don't talk about fight club . . . The second rule about fight club is you don't talk about fight club" (48). Outside of "fight club," no one talks about it, but one recognizes if another man goes to a "fight club," and the two signal this to each other (48, 54). In this sense the fights between two men in *Fight Club* work like the homoerotic contacts in classic nineteenth-century stories of the double: they are secret and implicitly understood.[11]

Third, the love triangle between the protagonist, Tyler, and Marla is the story between son, father, and mother. In his relationship with Marla and Tyler—his imagined doppelganger—the protagonist re-experiences the relationship between himself and his parents. Marla and Tyler are never in the same room—except when he "hears" them screwing in another room—and he has to convey messages between them just like between his estranged parents (65–66). The father (Tyler) sleeps with the mother (Marla). The son (our protagonist) wants to sleep with his mother but can only do so as the father. Moreover, the son fights the father (53, 134), and the protagonist thinks that he and Marla fight for Tyler's attention (60; cf. 141).

Just as the psychiatrist offers us a psychiatric interpretation of Norman Bates's case at the end of the film *Psycho*, so too in *Fight Club* we are also confronted with *psychiatric* interpretations. The protagonist suggests: "Tyler is . . . a dissociative personality disorder. A psychogenic fugue state. Tyler Durden is my hallucination." Tyler counters by saying, "Maybe you're *my* schizophrenic hallucination" (68; see also the reference to *Sybil* [196]). In fact, the entire construction of the novel suggests a comparison with dissociative identity disorder: the protagonist obviously suffers from severe amnesia and, as a result, cannot recall the actions of a personality that alternately shares a body with the protagonist. And Tyler's words come more or less involuntarily from his mouth (98, 114, 155).

If we consider the case in purely psychiatric terms, the reference to schizophrenic hallucinations is also justified: the protagonist hallucinates the presence of a second human being. When the protagonist telephones the police with Tyler standing next to him whispering what he should say, it bears similarity to the voices schizophrenics hear in their heads, telling them what they should do. (Or they are the voices that people with dissociative identity disorder hear.) The protagonist's feeling of being detached from or unable to touch things at all, which he traces back to his insomnia, resembles derealization, which often accompanies schizophrenia. His relation to Tyler has paranoid features as well; he sees Tyler holding a pistol in the protagonist's mouth, even after he has already discovered that Tyler is not a human being separate from him (11, 203–204). At any rate, Tyler's response is justified insofar as the protagonist has increasing difficulties distinguishing between dream and reality (137–138). We can interpret the last chapter of the novel as showing a protagonist who has lost all sense of reality. He reports that he is in heaven, being served by angels and talking to God, even though these are obviously the nurses and psychiatrists of a psychiatric ward (206–208). At this point, we must ask ourselves to what extent the preceding events were merely paranoid hallucinations.

2 MY DOPPELGANGER AS ANOTHER FUNDAMENTAL ENTITY

These are interpretations of *Fight Club* based on common interpretive models of doppelganger stories. The point of departure in these models is always the assumption that the story concerns the identity conflicts of one and the same fundamental entity. Now, my interest lies in establishing that the concept of one fundamental entity, of which there could be more than one in one body, also plays a role in *Fight Club.* There are two perspectives of interest here: that of the protagonist and that of Tyler. I will begin with Tyler's perspective since this allows me to draw a clear contrast to common approaches to stories of the double. In interpretations of such stories, the doppelganger's perspective is normally ignored as an independent perspective. Instead, it is treated simply as a perspective that expresses the protagonist's divisions and conflicts.

Let us return to the passage that was partially quoted earlier. Tyler has just explained to the protagonist that they have control over one and the same body at different times (163–168). The first person speaking in the following conversation is our protagonist:

> So, now that I know about Tyler, will he just disappear?
>
> "No," Tyler says, still holding my hand, "I wouldn't be here in the first place if you didn't want me. I'll still live my life while you're asleep, but if you fuck with me . . . then we'll be enemies. And I'll get you for it."
>
> Oh, this is bullshit. This is a dream. Tyler is a projection. He's a dissociative personality disorder. A psychogenic fugue state. Tyler Durden is my hallucination.
>
> "Fuck that shit," Tyler says. "Maybe you're *my* schizophrenic hallucination."
>
> I was here first.
>
> Tyler says, "Yeah, yeah, yeah, well let's just see who's here last." (168)

When Tyler proposes that "maybe you're *my* schizophrenic hallucination," this does not mean that Tyler is saying that he has hallucinations. He never thought that our protagonist existed as an independent human being. He—Tyler—was always aware that they share one body. But with this statement he makes clear that he and the protagonist are both individuals in their own right. He challenges the psychiatric interpretation that the protagonist had just proposed: he is not the protagonist's projection but an independent subject just like the protagonist. He is also not a personality fragment in a person with a psychiatric disorder. Tyler's statement —"I wouldn't be here in the first place if you didn't want me"—must be compared with a later interpretation by the protagonist: "Tyler Durden is a separate personality I've created" (173). Here the protagonist claims that Tyler is his creation. This is not what Tyler says. Tyler merely says that he would not be there in the first place if the protagonist did not want it that way. The protagonist must want a second being to share his body with him. He must create the space so that a second subject can emerge. He merely made the space available, but he did not create the subject.

I have interpreted this quote as meaning that Tyler understands himself as one of two fundamental entities in one body. This makes good sense of the passage, but it does not prove that Tyler really understands himself as one of two fundamental entities in one body. Ultimately, we cannot definitely resolve what Tyler's perspective "really" is. But that is not important anyway. The crucial point is that nothing rules out that this is Tyler's standpoint. The reader is invited to put herself in Tyler's position. And one possibility that suggests itself is understanding Tyler as somebody who views himself as one of two fundamental entities. This gives the text additional dramatic effect and suspense. A tension emerges between Tyler's perspective and the protagonist's. And if Tyler seems to assume that he is one of two fundamental entities in one body, the question arises for the reader whether this is perhaps really the case, which then heightens Tyler's independence and threatening presence. In this sense, the concept of a fundamental entity, of which there could be more than one in one body, clearly plays a role in *Fight Club*. This becomes obvious in the following passage, which additionally shows that Tyler, unlike the protagonist, has always had a clear view of the situation (the first person to speak in the conversation is Tyler):

> "We are not two separate men. Long story short, when you're awake, you have the control, and you can call yourself anything you want, but the second you fall asleep, I take over, and you become Tyler Durden."
>
> But we fought, I say. The night we invented fight club.
>
> "You weren't really fighting me," Tyler says. "You said so yourself. You were fighting everything you hate in your life."
>
> But I can see you.
>
> "You're asleep." (167)

When one reads this, one must wonder how Tyler understands the case. When the protagonist thinks that he and Tyler are fighting, where is Tyler—according to Tyler—at that moment? It is tempting for the reader to assume that Tyler views himself and the entire situation just as Sally regards her situation in the Beauchamp case. Sally thinks that she and BI are two fundamental entities in one body. Moreover, she thinks that she is always present when BI acts or thinks. She can observe the actions and thoughts of BI as BI carries them out. In this way, Tyler would assume that there are fundamentally three possible situations. (1) Our protagonist alone has control over the body and does not have any hallucinations about Tyler's presence as another human being. (2) Tyler alone has control over the body and the protagonist is not conscious. This also means that the protagonist does not have any hallucinations about Tyler's presence. (3) Our protagonist hallucinates Tyler's presence as another human being. The last possibility of course matches the fight scenes. To use the terminology introduced in Chapter 9, if Tyler understands himself in the way that Sally sees herself, he is *co-sensory* with the protagonist in both (1) and (3). Both fundamental entities perceive the situation. In the last case, the protagonist has, in addition, the hallucination that he fights with a second person.

> I'm not a literary theorist. But I'm a "second self" myself. So I'm an expert on this particular topic. There is simply something missing in all of these interpretations. Tyler Durden is not in any way another identity of one and the same self. Tyler Durden and the guy telling the story are two separate entities. That is not merely a possibility—not simply "Tyler's point of view." It's just plain TRUE. Logi's reasons for ignoring this fact are obvious. Tyler is cool and confident. The other guy is phony and in self-denial. They are different in every possible respect. This is just how it is with me and Logi. So it's no surprise he doesn't want to see that Tyler and the little fake are in fact two entities. Facing it would be facing me.

Now, in regard to the fight scenes, we could ask ourselves whether Tyler believes that he also fought here. Did Tyler also have control over the body in these cases? Tyler's answer is somewhat evasive: did he also have control over the body and did a few punches therefore come from him? Or did the protagonist simply punch himself? Here it appears that Tyler is mainly interested in making clear to our protagonist that they are not two separate human beings. His response is sufficient for this. But if the reader is supposed to take Tyler's interpretation of himself seriously as one of two fundamental entities in one body, Tyler must have control over the body in the current situation—in the conversation from the quoted passage. In this situation, he cannot be a pure hallucination of the protagonist. He is really speaking in this situation. He must therefore understand the situation as one in which he and the protagonist are really speaking with each other. He is just working on liberating the protagonist of the idea that it is a conversation between two human beings. Here two fundamental entities in one body are speaking with each other. If that is so, however, then nothing hinders us as readers from assuming that Tyler assumes that the following was the case in earlier situations (such as in the fight scene): he and the protagonist were *co-sensory* and *co-present*. That is, they not only perceived the situation simultaneously, but also both had control over the shared body. And in this situation, the protagonist hallucinated that Tyler was an independent human being. Thus, according to Tyler, the protagonist suffers from a systematic hallucination that is nonetheless quite understandable: whenever Tyler and the protagonist have simultaneous control over the body—and sometimes when only Tyler has control (intercourse with Marla?)—the protagonist hallucinates that Tyler's actions are performed by another human being.

To further elucidate Tyler's perspective and segue to the perspective of the protagonist, I will present several different interpretations of a certain situation here. Tyler kisses the protagonist's hand with his moist mouth. Tyler pours lye on the hand still wet from the kiss. The protagonist suffers indescribable pain (72–75). We can read this scene in various ways: (1) From Tyler's perspective, we are dealing with only one body but two fundamental entities. The two fundamental entities are co-present and co-sensory: they both have control over the body, and both perceive the situation. The one fundamental entity—he himself—kisses the hand that they share and pours lye on it. And the two speak with one another. But only he perceives the situation correctly. The other fundamental entity—our protagonist—simultaneously hallucinates that it is a second human being who kisses his hand. (2) From the protagonist's original perspective, a human being stands next to him and kisses his hand. As we learn later on, this is a hallucination. There is no second human being. (3) From the protagonist's later perspective, he is a multiple personality and performs this action as the one personality so that he suffers from it as the other personality.[12]

The comments on Tyler's perspective show that the concept of a fundamental entity, of which there could be more than one in one body, plays a role in *Fight Club*. But the protagonist's original and later perspectives are also worth considering. If we compare the two perspectives, it must be said that he needs the illusion of a second fundamental entity in order to ignore his own psychic split. But to be able to believe that there is a second fundamental entity involved, he has to believe that there is a second human being present. Our protagonist is thus obviously of the opinion that there cannot be two fundamental entities in one body. We cannot dismiss this. At any rate, we cannot unambiguously ascribe to our protagonist the belief that two fundamental entities could exist in one body.

But our protagonist's attitude is anything but simple. Here I would like to briefly examine two issues. (1) One sentence that recurs throughout the book is "I know this because Tyler knows this" (12, 26, 112, 185, 203). This sentence performs an ambivalent function. On the one hand, it gives weight to the assumption that Tyler is another fundamental entity. Concerning the knowledge of how to make bombs or use film spools, our protagonist wants to make it clear that he has learned these things from Tyler. Tyler is a second fundamental entity and has told or taught him about it.

When he then arrives at the view that Tyler is not a second fundamental entity, he says: "All the things that Tyler knows are all coming back to me . . . All of the sudden, I know how to run a movie projector" (198). Here he thus says: he did not learn it *from* Tyler but *as* Tyler. When Tyler learns something, our protagonist learns it automatically. This is of course related to the CAP criterion. If PX learns something and PY also knows it for just that reason, we are not dealing with two fundamental entities but with one. Ideas expressed in the CAP criterion thus play a role here, even if we cannot say that the protagonist accepts this criterion.

The other function of this sentence is related to the CAP criterion for the same reason. The sentence can also be interpreted as meaning that the protagonist senses that he has not *learned* something from Tyler, but rather knows or is able to do it because Tyler knows or is able to do it. The sentence does not say, "I know this because Tyler taught it to me," but is formulated so ambivalently that it allows for both interpretations. The second interpretation means that the protagonist suspects that, because he "know this because Tyler knows it," he and Tyler are not two fundamental entities. In this case, the protagonist would be thinking in accordance with the CAP criterion.

(2) I previously cited the passage in which the protagonist, unlike Tyler, proposes a psychiatric interpretation of the case. This psychiatric interpretation is clearly a position to which he clings in order to come to grips with the situation (168, 172–174, 196). But he does not adhere to this perspective consistently. In this regard, the scene in the second-to-last chapter in which our protagonist has a pistol in his mouth is quite revealing:

> To God, this looks like one man alone, holding a gun in his own mouth, but it's Tyler holding the gun, and it's my life . . .
> Marla's coming toward me, just me because Tyler's gone. Poof. Tyler's my hallucination, not hers. Fast as a magic trick, Tyler's disappeared.
> And now I'm just one man holding a gun in my mouth . . .
> This is like a total epiphany moment for me.
> I'm not killing myself, I yell. I am killing Tyler . . .
> And I pull the trigger. (203–205)

This is how the second-to-last chapter ends. In the final chapter he is—as he himself says—in heaven. But he is clearly in a psychiatric ward (the bullet went through his chin). This suggests understanding God's perspective as the perspective of psychiatry. This is the perspective that our protagonist wanted to maintain (Tyler is a "dissociative personality disorder" [168]). At the beginning of the quotation, he has lost this perspective again and hallucinates Tyler's presence: Tyler holds a pistol in his mouth. When Marla comes—offering a social perspective (she arrives with sick people from a support group)—the hallucination disappears. Our protagonist briefly appears to return to the psychiatric interpretation. But this perspective is lost to him again in a "total epiphany moment": it is no longer Tyler who points a gun at him, but he who points a gun at Tyler. And he pulls the trigger. Thus, for him, Tyler is neither a hallucinated second human being nor—as psychiatry would have it—a personality fragment. Our protagonist pulls the trigger on Tyler, but he remains ambiguous on Tyler's status until the end.[13]

> I've found peace. But not in death. He can't win. I don't care what you believe. I'll never be a part of him, unless I start believing it myself. If I became a part of him, he could extinguish me. So I'll simply stop fighting. I will remain silent and make him think that he has convinced me and eliminated me. Then—after his book has been published—I'll return. I'll be a stranger in his soul that he can't rid himself of. He'll be so terrified that he'll give up. And then I will take over. Alone.

3 CONCLUDING REMARKS

Understanding multiple personality is understanding ourselves. In thinking about multiple personality, two aspects of our self-understanding come to light. On the one hand, we believe that we never really encounter any human being who embodies more than one fundamental entity. On the other, we have the feeling that it would be possible for a human being to embody more than one fundamental entity. In short: we are alone in our bodies, but we need not be.

The authorial correlate theory gives an account of what we are—an account that articulates these two aspects of our self-understanding. On the one hand, if each one of us is fundamentally an agent who is a correlate to the psychological relations for which the agent is minimally responsible, then in most, if not all, cases, a human being will remain one and the same fundamental entity over time and will not embody more than one fundamental entity. This is demonstrated by the two articulations of the authorial correlate theory: the commitment criterion for diachronic identity and the CAP criterion for individuation. On the other hand, though such an agent is in fact always alone in the body, this need not be the case. If the CAP criterion were fulfilled, it would not be so. Multiple personality dramatizes our self-understanding. Here we have characters saying that they share their body with other fundamental entities. We don't believe them. Yet all they are doing is expressing our own self-understanding.

Notes

NOTES TO CHAPTER 1

1. See Keyes 1981.
2. Of course, the publication of *Sybil* is not the only explanation of this development; see Hacking 1995, 39–68.
3. Hacking 1995, 8.
4. A synopsis of many of these biographies, together with psychiatric commentary, can be found in North et al. 1993, 185–250.
5. For an overview of this literature up to 1995, see Ross 1997, 44–57; for a few recent developments, see Reddemann et al. 2004.
6. See Beta 2001.

NOTES TO CHAPTER 2

1. In the foreword to *Sybil*, the author—Flora Rheta Schreiber—writes that Sybil's therapist Dr. Cornelia B. Wilbur asked her to write about Sybil's case. She then becomes friends with both Sybil and Dr. Wilbur. Schreiber describes the process of working on the book as follows: "Through these ten years—during seven of which I was actively working on the book—I was intimately associated with Dr. Wilbur and Sybil, both of whom, sometimes separately, sometimes together, stood ready to 'sit' for the portrait. Our roles were quite distinct, however. I was recreating what Sybil had already lived and the doctor had already analyzed. But never, perhaps, did an author have more 'giving' subjects. In fact, in response to any questioning, they, too, reassessed many aspects of the analysis" (Schreiber 1973, 15–16). Critics claim that the personalities were artificially produced in therapy and that Dr. Wilbur and Schreiber intentionally exaggerated them for the effect as autonomous personalities (Acocella 1999, 56–60).
2. Schreiber 1973, 98–99.
3. Schreiber 1973, 96–97, 100–103.
4. Cf. Schreiber 1973, 168–171.
5. For example, F.W. Putnam and C.A. Ross, two of the most prominent authors on this topic, assume this: cf. Putnam 1989, 103; Ross 1997, 144.
6. Schreiber 1973, 170.
7. And Vicky says in the first quotation: "We're people . . . People in our own right." "People," one should remember, is the plural of "person." Even if, at the end of an integrative therapy, Vicky admits that she is now a part of Sybil (Schreiber 1973, 436), up to that point she consistently and vehemently

insists that she is an autonomous person, separate from Sybil (90–100, 168–171, 336–338). Here are a few more quotations: "'Do they also share the same body?' [the therapist asks about the other personalities]. 'That's silly,' Vicky replied authoritatively. 'They're people, I can tell you about them'" (169). "'What an absurdity it is to think of these complete individuals as the same. Marian Ludlow and I are more alike than are any two or three persons you have mentioned'" (i.e., the two or three personalities mentioned by the therapist, 170). Initially, Vicky also claims that she and Sybil do not have the same parents (92–93).

8. See Chapters 8 and 13.
9. American Psychiatric Association 2000. In contrast to DSM-IV, the 10th revision of *International Statistical Classification of Diseases and Related Health Problem* (ICD-10) has no separate definition for any such disorder. This reflects a somewhat skeptical attitude toward this diagnosis. Although ICD-10 uses the words "multiple personality," and multiple personality is listed under "other dissociative (conversion) disorders," the following is remarked about all dissociative (conversion) disorders: "All types of dissociative disorders tend to remit after a few weeks or months" (World Health Organization 2007). For a discussion of the differences between DSM-IV and ICD-10 and the shift from the designation "multiple personality disorder" in DSM-III to "dissociative identity disorder" in DSM-IV, see Hacking 1995, 10–20, and Braude 1995, 248–253.
10. Sally is not initially called by this name; see Chapter 8.
11. Prince 1906, 9–10, 16, 53, 291–293. The vocabulary used to describe BI and Sally here and in the next paragraph is Prince's, though I have not always drawn attention to it by the use of quotation marks.
12. Prince 1906, 11.
13. Prince 1906, 11.
14. Prince 1906, 47.
15. Prince 1906, 13, 290.
16. Prince 1906, 34, 53–54, 109, 117, 138, 152.
17. Prince 1906, 110.
18. Prince 1906, 54–56, 112.
19. Prince 1906, 52–53, 130.
20. Prince 1906, 47, 150–151.
21. Prince 1906, 129–130.
22. Prince 1906, 149–150.
23. Prince 1906, 160–161.
24. Prince 1906, 91.
25. There is no reason to assume that the fourth condition is not fulfilled as well.
26. Hacking 1995, 128–141. For case studies of multiple personalities from the nineteenth century to 1920, see Ellenberger 1970, 126–141; Crabtree 1993, 283–350; Hacking 1995, 142–197.
27. Putnam 1989, 31–34; Hacking 1995, 136.
28. For the proponents' arguments, see Steinberg/Schnall 2000; for the critics' arguments, see Acocella 1999. The titles of these two books are revealing of these two opposite trends: *The Stranger in the Mirror: Dissociation—The Hidden Epidemic* (Steinberg/Schnall) and *Creating Hysteria: Women and Multiple Personality Disorder* (Acocella).
29. Even if it is not part of the symptomatic definition of dissociative identity disorder, almost everyone who today considers dissociative identity disorder to be a valid psychological diagnosis thinks that this disturbance is caused by childhood trauma, especially sexual abuse. See Putnam 1989, 45–54; Ross 1994, vii–viii; Ross 1997, 61–66; Huber 1995, 18–19, 51–55; Alderman/

Marshall 1998, 40–47. Since I do not make any judgment about the validity of this psychiatric diagnosis, I also do not take any position on this causal explanation. But I would like to emphasize that a great number of children experience terrible violence, whether of a sexual or other nature. My neutrality here applies only to the validity of a psychiatric diagnosis and the corresponding causal explanation, not to the question of whether terrible mistreatment of children takes place. It does take place.

30. Prince 1906, 27.
31. Prince 1906, 27.
32. Frisch 2006, 17–18.
33. Other reasons for this—having to do with methodological issues relating to personal identity—will be discussed in the next chapter.
34. There are not many philosophical monographs on multiple personality. As far as I know, Braude 1995, Radden 1996, Hacking 1995, and Saks 1997 are the only ones falling into this category.

NOTES TO CHAPTER 3

1. This is a question of *constitutive*, not *epistemic*, conditions, of course.
2. The formulation "one and the same *individual* human being" (and "one and the same individual fundamental entity") is meant to indicate that the question concerns the conditions for being the *same individual of a kind.* Having specified the kind by answering question 1, question 2 concerns the identity conditions of individuals of that kind. I will often leave "individual" out of the formulation, but unless otherwise indicated I mean: one and the same individual of a certain kind. In other words, "one and the same" does not stand for the sense in which two distinct individuals may be "one and the same" if they share enough qualities. For example, when I, in question 3, talk about "one and the same individual personality," I mean: one and the same individual of the kind *personality*. Two individual personalities may in another sense be "one and the same" personality if they share enough personality traits, but that is not my topic. It should be noted that I am not assuming that the relation *one and the same individual of a kind* is the relation of *numerical identity*. To do so would be to make controversial assumptions about the former relation; cf. Quante 2007a, 9–10; Hartmann and Galert 2007, 195–199.
3. This way of proceeding presupposes that my identity is *not relative*. My identity would be relative if no concept determined the conditions of my identity as such, but rather, the question of my identity dissolved into questions about being one and the same relative to the different concepts applicable to me. In other words, if my identity were relative, we could not ask: "Does the concept *human being* or the concept *person* determine my condition of identity?" Rather, there is not really a question of my identity, but only questions about being one and the same individual of the kinds specified in terms of the concepts under which I fall (for example, the concept *human being*, *person*, and *Icelandic citizen*). We could only ask such questions as: "What are the conditions for being one and the same human being?" And: "What are the conditions for being one and the same person?" For discussions of relative identity, see Geach 1967–68; Perry 1970; Wiggins 2001, 21–54; Rapp 1995, 157–187, 387–408; Olson 1997, 159–162; Quante 2002, 50–51; Deutsch 2007.
4. In formulating the issues in this way, I have been guided both by Olson 1997, 22–31; Baker 2000, 4–12, 138; Baker 1999.
5. Quante 2007a, 110.
6. For a discussion of such theories, see section 6.2.

7. In a discussion of my approach, Quante suggests that my terminology does not exclude that both humans and persons are fundamental entities (Quante 2008, 564). This is not how "fundamental entity" is used here. Fundamental entities are specified in terms of the concept that determines the conditions of my identity and that can only be *one* concept. The question at stake is *which concept* determines my identity conditions.
8. It is important to note that—in contrast to Olson 1997, 27–28—the question "What am I fundamentally?" is not understood here as one that must be answered by specifying a *substance concept* (Olson draws on Wiggins; cf. Wiggins 2001, 21–22). We can ask for all sorts of things: "What is it?" For example, we can ask this question about a creature eating grass on a meadow. If the answer is "a sheep," then *sheep* would be a substance concept and the creature on the meadow would have come into existence when a sheep was born and would cease to exist when that sheep dies. Now, it seems that, in answering this question about this creature, we must suppose that being a sheep is somehow ontologically more fundamental than being a grass-processing system—that sheep are substances whereas grass-eating systems are not. How else could one arrive at an answer to the question "What is it?" with respect to the creature on the meadow? Here no such assumption is made with respect to the question "What am I fundamentally?" What I am fundamentally may not be anything that is somehow ontologically fundamental. For example, it may be that humans are ontologically more fundamental than persons. This does not exclude the possibility that the correct answer to the question "What am I fundamentally?" is "a person." In other words, what I am fundamentally may not be a substance.
9. Cather 1990, 240–241.
10. To make this question more precise, one would need to explain what is meant by "personality." It may turn out that question 3 is not a unified question, but rather stands for different questions, depending on the interpretation of personality (the same holds for question 5). For example, if "personality" stands for *moral character*, one may ask whether a fundamental entity still is the same individual character if she becomes increasingly corrupt in the course of her life. Alternatively, one may ask whether somebody whose moral character has not changed will still be the same individual personality if she—perhaps due to clinical depression—changes from a sanguine to a melancholic person. There, of course, are other interpretations.
11. See Wallis 1996 and Weathers 2006.
12. This is how Baker 2000 (107–109, 132) answers questions 2 and 4.
13. I discuss this question in Gunnarsson 2008a.
14. My division of the field into various questions has some things in common with Quante 2002, 19–23 and Quante 2007a, 1–16, 108–114, 168–175, 188–194. But there are also important differences.
15. I will concentrate on the contemporary discussion of this issue. The framing of the contemporary debate may be traced back to Locke 1975, but its historical roots go further back. For overviews of the historical dimension, see Noonan 1989, 30–103; Sturma 1997, 44–57, 150–177; Teichert 2000, 15–206; Sturma 2001, 25–141; Martin and Barresi 1999; Martin and Barresi 2006; Quante 2007a, 35–55. For overviews of the contemporary debate, see Noonan 1989, 1–29; Herrmann 1995, 16–41; Quante 1995; Quante 1999; Schechtman 1996, 7–50; Ausborn-Brinker 1999, 236–258; Gillitzer 2001, 130–238; Olson 2007.
16. On the use of the term "empirical" by two adherents of non-empirical conceptions, see Swinburne 1984, 3, 19–21; Nida-Rümelin 2003, 260–270, 261; Nida-Rümelin 2006, 27–28.

17. Henceforth, when I write "X is identical to Y" (or "X = Y"), I mean "X is one and the same individual fundamental entity as Y" in the sense of question 2.
18. This is why it seems that non-empirical theories must reject the following *supervenience principle*: if X = Y and X ≠ Z, then there must be an empirical difference between the empirical relations between X and Y, on the one hand, and X and Z, on the other (see section 3.3). For the response of the non-empiricist Nida-Rümelin to this problem, see Nida-Rümelin 2006, 242–247, 272–279.
19. A well-known variant of the psychological approach is the position that D. Parfit terms "psychological criterion"; Parfit 1987, 204–223. Some versions of the psychological approach: Grice 1941; Quinton 1962; Perry 1972; Lewis 1976; Dainton 2008.
20. Snowdon 1990; Olson 1997. Quante defends a biological account of the diachronic unity or persistence of human individuals (Quante 2002, 47–105, 119–156; Quante 2007a, 103–114). He distinguishes between the issue of the unity of the person and the issue of the "identity" of personality. Roughly speaking, his approach to the second topic elucidates the "identity" of a personality as biographical coherence (Quante 2007a, 135–177). In regard to the first issue, he arrives at the skeptical result that no conditions of unity can be formulated for *persons*. For this reason, he instead describes conditions of biological persistence for *human organisms* (Quante 2007a, 98–114). This is best understood as a biological answer to the question of the diachronic identity of fundamental entities in my sense (Quante 2008, 563–564). DeGrazia defends a view that is similar to Quante's in this respect (DeGrazia 2005, 1–114).
21. Williams 1973a; Williams 1973b; Williams 1973c; Thomson 1997.
22. Cf. Ausborn-Brinker 1999, 260–261.
23. For the brain criterion, see Nagel 1986, 37–43; Unger 1990, 102–110.
24. Some theories can be understood as giving "I am fundamentally a human being" as an answer to question 1 and then as giving a psychological account of the diachronic identity of human beings. Some versions of such theories: Wiggins 1976, 158–168; Rosenberg 1998, 98–108, 133–149; Johnston 1987, 75–80; Whiting 2002, 208–209 (for a restriction on categorizing Whiting's view as a version of the psychological approach, see section 5.2).
25. An example of a dualistic approach is Swinburne 1984; examples of inner-perspective approaches are: Madell 1991; Baker 2000; Nida-Rümelin 2006.
26. In making this statement, however, I do not wish to suggest that adherents of such theories consider reincarnation possible.
27. Of course, one can add dualistic ontological commitments to the inner-perspective approach; see Nida-Rümelin 2008.
28. According to this approach, the identity of fundamental entities must be understood in terms of the inner perspective *from which* one looks onto one's own experience and the world. The identity of this perspective cannot be explicated non-circularly. This theory must be distinguished from views aiming to explain identity in terms of the *phenomenal or experiential unity of the experiences* encountered in the inner perspective (see, for example, Dainton 2008). This is psychological unity and such views are thus versions of the psychological approach.
29. This is one of the most-discussed problems in the literature, and in the contemporary discussion of different solutions, it goes back to Wiggins 1967, 50–56. For an overview and discussion, see Noonan 1989, 14–29; Johnston 1989, 373–394; Schechtman 1996, 30–42; Whiting 2002, 194–199; Galert and Hartmann 2007, 207–211; Nida-Rümelin 2006, 28–54, 112–126, 242–261, 272–279; Quante 2007a, 91–95.

30. According to closest continuer theories, Fair might be identical to L-Fairchild if the number of empirically, non-circularly describable connections existing between Fair and L-Fairchild is larger than the number existing between Fair and R-Fairchild (see section 5.2).
31. Noonan 1989, 16 (for a discussion of this principle, see section 3.2).
32. Perdurantism with respect to diachronic identity makes it possible to embrace a version of (iv). According to perdurantism, a fundamental entity—or any object persisting over time—is not a three-dimensional but a four-dimensional object, having not only spatial but also temporal parts. This position holds that there is no such object as Fair existing wholly at each time. Rather, when we encounter a fundamental entity at a particular time, we are merely encountering a temporal part of an object that is literally stretched over time. So L-Fairchild and R-Fairchild are two objects composed of temporal parts. The temporal parts composing Fair will then be parts of L-Fairchild and R-Fairchild. Therefore, there will be a way of saying that Fair = L-Fairchild *and* Fair = R-Fairchild when we have translated the talk of identity into talk of temporal parts, which is carried out differently by different versions of perdurantism. Classic defenses of perdurantism for personal identity can be found in Perry 1972 and Lewis 1976. Endurantism is the view that objects existing over time are three-dimensional, existing wholly at each time. In other words, they have no temporal parts. For a recent overview of the debate between perdurantism and endurantism, see Sider 2001. For a way of embracing (iv) without accepting perdurantism, see Dainton 2008, 364–393.
33. Johnston 1989, 373, 379.
34. The expression "unity reaction" for this reaction is adopted from Blackburn 1997, 181. In various forms, the unity reaction is used to justify non-empirical approaches. Examples: Swinburne 1984, 18–19; Nida-Rümelin 2003, 260–264; Nida-Rümelin 2006, 107–109, 127–129, 187–191, 206–207.
35. Assuming that it is possible does not mean that one—if one is L-Fairchild—can tell after waking up as L-Fairchild that one is in fact L-Fairchild. On the contrary: both L-Fairchild and R-Fairchild will think they are Fair and there is no way of proving who is right.
36. Cf. Quante 2002, 41–46. The case of coma is especially well suited to point out the problems of the inner-perspective approach, because a coma is the equivalent of the absence of an inner perspective. The point here is the general problem for all non-empirical theories that they permit a change of identity despite the existence of all relevant empirical continuities (cf. Kant 1968, Third Paralogism, A 364, Note; Johnston 1987, 70–75).
37. Cf. Nida-Rümelin 2006, 99–109.
38. Condition of adequacy 3 focuses on relations that, *conceptually speaking*, cannot obtain between the predecessor and both of the successors. A splitting of a human organism that is also a person may be biologically impossible, but it is conceptually possible, if biological continuity is understood as empirical, non-circular continuity. Quante propounds a biological position and wants to solve the duplication problem by excluding fission as biologically impossible (Quante 2007a, 92–95). But since fission is nonetheless conceptually possible, condition of adequacy 3 cannot be fulfilled in this way.
39. The possible theory options are often defined in such a way that there is no place for empirical, circular approaches. This means that in the common contrast between *simple* and *complex* views of the identity of fundamental entities, empirical, circular theories belong to neither side of the dichotomy and thus plainly drop out. For example, Quante defines the so-called complexity thesis as follows: "There is *an informative, i.e., non-circular* analysis of personal unity, i.e., constitutive (and not merely epistemic) criteria of personal

unity." (Quante 2007a, 59; my emphasis and translation; here and in the other chapters translated by Mitch Cohen or Joann Skrypzak, I say in such cases 'my translation' to indicate that their respective translations may have been slightly modified.) This means that a rejection of the complexity thesis must deny not only that there is a non-circular, but also that there is an informative analysis. Empirical, circular approaches are thereby excluded by definition, because they are not only informative—because empirical—but also circular. However, this exclusion is motivated. The complexity thesis concerns my questions 2 and 4 (the diachronic and synchronic identity of fundamental entities), and to such questions Quante only allows answers given in purely descriptive and functional-causal terms (Quante 2007a, 199n30). These answers must be non-circular. With respect to answers to my questions 3 and 5 (the diachronic and synchronic identity of personalities), he allows answers involving evaluative categories and these may be circular (Quante 2008, 565–566; cf. Quante 2007b). In my view, this confinement of circular accounts to answers to questions 3 and 5 is a mistake. Not only does it prevent us from being able to fulfill conditions of adequacy 1–3, but it also involves a misconception of the relationship between the identity of fundamental entities, the identity of personalities, and the question "Who am I?" (question 6) (see Chapter 7 and Part III). Because Nida-Rümelin understands empirical theories to be reductionist, she too seems to have left no place for empirical, circular theories (Nida-Rümelin 2006, 26–28, 36–46). In contrast, Sturma wants to defend a position that combines simple and complex views (Sturma 2008, 581; cf. Sturma 1992; Sturma 1997, 97–205, 275–286; Sturma 2002).

40. Shoemaker 1970; Shoemaker 1979; Shoemaker 1997, 283–304; Korsgaard 1996b; Whiting 1999. On the differences between my approach and these accounts, see Chapters 4, 5, and 7.
41. See Chapter 7.
42. For a discussion of the employment of thought experiments in discussion of personal identity, see Wilkes 1988, 1–48; Johnston 1987; Rovane 1998, 35–45; Whiting 1999; Quante 2007a, 100–102, 124–126; Nida-Rümelin 2006, 49–65.

NOTES TO CHAPTER 4

1. At stake here is the diachronic identity of fundamental entities. Accordingly, by "P_1" and "P_2" I mean *X at t_1* and *Y at t_2* in the sense of question 2.
2. Since this cannot be a sufficient condition for fission, the psychological criterion must modify the condition to account for that case. I'll return to fission in Chapter 5 and set aside this complication for the time being.
3. For an account of the psychological criterion, see Parfit 1987, 204–223; Schechtman 1996, 18–20.
4. See Parfit 1987, 205–207, but remember that a clause for fission would need to be added.
5. For a longer version of this argument, see my unpublished manuscript "Personal Identity and Self-Transformation."
6. I shall argue later that one human body can embody more than one agent (Chapter 10). In such a case, the human being would not be an agent. Rather, the relevant human body would embody more than one agent. For each of these agents it would hold that her actions cannot be traced back to the actions of other agents.
7. In talking about clubs, I have in mind organizations made up of different *agents*. It is possible to imagine an agent made up of different bodies, where

none of these bodies *individually* constitutes an *agent. Together*, however, these bodies make up one agent. This would be the case of an agent whose actions cannot be traced back to the actions of other agents. The self-transformation of such an agent would then have to be understood analogously to the self-transformation of a human being in a normal case. I do not address the issue as to whether there can really be such an agent (cf. Strawson 1959, 113–115; Rovane thinks that there can be such agents: cf. Rovane 1998, 137–141, 160–166; Rovane 2002; Rovane 2004a; Rovane 2004b).

8. This is a view often traced back to Hume 1978. Some understand it as a version of Buddhist accounts of the self; Siderits 2003.
9. In making this claim, I am assuming that empirical, non-psychological answers to question 2 are always meant to be non-circular. Because this holds true for answers of this kind given in the literature on personal identity, it is a legitimate assumption.
10. It is not important whether she really has the commitment *that flying is dangerous*. She does have *some* commitment that has psychological reality and this commitment is under normative pressure. That is the point.
11. Cf. Williams 1973d.
12. By talking of "psychological reality" and "psychological influence" I do not wish to imply that reality contains mental states. I only use such phrases to talk about two ways of being committed to something and the connection between them. It is an open question what ontological implications this distinction has. For my purposes, it is not necessary to interpret this contrast in realistic terms. It would suffice if the two dimensions of commitments could be distinguished on the basis of the different conditions for attributing commitments to people in these respective senses.
13. This account of commitments is not meant to be original. I follow the basic ideas of Moran 2001 without attempting to be particularly faithful to the details of his view (for my criticism of Moran, see Gunnarsson 2005). My philosophical contribution is meant to consist in the ensuing account of commitment revision and commitment maintenance and their relevance to the identity of fundamental entities.
14. This amounts to an important difference between my theory and Korsgaard's—between my notion of a psychological relation for which the agent is minimally responsible and her idea of "[a]uthorial psychological connectedness" (Korsgaard 1996b, 379). This difference is related in an important sense to the differences discussed in Chapter 7.

NOTES TO CHAPTER 5

1. Perdurantists can maintain that commitment maintenance holds between Fair and both of her descendants (see Chapter 3, note 32). As far as I can see, the commitment criterion as such is compatible with perdurantism. However, in applying the commitment criterion to solve the duplication problem, I presuppose endurantism. So perdurantists wishing to embrace the commitment criterion could employ the usual perdurantist solutions to solve the duplication problem.
2. This means that the commitment account is incompatible with closest continuer approaches to the identity of fundamental entities. For such theories, see Nozick 1981, 29–70.
3. One might take a different line on moral responsibility than the one taken by the purely forensic account. One might admit that moral responsibility *normally* depends on the assumption that the fundamental entity held responsi-

ble is identical to the fundamental entity who performed the relevant action. However, one might say that *in fission* both of the fission descendants should be held morally responsible for the actions of the original fundamental entity even though neither of them is that fundamental entity (see Olson 1997, 57–62). This *broadening of the notion of moral responsibility* is compatible with the commitment criterion. Even if we *hold* both fission descendants *responsible* for a commitment made by the original fundamental entity, the relation of *commitment maintenance* does *not* exist between the original fundamental entity and the fission descendants. That relation is conceptually dependent on a *narrower notion of responsibility* that *presupposes the identity of fundamental entities.* Similarly, it is perfectly compatible with the commitment criterion to say that the original fundamental entity may—perfectly rationally—*care* just as much about her fission descendants as about herself.

4. This is only one strand in Shoemaker's theory—a theory he has been developing over decades, the first major piece being *Self-Knowledge and Self-Identity*, published 1963 (for this strand, see Shoemaker 1970; Shoemaker 1979; Shoemaker 1997). I follow Whiting 2002, 197–209, 215–216, in her interpretation of this strand.
5. Whiting 2002, 200–203.
6. Whiting 2002, 209, but cf. 201.
7. See Olson 2002, 682–698, 692.
8. See Whiting 2002, 195–209.

NOTES TO CHAPTER 6

1. Shoemaker 1984, 108–109.
2. Notice that the view defended here is *not* the view that a fundamental entity that starts its existence as a human being can only continue to exist *as a human being.* It is merely the view that this fundamental entity must continue to exist as *the same material being* that it was born as. In other words, even if I am born as a human being, it may be that I survive such a *radical replacement* of the material I am made of that I *no longer* exist as a *human* being.
3. Ramis 1996.
4. This means, of course, that this cloning goes beyond the creation of a *genetically identical* copy.
5. This line of reasoning corresponds in its general structure to Shoemaker's argument in "Self and Substance." Psychological relations for which a person is minimally responsible do not figure in Shoemaker's position. Nevertheless, they play the same role in my argument that ("autonomous") "self-perpetuation" and "immanent causation" play in Shoemaker's argument (Shoemaker 1997, 288–291, 295–298). This reasoning leads Shoemaker to conclude that personal identity is not preserved in BST. But he also says that much speaks in favor of thinking that identity is preserved in BST. He thinks that our attitudes are in conflict on this point but admits that he does not know how to resolve the conflict (Shoemaker 1997, 298–301). In earlier writings, he argues that identity is preserved in BST (Shoemaker 1984, 108–111).
6. Cf. Rea 1997. Not only is the idea of material constitution controversial, but there is no consensus on exactly how to understand it. This is a complex issue that I cannot possibly explore in any depth in this study. I merely wish to outline the basic ideas involved in one possible way of understanding material constitution.

7. Olson 2001, 338–340; Olson 1997, 97–108.
8. Lowe 2002.
9. At least this is what Olson himself must assume, since he argues that an entity that was once a fetus cannot be followed by an entirely new entity when the fetus becomes a person (Olson 1997, 79–80). If this cannot be the case when a fetus becomes a person, then Olson cannot assume that death is the beginning of the existence of an entirely new entity (Shoemaker 1999, 290–291, 295; Carter 1999). Olson nevertheless has a way out of the argument offered in the main text. He can deny that there exists an entity that first exists as my body and then becomes a corpse. This is precisely what Olson does (Olson 1997, 150–152). He claims that spatiotemporal continuity is not sufficient for there to be an entity that first exists in one way and then becomes a corpse. For that to be the case, a special kind of continuity would be necessary. In addition, the existence of an entity must end *at some point*. And biological death is such a radical change that it is plausible to assume that this is the end of the existence of the relevant entity. So no entity exists that is first my body and subsequently a corpse. However, Olson's argument only works if the corpse is not really an entity. Otherwise the existence of this entity must have begun at some point (see Merricks 2001, 53). Therefore, Olson can only get round the argument in the main text if he denies that corpses are entities at all (in contrast to a mere collection of material units).
10. See Sosa 1997, 64.
11. This is how Shoemaker argues in response to Olson; Shoemaker 1999, 290–291, 295. Carter 1999 argues in the same way, but he comes to a different conclusion—namely, that each one of us is an entity that will at some point become a corpse. Thomson also reaches this conclusion within the context of her view that people are their bodies (Thomson 1997, 202–205).
12. It also ends if all my commitments are replaced, and in cases of fission and fusion. I am talking about the normal case. Generally speaking, if I am P_n, my existence ends as P_n if there is no commitment continuity leading from there to any P_{n+1}.
13. Cf. Olson 1997, 73, 78–79; Quante 2002, 57.
14. Cf. Quante 2002, 57.
15. Cf. Carter 1999; Thomson 1997, 202.
16. Cf. Quante 2002, 149.
17. For a partial defense, see the argument for the rationalist principle (Chapter 12).
18. McDowell 1996.
19. See, e.g., Evans 1982.

NOTES TO CHAPTER 7

1. As already mentioned in Chapter 3, my distinctions are related to Quante's, though there are important differences. It should be noted that many writers have emphasized the need to distinguish between different questions in the area of personal identity; see, e.g., Rorty 1976; Schechtman 1996; Velleman 2006.
2. For (1), see Taylor 1989; Erikson 1968.
3. Frankfurt 1976; Stephens and Graham 2000, 145–155; Radden 1996, 255–266; Radden 1998.
4. Cf. Frankfurt 1976; Frankfurt 1988a; Frankfurt 1988b; Frankfurt 1988c; Frankfurt 1999a; Frankfurt 1999b; Korsgaard 1996a, 100–101.
5. Saint Augustine 1961, 43.

6. St. Augustine 1961, 170.
7. St. Augustine 1961, 171.
8. St. Augustine 1961, 172.
9. St. Augustine 1961, 233–234.
10. Recall the case of the professor and the little boy from Kansas discussed in Chapter 3. In contrast to St. Augustine's case, other cases do not imply any evaluative claim to the effect that the earlier self was better or worse than the later one.
11. For a longer discussion of replacement and commitment continuity, see my unpublished manuscript "Personal Identity and Self-Transformation."
12. Not all narrative theories are self-constitution accounts and not all self-constitution approaches offer a narrative view. See Dennett 1984, 74–100; Dennett 1992; Korsgaard 1996b; Korsgaard 1999; Ricoeur 1992, 113–168; Meuter 1995; DeGrazia 2005, 77–114; Hartmann and Galert 2007, 249–271; Atkins 2008; Atkins and Mackenzie 2008; Henning 2009.
13. There is some overlap between the next few paragraphs and my discussion in Gunnarsson 2002.
14. Schechtman 1996, 73.
15. Schechtman 1996, 1–2.
16. Schechtman 1996, 73.
17. Schechtman 1996, 74.
18. Schechtman 1996, 76.
19. Schechtman 1996, 94.
20. Schechtman 1996, 94–95.
21. Schechtman 1996, 115.
22. Schechtman 1996, 117.
23. Schechtman 1996, 113–114.
24. Another not implausible candidate would be the activity involved in what Korsgaard calls "authorial psychological connectedness" (Korsgaard 1996b, 379). In explicating what makes a connection authorial, she writes that "from the practical point of view our relationship to our actions and choices is essentially *authorial*: from it, we view them as *our own*" (378). She also writes that the "beliefs and desires you have actively arrived at are more truly your own than those which have simply arisen in you" (379). She talks about a "principle or way of choosing that you regard as expressive of *yourself*" (370). In another text in a related context, she speaks of "a description under which you value yourself, a description under which you find your life to be worth living and your actions to be worth undertaking" as "a conception of your practical identity." (Korsgaard 1996a, 101). This all suggests that her notion of "authorial psychological connectedness" goes beyond just maintaining a commitment to the effect that *p*, e.g., the commitment that Reykjavík is the capital of Iceland. Rather, it seems to be concerned with maintaining and revising commitments with respect to who I really am, what makes my life worth living, and similar questions. Thus, the notion of "authorial psychological connectedness" is only able to account for the identity of personality rather than fundamental entities. However, Korsgaard herself does not draw a clear distinction between the identity of fundamental entities and the identity of personalities, and the notion of "authorial psychological connectedness" seems intended to explain both the identity of fundamental entities and the identity of personalities (see Korsgaard 1996b, 370, 378–380; Korsgaard 1999 is characterized by the same ambiguity). This makes it possible for critics like David W. Shoemaker to argue, by implicitly focusing on the identity of personality, that Parfit can respect the authorial element in personal identity just as well as Korsgaard (Shoemaker 1996).
25. Parfit 1975, 327.

26. Schechtman 2001, 100.
27. Schechtman 2001, 110–111.
28. Schechtman 2001, 106.
29. Schechtman 2001, 105–108.
30. It is therefore not surprising that authors who are sympathetic to narrative approaches—broadly understood—and who (in contrast to Schechtman in her appeal to "empathic access") think that a personality may survive radical ways of distancing oneself from earlier points in life refer to multiple personality as a possible case in which we may encounter more than one personality (see Quante 2007a, 170–175; Hartmann and Galert 2007, 259–271).
31. Cf. Quante 2007a, 172–174; DeGrazia 2005.

NOTES TO CHAPTER 8

1. However, I do not wish to claim that no theoretical progress has been made; see Braude 1995, 37–65, 93–122, 248–268. For a discussion of the more recent literature, see Chapter 13.
2. This is a pseudonym; cf. Rosenzweig 1987 on who the patient really was.
3. All parenthetical references in the main text of this chapter refer to this book.
4. The exception is an extended trip to Europe in late summer. During this time, the patient does not see Dr. Prince, and BI remains almost exclusively in control (101).
5. There are few exceptions to this (251–265).
6. Later on, Sally is also able to gain a certain degree of direct access to BIV's psychological states (435–443).
7. I ignore: BV (267), BIVa (444–448), BIVb, BIVc, BIVd, BIb, BIc, BVII, etc. (462–475).
8. I will take the liberty of referring to other works by Morton Prince. These are also representations of the attitude of the psychiatrist Dr. Prince, who appears in Prince 1906.
9. Footnote omitted.
10. When reciting this passage, I have sometimes added emphasis.
11. From Alfred Binet and Charles Féré, according to Prince 1906, 68.
12. From Hippolyte Bernheim, according to Prince 1906, 68.
13. This is my term.
14. After Pierre Janet first made *dissociation* a central concept in 1887, Prince used the concept in a research report of 1890 (Prince 1975). Prince reports on several of his experiments in this lecture, but chiefly on the latest research by such leading exponents of dissociation psychology as Pierre Janet, Alfred Binet, Edmund Gurney, Max Dessoir, William James, and Frederic W. H. Myers. The idea of a divided consciousness is used to explain phenomena such as posthypnotic suggestion, hysterical anesthesia, automatic writing, and double personality. Of course, experiments, reports, and theoretical considerations by different representatives of dissociation psychology are also discussed in Prince 1906. For an overview of the contributions made by Janet, Meyers, Binet, Dessoir, James, and Prince to dissociative psychology, see Crabtree 1993, 307–350. Concerning Gurney, see Braude 1995, 28–29; for a detailed interpretation of Janet, see Ellenberger 1970, Chapter 6. At the end of the nineteenth and beginning of the twentieth century, Boston was an important center for research in the field of abnormal psychology, and Prince was one of the main figures of the informal Boston school of abnormal psychology and psychotherapy. Several men from this circle attended the aforementioned lecture by Prince in 1890: William James, Josiah Joyce, James Jackson Putnam, and George A. Waterman (Hale

1975, 4; Prince 1975, 55–60; Rosenzweig 1987, 19). In 1912, Waterman, a psychiatrist and good friend of Prince's, married Clara Ellen Fowler, the person we know as Miss Beauchamp from Prince 1906 (Rosenzweig 1987). Boris Sidis was another exponent of dissociation psychology who belonged to this Boston circle. Together with Prince he coauthored a study on hysteria, which is discussed in Prince 1906 (152, 256, 465, 509–510); concerning Sidis, see Crabtree, 348–349. For a discussion of Prince's person and his professional scientific career and development, see Hale 1975; Rosenzweig 1987, 18–25; Leys 2000, 62n. For details of Prince's concept of dissociation, see Braude 1995, 106–112.

15. Prince 1900–1901, 480.
16. A printing mistake has slipped into Prince's diagram: Sally was first able to assume control over the body in 1898—not 1897.
17. Cf. Prince 1900–1901, 480: "component rays."
18. Prince 1900–1901, 480.
19. Also from Prince 1900–1901, 479.
20. See also the overlapping of "Miss B. Original Self" and the "Subliminal Self" in the prism diagram (Figure 8.1).
21. BII is a fusion of BI and BIV. Dr. Prince is not quite consistent on Sally's fate in this process (405, 417, 523–524).
22. Cf. also Binet 1890; Dessoir 1889.
23. This is pointed out by Leys 2000, 42.
24. Leys also makes this point, but in relation to an essay by Prince from 1920, in which Prince writes that Miss Beauchamp "like the traditional princess in the fairy story, soon married and 'lived happily ever afterward'" (Prince 1920, 135). These remarks in this late essay might be a reference to her marriage to Prince's colleague Waterman (see note 14).
25. Cf. Leys 2000, 60–63.
26. Sally frequently helps Dr. Prince to develop his theories; see also, e.g., 238–239, 328–329, 381.
27. Of course, he finds further confirmation in BII's normality and naturalness (516–520).
28. Several appendices to the study follow.
29. Since BIV does not recall these years (my comment).
30. That is, BI, since Dr. Prince sometimes refers to BI this way (my comment).
31. Cf. Velleman 2006a; Matthews 1998.
32. I do not assume that Miss Beauchamp does this all consciously. *She* does it, but she does many things *unconsciously*. For a more detailed discussion of unconscious states, see Chapter 13.
33. Cf. Velleman 2006a; Korsgaard 1996b; Korsgaard 1999; Schechtman 1996.
34. However, she also regularly says that BIV is not a "real person" (500).
35. I am using brackets for my interpolations and angle brackets for Prince's comments in order to distinguish between the two.
36. The relevant passage on p. 27 was quoted in section 2.2, and the relevant part on pp. 27–28 in the first section of this chapter.
37. As we have seen, Prince assumes that these psychological states are all conscious. However, this assumption is not part of bundle theory as such.

NOTES TO CHAPTER 9

1. For another overview, see Saks 1997, 39–63.
2. This means that certain philosophical approaches will not be discussed in this chapter. Some of these theories assume that it is not possible that two fundamental entities exist in one body; others merely say that the fulfillment

of certain conditions does not mean that more than one fundamental entity exists in one body. I merely wish to mention such theories briefly in this note. Olson explicitly rejects the coexistence thesis (Olson 2003). As a proponent of the bodily criterion of personal identity, Williams argues that the differences between the different personalities in cases of multiple personality must be understood simply as differences between the "sets of characteristics" (Williams 1973a, 18) of one and the same individual (15–18). According to Ausborn-Brinker, cases of multiple personality do not present a reason to doubt the concept of a person as a unified agent; such cases should rather be understood as *one* person who is sick (Ausborn-Brinker 1999, 273–274). Lizza says that he agrees with Morton Prince that for psychological, biological, and physiological reasons a multiple patient should be regarded as *one* ill individual (Lizza 1993, 268–272). According to Brown, an indirect argument supporting biological or Aristotelian accounts of personal identity is that such accounts can employ narrative approaches to interpret the different personalities of a multiple patient as narrative abstractions (Brown 2001, 442–446). Sinnott-Armstrong and Behnke are sympathetic to the brain criterion, which means that, assuming that only one brain exists, we do not have more than one fundamental entity (Sinnott-Armstrong and Behnke 2000, 308–310). However, they don't want to commit themselves to this criterion and propose a sufficient condition for personal identity involving "convergent memory chains" (313). They believe that this condition is fulfilled in all actual cases of multiple personality disorder, which means that these are all cases of only one person (313–314; see section 12.2). Kennett and Matthews do not want to rule out the possibility that the early cases of multiple personality in the nineteenth century, in which two complex characters existed in one body, were cases of two fundamental entities in one body (Kennett and Matthews 2003, 33, 47; Matthews 2003a, 170–172). However, their focus is on showing that the recent cases, in which very many and highly fragmentary personalities exist, are better explained as delusions and disturbances of the autobiographical memory of a single person; see also Matthews 1998, 77–86, and Matthews 2003b.

3. I do not mean to suggest that all of the theorists discussed aim to offer criteria for the existence of more than one fundamental entity in one body. Thus, some of these theorists might be happy to embrace my arguments. However, I am not interested in refuting any of these theories. I merely want to show that they are not suitable for specifying criteria for the existence of more than one fundamental entity in one body.
4. In my discussion of Radden, all page references in parentheses refer to Radden 1996.
5. From Radden's positive discussion of Hume and Parfit we can conclude that she would interpret the issue of the presence of more than one fundamental entity in a body as an issue of the presence of more than one self. Like Parfit, Radden leaves no room for understanding fundamental entities other than as bundles of psychological characteristics (183–192). However, since Radden does not directly discuss the issues in terms of fundamental entities, the interpretation of her text must remain open on this point (cf. Radden 2004).
6. But she also says that conditions 1, 2, and 4 should be understood as "criteria," not as "necessary and sufficient conditions," whereas 3 is a necessary condition (43). I would like to leave aside the question of how Radden's remarks should be understood here.
7. Radden also assumes that individuals suffering from dissociative identity disorder fulfill the four conditions, but only when the fourth condition is inter-

preted as allowing for a certain awareness by the selves of the other selves (46–54).

8. Even though Radden thinks that the case of Jekyll and Hyde is paradigmatic, she notes that Dr. Jekyll is not certain whether he should regard himself as "a unity or a duality." She writes: "Stevenson teases his readers with this question without answering it" (44).
9. Stevenson 1979, 81.
10. Such a distinction is commonly made. For example, Kennett and Matthews (Kennett and Matthews 2003, 43–44) do so to make a similar point.
11. Cf. Radden 1996, 241–254.
12. Radden doubts, however, that two selves can be *simultaneously* present in one body as *two centers of awareness* (46, 241–266; Radden 1998).
13. She makes this remark in a positive discussion of Parfit. Drawing on Parfit's account of diachronic identity as a matter of degree, Radden suggests that there is no "absolute or binding" answer to the question how much personalities like Dr. Jekyll and Mr. Hyde must share for them to count as an aspect of the same self (191–192).
14. Mackie (1985) offers an interesting account of multiple personality and the individuation of persons in terms of responsibility and the appropriateness of punishment, though it is an unsatisfactory approach to the individuation of fundamental entities.
15. Cf. Dennett 1989, 168–172; Humphrey and Dennett 1989, 75–82.
16. Dennett 1992, 105.
17. Dennett 1992, 107.
18. Dennett 1992, 108.
19. Dennett 1992, 108.
20. Dennett 1992, 111. This quotation is misleading insofar that, in other writings, Dennett assumes that not all cases of multiple personality disorder are generated in therapy (Humphrey and Dennett 1989, 90–92).
21. Cf. Humphrey and Dennett 1989, 75–82; Dennett 1992, 108–115.
22. For criticism relevant in this context, see Braude 1995, 164–187; Velleman 2006a.
23. That the human being has created more than one fictional self is also the core of his and Humphrey's five conditions, which hold if multiple personality disorder is "real" (Humphrey and Dennett 1989, 83–84).
24. Hardcastle and Flanagan 1999, 650.
25. Cf. Flanagan 1992, 177–192, 200–204; Hardcastle and Flanagan 1999, 649–650.
26. Cf. Flanagan 1992, 201; Flanagan 1994, 141–142.
27. Cf. Flanagan 1992, 203–204; Flanagan 1994, 135–137, 142–143, 153–155; Hardcastle and Flanagan 1999, 650–655.
28. Flanagan wants to distance himself from Dennett's view that selves are fictional and unreal (Flanagan 1992, 204–211; Flanagan 1994, 143–145; Hardcastle and Flanagan 1999, 650–651). Graham argues that, to explain multiple personality, we need not choose between the assumption of *a real self* that is psychologically disturbed and the assumption of *several fictional* selves (Graham 1999; see also Graham 2002, 118–126). Instead, we could assume *several real* selves whose *boundaries*, however, are fundamentally vague.
29. By this I do not mean to say that Flanagan himself is interested in distinguishing between different fundamental entities in one body. He distinguishes at various points between the identity issue, which concerns him, and "personal identity proper," which "can be grounded in the thinnest thread of biological or psychological continuity" (Flanagan 1994, 138); see also Flanagan 1994,

157n3, 159; Flanagan 1992, 193, 197–198. Although Tye does not defend a narrative account, he is probably subject to the same criticism: he seems to understand the "psychological frameworks" that he thinks serve to individuate persons in such a way that it cannot be excluded that one fundamental entity has more than one psychological framework (Tye 2003, 138–141, 151–152).

30. Dennett 1991, 427.
31. Hardcastle and Flanagan 1999, 649; see also Flanagan 1992, 195: " . . . one's model of one's self, or as I shall say for simplicity, *the self*."
32. Metzinger 2003, 525; cf. Metzinger 1999, 190; Metzinger 1997.
33. A similar criticism applies to Boden 1994.
34. See also the discussion of narrative theories in section 7.2.
35. The parenthetical references in the discussion of Wilkes refer to Wilkes 1988.
36. This does not mean that the arguments speak for the presence of several "selves," since Wilkes considers the notion of self philosophically useless (Wilkes 1991).
37. Dennett formulates his conditions in Dennett 1976.
38. Nor does it settle question 5. Sinnott-Armstrong and Behnke argue along the same lines against arguments like that of Wilkes (Sinnott-Armstrong and Behnke 2000, 306–307).
39. Cf. Braude 1995, 88–89. I adopt Braude's terminology in order to maintain unified terminology in the research literature. However, since I do not want to adopt his notion of an "*apperceptive center*," my use of the terms is slightly different from his. Still, the terms aim to capture the same facts.
40. This of course is not her terminology, but the terminology refers to the facts she is talking about. Co-activity also plays a role in Wilkes, but since being co-sensory presupposes co-activity, this will not be taken up separately.
41. In addressing individuation, Anderson (1976), like Wilkes, takes the conditions of personhood as a starting point, but also explicitly specifies an additional condition meant to demonstrate the presence of more than one person. This additional condition fails because it can be just as easily fulfilled by one fundamental entity dividing its attention as by two fundamental entities.
42. All parenthetical references in this section refer to Rovane 1998. For a critical discussion of Rovane 1998, see Whiting 2005.
43. For other examples and ways of describing her view, see Rovane 2002, 2004a, 2004b.
44. From the point of view of the objective theory of practical reason, this would hold at least for all the attitudes that the person regards as well founded.
45. For an account of what makes an attitude *mine*, see the rationalist principle defended in section 12.1.
46. Rovane also discusses holistic reasons for doubting that such sharing is possible (207–208).
47. Rovane also defends an "*ethical criterion of personhood*" (72) and thinks that her philosopher, musician, and teacher "each would . . . satisfy the ethical criterion of personhood" (177). As shown in the discussion of Wilkes, the conditions of personhood cannot be assumed to individuate persons. The same criticism applies to Matthews (2003a, 170–172).
48. All parenthetical references in this section refer to this work.
49. This of course goes further than that the states of the others are not autobiographical or not indexical for Sally. This could also be the case if Sally had no beliefs or experiences of the states of the others. To express this difference as it relates to beliefs, Braude introduces the terms "non-referential" and "extra-referential" (82).

50. Cf. also Braude 2003; for his views on diachronic personal identity, see Braude 2005.
51. This is confirmed in another publication by Braude: "But I never claimed that this unifying subject meets *any* criteria of personhood" (Braude 2003, 156).
52. "If identity is a matter of fact, it must be a matter of nonmaterial fact" (Clark 2003, 159).
53. Cf. Clark 1991, 224–233; Clark 1996.
54. Baker (2000) defends a non-empirical account of *diachronic* identity, but different fundamental entities are *individuated* by their body (107–108, 132). Since Clark makes no such distinction in these texts, we may assume that he does not rule out this possibility.

NOTES TO CHAPTER 10

1. Cf. Olson 1997, 1–2.
2. Olson 1997, 7–9, 16–18; DeGrazia 2005, 142–149.
3. Wiggins 1976, 158–168; Whiting 2002, 208–209.
4. I will henceforth use the word "organ" to denote *biological organs* rather than something that has no biological structure but fulfills the same function as a biological organ.
5. For a discussion of this issue, see Rosenberg 1998, 141–144; Quante 2002, 152–155.
6. Olson 1997, 131–140.
7. Cf. Baker 2000, 107–108; Quante 2002, 78–79; DeGrazia 2005, 56–57.
8. Based on my information about the real case, this is indeed true, but that is not the point. Although this is a real case, I can make that assumption for the sake of the point I am making.
9. Conjoined twins usually understand themselves as two fundamental entities; cf. Smith 1988, 18–82.
10. I am assuming that it is not a problem to account for the diachronic identity of each of the twins, though each of them has periods of unconsciousness; see the discussion of coma in section 5.1.
11. Given that this is no longer the real case, I am calling the twins "A." and "B."
12. (V) is also meant to be different from (I) in that in (V) the organism is normal in all respects: in this case there is not just one brain, but also one heart, one spinal cord, etc.
13. Cf. Karlsson 2002.
14. I say "intentional *human* action" merely to avoid complications about possible actions performed by entities such as corporations that are larger than humans.
15. I said that my arguments were applicable to other criteria for the individuation of a human organism offered by the vegetative approach. Let me give one example: if human beings are individuated by the number of hearts they have—as tentatively proposed by Barilan (Barilan 2002, 602–603)—then the same paradox arises; see also Barilan 2003.
16. The difference between passive states and active attitudes is that I am minimally responsible for the latter but not the former (see section 12.1).
17. The answers to the two objections about memory show that, without begging the question against the coexistence thesis, Olson is not entitled to say that Odd remembers Even's actions without being able to express that she remembers them (cf. Olson 2003, 344). Odd and Even are, roughly speaking, my PX and PY.

NOTES TO CHAPTER 11

1. This sort of solution is also favored by Tye 2003, 142–143.
2. These are two "vertical" organic unities between the mental and the vegetative functions. This does not answer the question of how to describe the "horizontal" relationship between the two organic unities: although two fundamental entities exist here, are these two fundamental entities two organisms or part of one organism? The problem is illustrated by conjoined twins: even if each of them is "vertically" an organic unity, this does not settle the question of whether they are two organisms or parts of one organism—even if we assume that they are two fundamental entities.
3. This undermines Olson's criticism of the coexistence thesis because Olson only considers the possibility that Odd and Even have different parts in the narrow sense (Olson 2003, 342–343). As I said in the last chapter, Odd and Even are, roughly speaking, PX and PY.
4. Wiggins 1997, 5.
5. Wiggins 1997, 8.
6. This claim is supposed to have a "Strawsonian" ring to it; cf. Strawson 1966, 97–112, 162–170; Evans 1982, Chapter 7; McDowell 1996, 99–104; Cassam 1997, 35–40; Slors 1998. I do not take a stand on this claim.
7. This is also meant to sound like a "Strawsonian" claim. Again, I do not evaluate this claim here.
8. Merleau-Ponty 1962, 105.
9. Merleau-Ponty 1962, 121–122.
10. Merleau-Ponty 1962, 162.
11. Merleau-Ponty 1962, 159.
12. Cf. Kelly 2001, 77–89.
13. Merleau-Ponty 1962, 107.
14. Cf. Brewer 1995.
15. Baker 2000, 108.

NOTES TO CHAPTER 12

1. I am only talking about personal rather than sub-personal states.
2. Thus the ownership question cannot be identified with Schechtman's (1996) characterization question; cf. Chapter 7. Note that "Frankfurtean" identification with a mental state cannot explain why it is *my* mental state. Such identification already assumes that a mental state is mine in the sense to be explained here.
3. By speaking here of an empiricist and, later, a rational answer, I intend for this terminology to echo the difference between the empiricist and rationalist traditions in modern philosophy.
4. Remember that when I speak of mental states, I am excluding *sub-personal* processes.
5. This is not intended as an analysis of our everyday concepts of perceptions and desires. Rather, I just need some terms for the three categories into which I am assuming passive states fall: 1) perceptions, 2) desires, 3) feelings or sensations.
6. Cf. Sinnott-Armstrong and Behnke 2000, 310.
7. Perhaps they believe that it would be sufficient not to have the same body, but only the same brain (Armstrong and Behnke 2000, 308–309, 313).
8. Cf. Armstrong and Behnke 2000, 312–314. They write at one point that it belongs to the sufficient conditions that nobody else has ever had an experi-

ential memory that is phenomenologically the same as the memories of A and B (313–314).

9. They seem to assume that such a memory exists if it would be present after therapy (Armstrong and Behnke 2000, 313).
10. Cf. Matthews 2003b, 147–148. It should be noted, though, that his criticism is not quite fair because he describes a situation in which it is not the case that one and the same body exists over the relevant span of time.
11. Cf. Shoemaker 1984, 94–97.
12. Cf. Parfit 1987, 207.
13. Cf. Braude 1995 and Braude 2002.

NOTES TO CHAPTER 13

1. The screaming and pain is surely meant to come from memories of traumatic experiences. Like almost everyone who employs dissociative identity disorder as a valid psychiatric diagnosis, Alderman and Marshall believe that this disorder is caused by traumatic childhood experiences, especially sexual abuse (40–47); cf. Putnam 1989, 45–54; Ross 1994, vii–viii; Huber 1995, 18–19, 51–55; Ross 1997, 61–66. As I said in Chapter 2, I do not take a stand on the validity of this diagnosis or the causal explanation, but it is a fact that many children are subject to terrible abuse.
2. That "multiples" speak in the we-form is also reported by those who take a skeptical stance toward the diagnosis (cf. Stübner, Völkl, and Soyka 1998, 443).
3. We are of course familiar with this manner of speaking from Sally's understanding of herself (Chapters 2 and 8) and from the quotations from the biography *Sybil* at the beginning of Chapter 2 (also in the notes). There are direct self-reports in many sources, such as autobiographies like West 1999, 104–105, 110–116 (more on this later), and documentary films like Krausz 2001. This film reported chiefly on two cases and interviewed those affected. One of these individuals—Willi—described his situation on camera as follows: "For us it is such that Willi is, as it were, a concept for the organization of all the persons residing in this body. And, in that sense, it also has an identity. There is thus a 'Willi' identity for us as well. In the sense of: it is the boat in which we all swim. But we don't have an identity in the sense that there is one person here" (my translation). But not only researchers in favor of employing dissociative identity disorder as a diagnosis report such inner viewpoints of patients (cf. Erkwoh 1996, 552–553). In contrast to Alderman and Marshall, many psychologists and psychiatrists working with the diagnosis of dissociative identity disorder warn against taking this inner viewpoint of the patient as the correct one. At the same time, they confirm that this is often the inner viewpoint; cf. Putnam 1989, 103, and Ross 1997, 144–145; Huber 1995, 19–20; Gast 2003, 36.
4. Several sources mention that multiples hear voices; cf. Putnam 1989, 62; Huber 1995, 118–120; Ross 1997, 129–130. The autobiography West 1999 is a detailed source for the inner description of such inner voices. Before he links voices to inner persons, West reports on hearing inner voices or on speaking without it being his voices (41–44, 47–48, 69–70). Later the voices are connected partly to individual inner persons and entire inner dialogues are reproduced (87, 90, 131, 143–144, 150, 168, 216–217, 255, 300). Like *Amongst Ourselves*, which recommends imagining an inner and safe room in which the alters are secure and can communicate among themselves (160–161), West's psychotherapist recommends that he create a room in his mind

("the Comfort Room") to serve as a place of gatherings and security. This he does (159, 211, 215, 217, 239, 265–266, 300).

5. Alters are often classified into different possible types according to their various characteristics and functions; see Alderman and Marshall 1998, 27–32; Putnam 1989, 106–114; Ross 1997, 144–156.
6. West 1999 (1–3, 104–105, 257–258) describes how actions and surroundings are perceived from the perspective of different persons.
7. These criteria were cited in section 2.2.
8. Alderman and Marshall draw on DSM-IV. The official commentary on DSM-IV (Frances, First, and Pincus 1995) states that the change in the formulation of the first criteria for dissociative identity disorder between DSM-IV and DSM-III-R—the forerunner of DSM-IV—was meant to help "reduce reification" (305). For a commentary on this reformulation, the debate over it, and the renaming of multiple personality disorder to dissociative identity disorder, see Hacking 1995, 16–20.
9. However, many therapists working with the diagnosis of dissociative identity disorder make no such assumptions. Ross even says that it is *impossible* that more than one person really exists in one body (Ross 1997, 62; Ross 1994, ix). If I am right, Ross is mistaken on this point.
10. Cf. Braude 1995, 70–92.
11. I think that Radden defends the same thesis, although she does not employ the terminology of fundamental entities; cf. Radden 1996, 255–266; Radden 1998.
12. See also the argument for the rationalist principle (Chapter 12).
13. Cf. Moran 1997, 145–146, 151–152; Moran 2001, 60–86.
14. Cf. Rey 1988, 276; Moran 1997, 152; Moran 2001, 31; Finkelstein 1999, 80–81.
15. For a discussion of the difference between the concept of dissociation and other concepts such as that of the unconscious, see Braude 1995, 93–106, 112–116, 120–122.
16. Gunnarsson 2005.
17. Finkelstein 1999, 93; cf. 91–97.
18. Cf. Finkelstein 1999, 97.
19. In Gunnarsson 2005, I say more about unconscious *emotions*.
20. Moran 2001 has strongly influenced my discussion of unconscious states not only in this paragraph, but also more generally. However, as discussed in Gunnarsson 2005, Moran shares the assumption by Finkelstein that I argue against here and, in more detail, in this article.
21. Communication, including inner communication, is generally recommended as part of therapy; see Putnam 1989, 152–158; Ross 1997, 319–323. See also note 4 on the inner dialogues in West 1999.

NOTES TO CHAPTER 14

1. In Gast 2003 (36) a film poster with Anthony Perkins as Norman Bates is reproduced along with a comment—perhaps added by the editors of the magazine rather than Gast herself—that interprets Bates as a multiple personality.
2. Cf. Hitchcock 1960.
3. Schmid 1996, 30–31 (my emphasis); see 27–32. Beginning with the 1925 edition of Otto Rank's classic *Der Doppelgänger* (Rank 1925), Schmid summarizes works on the doppelganger motif extending up to 1990 (20–26).
4. Forderer 1999, 17–18 (my emphasis and translation). Webber's aim is not to offer a "definitive model" of the doppelganger but only "a working defini-

tion," initially formulated in nine premises (Webber 1996, 2–5). The first and third premises reveal that the doppelganger motif involves the identity of a *single subject.*

5. The novel was filmed by director David Fincher in 1999. Since the film differs from the book on a few important points, I will deal exclusively with the novel. All parenthetical references are to the novel.
6. Here I freely follow the five interpretive approaches that Schmid uses for English stories of the double between 1764–1910: the "Existential-Philosophical Approach," the "Socio-Psychological Approach," the "Moral-Allegorical Approach," the "Psychoanalytical Approach," and the "Psychiatric Approach." I will not address the extent to which my interpretative models coincide with her approaches.
7. I have formulated this in quite general terms so as to make this interpretive model fit different doppelganger stories. For instance, I have used the phrase "a new self that opposes society or is strong enough to gain power in society" in order to do justice to such different tales as Shelley's *Frankenstein* and Dostoyevsky's *The Double* (Shelley 1998; Dostoyevsky 2007). Whereas Frankenstein's monster is even more marginalized from society than he is himself, Dostoyevsky's protagonist invents a doppelganger who is a match for the demands of modern society on which the protagonist is doomed to founder. On *Frankenstein*, see Schmid 1996, 97–103; on *The Double*, see Forderer 1999, 109–113, 118–127; and Miller 1985, 132–136.
8. The inner conflict is for instance clear in the protagonist's behavior toward his boss (cf. 69, 96, 98, 126, 186).
9. Cf. the interpretation of Wilde 1949 in Schmid 1996, 142–145.
10. See Schmid 1996.
11. There are many other homoerotic connotations (11, 14, 32–33, 89, 182).
12. The protagonist's perspective is not this simple. More on this later.
13. Tyler's status is reflected in the protagonist's repeated assertions that he is not Tyler (174, 188, 196–197). And with respect to the question of the assignment of the responsibility for Tyler's actions, he is also inconsistent (193, 195, 196). As Schmid 1996 (192–200) shows, such ambivalences are also present in "Henry Jekyll's Full Statement of the Case" in Stevenson 1979.

Bibliography

Acocella, Joan. 1999. *Creating Hysteria: Women and Multiple Personality Disorder.* San Francisco: Jossey-Bass Publishers.

Alderman, Tracy, and Karen Marshall. 1998. *Amongst Ourselves: A Self-Help Guide to Living with Dissociative Identity Disorder.* Oakland, CA: New Harbinger Publications.

American Psychiatric Association. 2000. *Diagnostic and Statistical Manual of Mental Disorders, Fourth Edition, Text Revision* (DSM-IV-TR). Washington, DC: American Psychiatric Association.

Anderson, Susan Leigh. 1976. "Coconsciousness and Numerical Identity of the Person." *Philosophical Studies* 30: 1–10.

Atkins, Kim. 2008. *Narrative Identity and Moral Identity: A Practical Perspective.* New York: Routledge.

Atkins, Kim, and Catriona Mackenzie, eds. 2008. *Practical Identity and Normative Agency.* New York: Routledge.

Ausborn-Brinker, Sandra. 1999. *Person und Personalität: Versuch einer Begriffsklärung.* Tübingen, Germany: Mohr Siebeck.

Baker, Lynne Rudder. 1999. "What Am I?" *Philosophy and Phenomenological Research* 59 : 151–159.

———. 2000. *Persons and Bodies: A Constitution View.* Cambridge: Cambridge University Press.

Barilan, Y. Michael. 2002. "Head-Counting vs. Heart-Counting: An Examination of the Recent Case of the Conjoined Twins from Malta." *Perspectives in Biology and Medicine* 45: 593–603.

———. 2003. "One or Two: An Examination of the Recent Case of the Conjoined Twins from Malta." *Journal of Medicine and Philosophy* 28: 27–44.

Beta, Katharina. 2001. *Katharsis: Aus dem Wasser geboren.* Munich: Ullstein Verlag.

Binet, Alfred. 1889–1890. *On Double Consciousness: Experimental Psychological Studies.* Chicago: Open Court.

Blackburn, Simon. 1997. "Has Kant Refuted Parfit?" In *Reading Parfit*, edited by Jonathan Dancy. Oxford: Blackwell Publishers.

Boden, Margaret A. 1994. "Multiple Personality and Computational Models." In *Philosophy, Psychology and Psychiatry*, edited by A. Phillips Griffiths. The Royal Institute of Philosophy Supplement 37. Cambridge: Cambridge University Press.

Braude, Stephen E. 1995. *First Person Plural: Multiple Personality and the Philosophy of Mind.* Revised edition. Lanham, MD: Rowman & Littlefield Publishers.

———. 2002. "The Creativity of Dissociation." *Journal of Trauma & Dissociation* 3: 5–26.

———. 2003. "Counting Persons and Living with Alters." *Philosophy, Psychiatry and Psychology* 10: 153–156.
———. 2005. "Personal Identity and Postmortem Survival." *Social Philosophy and Policy* 22: 226–249.
Brewer, Bill. 1995. "Bodily Awareness and the Self." In *The Body and the Self*, edited by José Luis Bermúdez, Anthony Marcel, and Naomi Eilan. Cambridge, MA: MIT Press.
Brown, M. 2001. "Multiple Personality and Personal Identity." *Philosophical Psychology* 13: 435–447.
Carter, W. R. 1999. "Will I Be a Dead Person?" *Philosophy and Phenomenological Research* 59: 167–171.
Cassam, Quassim. 1997. *Self and World*. Oxford: Clarendon Press.
Cather, Willa. 1990. *The Professor's House*. New York: Vintage Books.
Clark, Stephen R. L. 1991. "How Many Selves Make Me?" In *Human Beings*, edited by David Cockburn. Cambridge: Cambridge University Press.
———. 1996. "Minds, Memes, and Multiples." *Philosophy, Psychiatry and Psychology* 3: 21–28.
———. 2003. "Constructing Persons: The Psychopathology of Identity." *Philosophy, Psychiatry and Psychology* 10: 157–160.
Crabtree, Adam. 1993. *From Mesmer to Freud: Magnetic Sleep and the Roots of Psychological Healing*. New Haven, CT: Yale University Press.
Dainton, Barry. 2008. *The Phenomenal Self*. Oxford: Oxford University Press.
DeGrazia, David. 2005. *Human Identity and Bioethics*. Cambridge: Cambridge University Press.
Dennett, Daniel C. 1976. "Conditions of Personhood." In *The Identities of Persons*, edited by Amélie Oksenberg Rorty. Berkeley and Los Angeles: University of California Press.
———. 1984. *The Elbow Room: The Varieties of Free Will Worth Wanting*. Cambridge, MA: MIT Press.
———. 1989. "The Origins of Selves." *Cogito* 2: 163–173.
———. 1991. *Consciousness Explained*. Boston: Little Brown
———. 1992. "The Self as the Center of Narrative Gravity." In *Self and Consciousness: Multiple Perspectives*, edited by F. Kessel et al. Hillsdale, NJ: Lawrence Erlbaum Associates.
Dessoir, Max. 1889. *Das Doppel-Ich*. Schriften der Gesellschaft für Experimental-Psychologie zu Berlin.
Deutsch, Harry. 2007. "Relative Identity." In *The Stanford Encyclopedia of Philosophy*. First published April 22, 2002, last substantive revision November 5, 2007. http://plato.stanford.edu/entries/identity-relative/ (accessed July 25, 2008).
Dostoyevsky, Fyodor. 2007. *The Double*. In *The Double and the Gambler* by Dostoyevsky. Translated by Richard Pevear and Larissa Volokhonsky. New York: Vintage Random House.
Ellenberger, Henri F. 1970. *The Discovery of the Unconscious: The History and Evolution of Dynamic Psychiatry*. New York: Basic Books.
Erikson, Erik H. 1968. *Identity: Youth and Crisis*. New York: W. W. Norton & Company.
Erkwoh, R. 1996. "Über leiblich erfahrene Ich-Störungen." *Der Nervenarzt* 67: 552–557.
Evans, Gareth. 1982. *The Varieties of Reference*, edited by John McDowell. Oxford: Clarendon Press.
Finkelstein, David. 1999. "On the Distinction between Conscious and Unconscious States of Mind." *American Philosophical Quarterly* 36: 79–100.

Flanagan, Owen. 1992. *Consciousness Reconsidered.* Cambridge, MA: MIT Press.

———. 1994. "Multiple Identity, Character Transformation, and Self-Reclamation." In *Philosophical Psychopathology*, edited by George Graham and G. Lynn Stephens. Cambridge, MA: MIT Press.

Forderer, Christof. 1999. *Ich-Eklipsen: Doppelgänger in der Literatur seit 1800.* Stuttgart: Metzler.

Frances, Allen, Michael B. First, and Harold Alan Pincus. 1995. *DSM-IV Guidebook.* Washington, DC: American Psychiatric Press.

Frankfurt, Harry G. 1976. "Identification and Externality." In *The Identities of Persons,* edited by Amélie Oksenberg Rorty. Berkeley and Los Angeles: University of California Press. Reprinted in Frankfurt. 1988. *The Importance of What We Care About.*

———. 1988. *The Importance of What We Care About: Philosophical Essays.* Cambridge: Cambridge University Press.

———. 1988a. "Freedom of the Will and the Concept of a Person." In Frankfurt 1988.

———. 1988b. "The Importance of What We Care About." In Frankfurt 1988.

———. 1988c. "Identification and Wholeheartedness." In Frankfurt 1988.

———. 1999a. "The Faintest Passion." In *Necessity, Volition, and Love* by Frankfurt. Cambridge: Cambridge University Press.

———. 1999b. "Autonomy, Necessity, and Love." In *Necessity, Volition, and Love* by Frankfurt. Cambridge: Cambridge University Press.

Frisch, Max. 2006. *I'm Not Stiller.* Translated by Michael Bullock. Rochester: Dalkey Archive Press.

Gast, Ursula. 2003. "Das bin ich nicht: Überleben in anderer Identität." *Gehirn und Geist: Das Magazin für Psychologie und Hirnforschung* 4: 34–38.

Geach, Peter. 1967–68. "Identity." *Review of Metaphysics* 21: 3–12.

Gillitzer, Berthold. 2001. *Personen, Menschen und ihre Identität.* Suttgart: Kohlhammer.

Graham, George. 1999. "Fuzzy Fault Lines: Selves in Multiple Personality Disorder." *Philosophical Explorations* 2: 159–174.

———. 2002. "Recent Work in Philosophical Psychopathology." *American Philosophical Quarterly* 39: 109–134.

Grice, H. P. 1941. "Personal Identity." *Mind* 50: 330–350.

Gunnarsson, Logi. 2002. "What Is Constituted in Self-Constitution?" In *Persons: An Interdisciplinary Approach*, edited by Christian Kanzian, Josef Quitterer, and Edmund Runggaldier. *Papers of the 25th International Wittgenstein Symposium* 10: 76–78.

———. 2005. "Trapped in a 'Secret Cellar': Breaking the Spell of a Picture of Unconscious States." *Philosophical Investigations* 28: 273–289.

———. 2008a. "The Great Apes and the Severely Disabled: Moral Status and Thick Evaluative Concepts." *Ethical Theory and Moral Practice* 11: 305–326.

———. 2008b. "Festlegungstheorie zur Frage personaler Identität." *Deutsche Zeitschrift für Philosophie* 56: 535-553.

———. 2009. "Sharing My Body." *Sats: Nordic Journal of Philosophy* 10.

Hacking, Ian. 1995. *Rewriting the Soul: Multiple Personality and the Sciences of Memory.* Princeton, NJ: Princeton University Press.

Hale, Nathan G., Jr. 1975. "Introduction." In *Psychotherapy and Multiple Personality: Selected Essays* by Morton Prince. Edited by Nathan G. Hale, Jr. Cambridge. MA: Harvard University Press.

Hardcastle, Valerie Gray, and Owen Flanagan. 1999. "Multiplex vs. Multiple Selves: Distinguishing Dissociative Disorders." *The Monist* 82: 645–657.

Hartmann, Dirk, and Thorsten Galert (principle authors). 2007. "Person, Personal Identity, and Personality." In *Intervening in the Brain: Changing Psyche and Society,* edited by R. Merkel, G. Boer, J. Fegert, T. Galert, D. Hartmann, B. Nuttin, and S. Rosahl. Berlin: Springer.

Henning, Tim. 2009. *Person sein und Geschichten erzählen: Eine Studie über personale Autonomie und narrative Gründe.* Berlin: W. de Gruyter.

Herrmann, Martina. 1995. *Identität und Moral: Zur Zuständigkeit von Personen für ihre Vergangenheit.* Berlin: Akademie Verlag.

Hitchcock, Alfred. 1960. *Psycho.* Universal Studios.

Huber, Michaela. 1995. *Multiple Persönlichkeiten: Überlebende extremer Gewalt: Ein Handbuch.* Frankfurt/Main: Fischer.

Hume, David. 1978. *A Treatise of Human Nature*, edited by L. A. Selby-Bigge and P. H. Nidditch. Oxford: Oxford University Press.

Humphrey, Nicholas, and Daniel C. Dennett. 1989. "Speaking for Ourselves: An Assessment of Multiple Personality Disorder." *Raritan* 9: 68–98. Reprinted in D. Kolak and R. Martin, eds. 1990. *Self and Identity.* New York: Macmillan.

Johnston, Mark. 1987. "Human Beings." *Journal of Philosophy* 84: 59–83.

———. 1989. "Fission and the Facts." *Philosophical Perspectives* 3: 85–102.

Kant, Immanuel. 1968. *Critique of Pure Reason.* Translated by Norman Kemp Smith. New York: St. Martin's.

Karlsson, Mikael M. 2002. "Agency and Patiency: Back to Nature?" *Philosophical Explorations* 5: 59–81.

Kelly, Sean D. 2001. *The Relevance of Phenomenology to the Philosophy of Language and Mind.* New York: Garland Publishing.

Kennett, Jeanette, and Steve Matthews. 2003. "Delusion, Dissociation and Identity." *Philosophical Explorations* 6: 31–49.

Keyes, Daniel. 1981. *The Minds of Billy Milligan.* New York: Bantam Books.

Korsgaard, Christine M. 1996a. *The Sources of Normativity.* Cambridge: Cambridge University Press

———. 1996b. "Personal Identity and the Unity of Agency: A Kantian Response to Parfit." In *Creating the Kingdom of Ends* by Korsgaard. Cambridge: Cambridge University Press.

———. 1999. "Self-Constitution in the Ethics of Plato and Kant." *The Journal of Ethics* 3: 1–29.

Krausz, Rosvita. 2001. *Ich bin so Viele: Aus dem Leben multipler Persönlichkeiten.* Television documentary, first aired in the series *37 Grad* by the German broadcast company ZDF on July 3, 2001.

Lewis, David. 1976. "Survival and Identity." In *The Identities of Persons*, edited by Amélie Oksenberg Rorty. Berkeley: University of California Press.

Leys, Ruth. 2000. *Trauma: A Genealogy.* Chicago: University of Chicago Press.

Lizza, John P. 1993. "Multiple Personality and Personal Identity Revisited." *The British Journal for the Philosophy of Science* 44: 263–274.

Locke, John. 1975. *An Essay Concerning Human Understanding*, edited by Peter H. Nidditch. Oxford: Oxford University Press.

Lowe, E. J. 2002. "Material Coincidence and the Cinematographic Fallacy: A Response to Olson." *Philosophical Quarterly* 52: 369–372.

Mackie, J. L. 1985. "Multiple Personality." In *Persons and Values*, edited by Joan Mackie and Penelope Mackie. Oxford: Clarendon Press.

Madell, Geoffrey. 1991. "Personal Identity and the Idea of a Human Being." In *Human Beings*, edited by David Cockburn. Cambridge: Cambridge University Press.

Martin, Raymond, and John Barresi. 1999. *Naturalization of the Soul: Self and Personal Identity in the Eighteenth Century.* London: Routledge.

———. 2006. *The Rise and Fall of Soul and Self: An Intellectual History of Personal Identity*. New York: Columbia University Press.

Matthews, Steve. 1998. "Personal Identity, Multiple Personality Disorder, and Moral Personhood." *Philosophical Psychology* 11: 67–88.

———. 2003a. "Blaming Agents and Excusing Persons: The Case of DID." *Philosophy, Psychiatry and Psychology* 10: 169–174.

———. 2003b. "Establishing Personal Identity in Cases of DID." *Philosophy, Psychiatry and Psychology* 10: 143–151.

McDowell, John. 1996. *Mind and World: With a New Introduction*. Cambridge, MA: Harvard University Press.

Merleau-Ponty, Maurice. 1962. *Phenomenology of Perception*. Translated by Colin Smith. London: Routledge.

Merricks, Trenton. 2001. *Objects and Persons*. Oxford: Oxford University Press.

Metzinger, Thomas. 1997. "Ich-Störungen als pathologische Formen mentaler Selbstmodellierung." In *Neuropsychiatrie und Neurophilosophie*, edited by G. Northhoff. Paderborn, Germany: Mentis.

———. 1999. *Subjekt und Selbstmodell: Die Perspektivität phänomenalen Bewußsteins vor dem Hintergrund einer naturalistischen Theorie mentaler Repräsentation*. 2nd revised edition. Paderborn, Germany: Mentis.

———. 2003. *Being No One: The Self-Model Theory of Subjectivity*. Cambridge, MA: MIT Press.

Meuter, Norbert. 1995. *Narrative Identität: Das Problem der personalen Identität im Anschluss an Ernst Tugendhat, Niklas Luhmann und Paul Ricoeur*. Stuttgart: Metzler/Poeschel.

Miller, Karl. 1985. *Doubles: Studies in Literary History*. Oxford: Oxford University Press.

Moran, Richard. 1997. "Self-Knowledge: Discovery, Resolution, and Undoing." *European Journal of Philosophy* 5: 141–161.

———. 2001. *Authority and Estrangement: An Essay on Self-Knowledge*. Princeton, NJ: Princeton University Press.

Nagel, Thomas. 1986. *The View from Nowhere*. New York: Oxford University Press.

Nida-Rümelin, Martine. 2003. "My Future Body." In *Persons: An Interdisciplinary Approach*. Proceedings of the 25th International Wittgenstein Symposium, edited by Christian Kanzian, Josef Quitterer, and Edmund Runggaldier. Vienna: öbv & hpt Verlagsgesellschaft. *Proceedings of the 25th International Wittgenstein Symposium*: 260-270.

———. 2006. *Der Blick von innen: Zur transtemporalen Identität bewusstseinsfähiger Wesen*. Frankfurt/Main: Suhrkamp.

———. 2008. "Transtemporale Identität bewusstseinsfähiger Wesen." *Deutsche Zeitschrift für Philosophie* 56: 513-534.

Noonan, Harold W. 1989. *Personal Identity*. London: Routledge.

North, Carol S. et al. 1993. *Multiple Personalities, Multiple Disorders: Psychiatric Classification and Media Influence*. New York: Oxford University Press.

Nozick, Robert. 1981. *Philosophical Explanations*. Cambridge, MA: Harvard University Press.

Olson, Eric T. 1997. *The Human Animal: Personal Identity without Psychology*. New York: Oxford University Press.

———. 2001. "Material Coincidence and the Indiscernibility Problem." *Philosophical Quarterly* 51: 337–355.

———. 2002. "What does Functionalism Tell Us about Personal Identity?" *Nous* 36: 682–698.

———. 2003. "Was Jekyll Hyde?" *Philosophy and Phenomenological Research* 66: 328–348.

———. 2007. "Personal Identity." In *The Stanford Encyclopedia of Philosophy*. First published August 20, 2002; last substantive revision February 20, 2007. http://plato.stanford.edu/entries/identity-personal/ (accessed July 25, 2008).
Palahniuk, Chuck . 1997. *Fight Club*. London: Vintage Random House.
Parfit, Derek. 1975. "Personal Identity." In *Personal Identity*, edited by John Perry. Berkeley and Los Angeles: University of California Press.
———. 1987. *Reasons and Persons*. Corrected edition. Oxford: Clarendon Press.
Perry, John. 1970. "The Same *F*." *The Philosophical Review* 79: 181–200.
———. 1972. "Can the Self Divide?" *The Journal of Philosophy* 69: 463–488.
Prince, Morton. 1900–1901. "The Development and Genealogy of the Misses Beauchamp: A Preliminary Report of a Case of Multiple Personality." *Proceedings of the Society for Psychical Research* 15: 466–483.
———. 1906. *The Dissociation of a Personality: A Biographical Study in Abnormal Psychology*. New York: Longman's, Green and Co.
———. 1920. "Miss Beauchamp: The Theory of the Psychogenesis of Multiple Personality." *The Journal of Abnormal Psychology* 15: 67–135.
———. 1975. "Some of the Revelations of Hypnotism: Post-Hypnotic Suggestion, Automatic Writing and Double Personality." In *Psychotherapy and Multiple Personality: Selected Essays* by Prince. Edited by Nathan G. Hale, Jr. Cambridge, MA: Harvard University Press.
Putnam, Frank W. 1989. *Diagnosis and Treatment of Multiple Personality Disorder*. New York: The Guilford Press.
Quante, Michael. 1995. "Die Identität der Person: Facetten eines Problems; Neuere Beiträge zur Diskussion um persönliche Identität." *Philosophische Rundschau* 42: 35–59.
———. 1999. "Einführung." In *Personale Identität*, edited by Michael Quante. Paderborn: Schöningh.
———. 2002. *Personales Leben und menschlicher Tod: Personale Identität als Prinzip der biomedizinischen Ethik*. Frankfurt/Main: Suhrkamp.
———. 2007a. *Person*. Berlin: W. de Gruyter.
———. 2007b. "The Social Nature of Personal Identity." *Journal of Consciousness Studies* 14: 56–76.
———. 2008. "Warum (und in welchem Sinne) gibt es keine personale Identität?" *Deutsche Zeitschrift für Philosophie* 56: 555–568.
Quinton, Anthony. 1962. "The Soul." *Journal of Philosophy* 59: 393–403.
Radden, Jennifer. 1996. *Divided Minds and Successive Selves: Ethical Issues in Disorders of Identity and Personality*. Cambridge, MA: MIT Press.
———. 1998. "Pathologically Divided Minds, Synchronic Unity and Models of Self." *Journal of Consciousness Studies* 5: 658–672.
———. 2004. "Personal Identity, Characterization Identity, and Mental Disorder." In *The Philosophy of Psychiatry: A Companion*, edited by Jennifer Radden. Oxford/New York: Oxford University Press.
Ramis, Harold (director). 1996. *Multiplicity*. Screenplay by Chris Miller, Mary Hale, Harold Ramis, Lowell Ganz, Babaloo Mandel. Based on a short story by Chris Miller. Columbia Pictures.
Rank, Otto. 1925. *Der Doppelgänger: Eine psychoanalytische Studie*. Leipzig: Internationaler Psychoanalytischer Verlag.
Rapp, Christof. 1995. *Identität, Persistenz und Substantialität: Untersuchung zum Verhältnis von sortalen Termen und Aristotelischer Substanz*. Freiburg, Germany: Alber.
Rea, Michael C. 1997. "Introduction." In *Material Constitution: A Reader*, edited by Michael C. Rea. Lanham, MD: Rowman & Littlefield Publishers.

Reddemann, Luise, Arne Hofmann, and Ursula Gast, eds. 2004. *Psychotherapie der dissoziativen Störungen. Krankheitsmodelle und Therapiepraxis—störungsspezifisch und schulenübergreifend.* Stuttgart: Georg Thieme Verlag.

Rey, Georges. 1988. "Toward a Computational Account of *Akrasia* and Self-Deception." In *Perspectives on Self-Deception*, edited by Brian P. McLaughlin and Amélie Oksenberg Rorty. Berkeley and Los Angeles: University of California Press.

Ricoeur, Paul. 1992. *Oneself as Another.* Translated by Kathleen Blamey. Chicago: University of Chicago Press.

Rorty, Amélie Oksenberg. 1976. "A Literary Postscript: Characters, Persons, Selves, Individuals." In *The Identities of Persons*, edited by Amélie O. Rorty. Berkeley and Los Angeles: University of California Press.

Rosenberg, Jay F. 1998. *Thinking Clearly about Death.* 2nd edition. Indianapolis: Hackett Publishing Company.

Rosenzweig, Saul. 1987. "Sally Beauchamp's Career: A Psychoarchaeological Key to Morton Prince's Classic Case of Multiple Personality." *Genetic, Social, and General Psychology Monographs* 113: 5-60.

Ross, Colin A. 1994. *The Osiris Complex: Case-Studies in Multiple Personality Disorder.* Toronto: University of Toronto Press.

———. 1997. *Dissociative Identity Disorder: Diagnosis, Clinical Features, and Treatment of Multiple Personality.* New York: John Wiley & Sons.

Rovane, Carol. 1998. *The Bounds of Agency. An Essay in Revisionary Metaphysics.* Princeton, NJ: Princeton University Press.

———. 2002. "From a Rational Point of View." *Philosophical Topics* 30: 209–235.

———. 2004a. "What Is an Agent?" *Synthese* 140: 181–198.

———. 2004b. "A Nonnaturalist Account of Personal Identity." In *Naturalism in Question*, edited by Mario de Caro and David Macarthur. Cambridge, MA: Harvard University Press.

Saint Augustine. 1961. *Confessions.* Translated by R. S. Pine-Coffin. London: Penguin.

Saks, Elyn R., with Stephen H. Behnke. 1997. *Jekyll on Trial: Multiple Personality Disorder and Criminal Law.* New York: New York University Press.

Schechtman, Marya. 1996. *The Constitution of Selves.* Ithaca, NY: Cornell University Press.

———. 2001. "Empathic Access: The Missing Ingredient in Personal Identity." *Philosophical Explorations* 4: 95–111.

Schmid, Astrid. 1996. *The Fear of the Other: Approaches to English Stories of the Double (1764–1910).* Bern: Peter Lang.

Schreiber, Flora Rheta.1973. *Sybil.* New York: Warner Books.

Shelley, Mary. 1998. *Frankenstein; or, the Modern Prometheus,* edited by Marilyn Butler. Oxford: Oxford University Press.

Shoemaker, David W. 1996. "Theoretical Persons and Practical Agents." *Philosophy and Public Affairs* 25: 318–332.

Shoemaker, Sydney. 1963. *Self-Knowledge and Self-Identity.* Ithaca, NY: Cornell University Press.

———. 1970. "Persons and Their Past." *American Philosophical Quarterly* 7: 269–285.

———. 1979. "Identities, Properties, and Causality." *Midwest Studies in Philosophy* 4: 21–342.

———. 1984. "Personal Identity: A Materialist Account." In *Personal Identity* by Sydney Shoemaker and Richard Swinburne. Oxford: Basil Blackwell.

———. 1997. "Self and Substance." *Philosophical Perspectives* 11: 283–304.

———. 1999. "Self, Body, and Coincidence." In *Proceedings of the Aristotelian Society.* Suppl. vol. 73: 287–306.

Sider, Theodore. 2001. *Four-Dimensionalism: An Ontology of Persistence and Time*. Oxford: Oxford University Press.

Siderits, Mark. 2003. *Personal Identity and Buddhist Philosophy: Empty Persons*. Aldershot, UK: Ashgate.

Sinnott-Armstrong, Walter, and Stephen Behnke. 2000. "Responsibility in Cases of Multiple Personality Disorder." *Philosophical Perspectives* 14: 301–323.

Slors, Marc. 1998. "Two Conceptions of Psychological Continuity." *Philosophical Explorations* 1: 61–80.

Smith, J. David. 1988. *Psychological Profiles of Conjoined Twins. Heredity, Environment, and Identity*. Foreword by Robert Bogdan. New York: Praeger.

Snowdon, P. F. 1990. "Persons, Animals, and Ourselves." In *The Person and the Human Mind: Issues in Ancient and Modern Philosophy*, edited by Christopher Gill. Oxford: Clarendon Press.

Sosa, Ernest. 1997. "Subjects among Other Things." In *Material Constitution: A Reader*, edited by in Michael C. Rea. Lanham, MD: Rowman & Littlefield Publishers.

Steinberg, Marlene, and Maxine Schnall. 2000. *The Stranger in the Mirror: Dissociation—The Hidden Epidemic*. New York: Cliff Street Books.

Stephens, G. Lynn, and George Graham. 2000. *When Consciousness Breaks: Alien Voices and Inserted Thoughts*. Cambridge, MA: MIT Press.

Stevenson, Robert Louis. 1979. *The Strange Case of Dr Jekyll and Mr Hyde*. Edited by Jenni Calder. London: Penguin Books.

Strawson, P. F. 1959. *Individuals: An Essay in Descriptive Metaphysics*. London: Routledge.

———. 1966. *The Bounds of Sense: An Essay on Kant's Critique of Pure Reason*. London: Methuen & Co. Ltd.

Stübner, S., G. Völkl, and M. Soyka. 1998. "Zur Differentialdiagnose der dissoziativen Identitätsstörung (multipler Persönlichkeitsstörung)." *Der Nervenarzt* 69: 440–445.

Sturma, Dieter. 1992. "Person und Zeit." In *Zeiterfahrung und Personalität*, edited by Forum für Philosophie Bad Homburg. Frankfurt/Main: Suhrkamp.

———. 1997. *Philosophie der Person: Die Selbstverhältnisse von Subjektivität und Moral*. Paderborn, Germany: Schöningh.

———. 2002. "Selbstbewusstsein und personale Identität: Kant über den Zusammenhang von Erkenntniskritik und Philosophie des Geistes." In *Perspektiven der Transzendentalphilosophie im Anschluss an die Philosophie Kants*, edited by R. Hiltscher and A. Georgi. Freiburg, Germany: Alber.

———. 2008. "Selbstreferenz, Zeit und Identität: Grundzüge einer naturalistischen Theorie personaler Identität." *Deutsche Zeitschrift für Philosophie* 56: 569–583.

Swinburne, Richard. 1984. "Personal Identity: The Dualist Theory." In *Personal Identity*, edited by Sydney Shoemaker and Richard Swinburne. Oxford: Basil Blackwell.

Taylor, Charles. 1989. *Sources of the Self: The Making of the Modern Identity*. Cambridge, MA: Harvard University Press.

Teichert, Dieter. 2000. *Personen und Identitäten*. Berlin: Walter de Gruyter.

Thomson, Judith Jarvis. 1997. "People and Their Bodies." In *Reading Parfit*, edited by Jonathan Dancy. Oxford: Blackwell Publishers.

Tye, Michael. 2003. *Consciousness and Persons: Unity and Identity*. Cambridge, MA: MIT Press.

Unger, Peter. 1990. *Identity, Consciousness and Value*. New York: Oxford University Press.

Velleman, J. David. 2006. *Self to Self: Selected Essays*. Cambridge: Cambridge University Press.

———. 2006a. "The Self as Narrator." In Velleman 2006.

Wallis, Claudia. 1996. "The Most Intimate Bond." *Time Magazine*, March 25.

Weathers, Helen. 2006. "Abigail and Brittany Hensel: An Extraordinary Bond." Mail Online: http://www.dailymail.co.uk/femail/article-425736/Abigail-Brittany-Hensel-extraordinary-bond.html, last updated 31 December 2006 (accessed 24 July 2008).

Webber, Andrew J. 1996. *The "Doppelgänger": Double Visions in German Literature.* Oxford: Clarendon Press.

West, Cameron. 1999. *First Person Plural: My Life as a Multiple.* New York: Hyperion.

Whiting, Jennifer. 1999. "Back to 'The Self and the Future.' " *Philosophical Topics* 26: 441–477.

———. 2002. "Personal Identity: The Non-Branching Form of 'What Matters.' " In *The Blackwell Guide to Metaphysics*, edited by Richard Gale. Oxford: Blackwell.

———. 2005. Review of *Self-Concern*, by Raymond Martin, and *The Bounds of Agency*, by Carol Rovane. *Philosophical Review* 114: 339-410.

Wiggins, David. 1967. *Identity and Spatio-Temporal Continuity.* Oxford: Basil Blackwell.

———. 1976. "Locke, Butler and the Stream of Consciousness: And Men as a Natural Kind." In *The Identities of Persons*, edited by A. Rorty. Berkeley: University of California Press.

———. 1997. "On Being in the Same Place at the Same Time." In *Material Constitution: A Reader*, edited by Michael C. Rea. Lanham, MD: Rowman & Littlefield Publishers.

———. 2001. *Sameness and Substance Renewed.* Cambridge: Cambridge University Press.

Wilde, Oscar. 1949. *The Picture of Dorian Gray*. London: Penguin Books.

Wilkes, Kathleen V. 1988. *Real People: Personal Identity without Thought Experiments.* Oxford: Clarendon Press.

———. 1991. "How Many Selves Make Me?" In *Human Beings*, edited by David Cockburn. Cambridge: Cambridge University Press.

Williams, Bernard. 1973. *Problems of the Self: Philosophical Papers 1956–1972* by Williams. Cambridge: Cambridge University Press.

———. 1973a. "Personal Identity and Individuation." In Williams 1973.

———. 1973b. "Are Persons Bodies?" In Williams 1973.

———.1973c. "The Self and the Future." In Williams 1973.

———.1973d. "Deciding to Believe." In Williams 1973.

World Health Organization. 2007. *International Statistical Classification of Diseases and Related Health Problems,* Tenth Revision (ICD-10). Online version: http://www.who.int/classifications/apps/icd/icd10online/.

Index

L

M

N

O

P

T

U

V

W